PHENOMENON

THE STALIN PHENOMENON

by

JEAN ELLEINSTEIN

1976
LAWRENCE AND WISHART
LONDON

First published in 1975 under the title Histoire du phénomène Stalinien
by Grasset, Paris

English translation by Peter Latham

In the English edition some of the chapter titles of the French text have been reworded and a few paragraphs near the end, directed specially to French readers, have been omitted.

Printed in Great Britain by
The Camelot Press Ltd, Southampton

Contents

Introduction

The Stalin phenomenon was not born with Stalin nor did it die with him. It is not limited to the Soviet Union, but that country constitutes its epicentre. It concerns all the socialist states born just after the Second World War and all Communist parties. It affects the fields of theory as well as practice, politics as well as economics and ideology. It was born in the Soviet Union in the nineteen-twenties just after Lenin's death, and there it began to fade after Stalin's death (1953) and after the 20th Congress of the Communist Party of the Soviet Union (1956). It is important to grasp the significance of the choice of the very expression 'Stalin phenomenon'. The word 'Stalinism' does not strike me as scandalous. However, it does, in my opinion, have certain disadvantages. Historically speaking, it is a word invented by the bourgeoisie, an ideological and political weapon, though it is a word which is in common usage (in Communist circles too), and which is simple and generally understood.

The expression 'personality cult', which was used by the Communist Party of the Soviet Union and later adopted by the international Communist movement, seems even less acceptable as it only stresses one aspect of the phenomenon – the cult of the leader. As for the expression 'Stalinist Period', it has the disadvantage of setting too narrow time limits to the phenomenon. Indeed, even the adjective 'Stalinist' creates problems. The phenomenon cannot be reduced to the personality of Stalin, and it is even less possible to explain it in that way. However, for quite clear historical reasons it is linked with him. As it is less restrictive in terms of time and space, the expression 'Stalin phenomenon' seems the most satisfactory to me.

This work, which completes my *Histoire de l'U.R.S.S.* published in four volumes by Editions Sociales (the fourth volume has just come out), is intended to describe and to explain.

First of all, I intend to study the Stalin phenomenon in

all its contradictory manifestations, a task more difficult than
might at first appear. My second aim, whose significance will
escape no one who thinks about the future of mankind, is to
understand its causes and thus its profound nature. In our time,
nobody can escape this tragic dilemma: either the Stalin
phenomenon is explained by the historical conditions under
which the first socialist revolution took place, and is therefore
an accidental product of Communism, or it is the natural,
inevitable product of it. This is the fundamental question which
we shall attempt to answer in the following pages.

1 Party and State after the Civil War

Immediately after the end of the Civil War the economic situation in Soviet Russia was dreadful. In 1913, Tsarist Russia was far from being a rich country. There had been real industrial development since 1880, but this was still limited. The production of energy producing raw materials (oil, coal) outweighed actual industrial production. Though Russia had become the fifth greatest industrial power in the world, she was still far behind the leading capitalist countries: the United States, Germany, Great Britain and France (taking their population into account).

The industrial output of France was two and a half times as great as that of Russia with a population four times smaller. Industrial output in the United States was fourteen times greater than that of Russia in absolute figures, and twenty-two times greater if population is taken into account. In any case these figures only show the position in quantitative terms. From the point of view of quality, the difference was even bigger. Moreover, this industrialisation had not profoundly changed the rural structures of this huge country. Industry was concentrated in a few big towns and in a few regions (St. Petersburg, Moscow, the Donbass, Baku and Ural regions), as if stuck veneer-like on the immense, rural body of Tsarist Russia.

Agriculture itself remained poor and old-fashioned because of the poor equipment, little use of chemical fertilisers and a generally unscientific approach. Yields were low and the rural population was large in relation to the amount of land under cultivation.

But the consequences of the Civil War (and of the First World War) were dramatic.

Industry (apart from arms production) virtually disappeared and agricultural output fell by half. The figures speak for themselves:

Percentage compared to *1913* (*in* %)

Industry	1920	1921
Coalmining	26·8	30·8
Oil	41·1	42·7
Iron	1·0	1·6
Engineering	8·7	9·3
Sugar	5·9	6·7
Cotton	5·2	7·5

Agriculture	1901–13 Average	1920	1921
Grain Harvests (in mn. poods)	4,079	1,738	1,617
Area cultivated (in mn. dessiatines)	81·2	56·8	49

1 pood = 36·11 lb.
1 dessiatine = 2·7 acres

The result of this drop in agricultural production was the famine in the winter of 1920–1, one of the worst in history: 24 million people were affected by the famine in an area of about 2 million square kilometres covering the Volga region as far as the Urals and the Caucasus (Samara, Ufa, Kazan, Tsaritsyn, Stavropol) and south to the Crimea. These areas were cast into the distant past when human beings quite literally starved to death. In addition to the famine there were typhus and cholera epidemics. (More than 20 million people had suffered typhus between 1917 and 1921.) The famine killed more than 7 million people. To these figures had to be added, 1,500,000 who died in the First World War, 1 million dead in the Civil War and 3 million victims of the epidemics. As a result of foreign and civil wars and their consequences, a total of 13,500,000 people died. About 2 million people emigrated. Tens of millions of beggars, vagrants and abandoned children roamed the countryside. Bandits flourished as they had in France during the 'Directoire'. Nowadays we all too easily forget the real situation in 1921, or we underestimate its seriousness and its consequences.

The economic development of the Soviet Union did not start from the 1913 situation. The building of socialism started from 1921 and from the actual situation at that precise time.

It would be hard to claim that the Bolsheviks were responsible for the First World War. As for the Civil War, they tried to avoid it and though they did not refuse to fight, they did not start the fighting. As early as mid-November 1917, the White Russians organised an army which tried to retake Petrograd and was beaten at Pulkovo. Until the armistice signed on 11th November 1918, the Germans intervened directly in the Ukraine despite the peace agreement signed by the Germans and Russians at Brest-Litovsk. In March 1918, 30,000 Czechs who had fought in the Austrian ranks, and who had been released, revolted against the young Soviet state. The White Russians raised several armies in order to bring down the Soviets, and troops from seventeen countries (France, Britain, Japan, Turkey, etc.) intervened against the Revolution.

'War Communism' had been nothing but a caricature of Communism, born out of penury and the Civil War. Massive requisitioning constituted one of the most spectacular elements of this policy, which was sustained by the utopian idea that it was possible to proceed immediately and directly to communist production and distribution.[1] Indeed in 1918 it had been announced that public services would be free. It is not hard to understand that in such circumstances the most urgent and fundamental task, as foreseen in the Party programme, was 'the development of the productive forces' (Lenin, *Collected Works*, Vol. 33, p. 67, report to the 2nd Congress of the Political Education Departments, 17th October 1921).

The New Economic Policy (N.E.P.)[2] arose from these objective requirements, but the development of the forces of production was hindered by two facts which were themselves inherited from the Civil War: the departure from Russia of most of the managerial staff, few enough even before the Revolution, and the virtually total foreign boycott. This meant that reconstruction would have to be carried out without technicians or foreign capital.

These circumstances were not without influence on the developments which took place in the nineteen-twenties. They

constitute one of the components of the historical environment
from which the Stalin phenomenon emerged. The situation in
which Soviet Russia found itself in 1921 demanded that
priority be given to industrial development.

In his recent work *Les Luttes de classes en U.R.S.S.*, Vol. 1,
1917–1923 ('Class Struggles in the U.S.S.R.'), Charles
Bettelheim quite simply omits to study economic conditions in
Soviet Russia immediately after the Civil War. Historical
research tends to be replaced by speeches about history. 'It is
up to the Bolshevik Party to take Russia along the road to
Socialism; its tasks are many, and were mostly pointed out by
Lenin. Above all, they concern the transformation of ideological and political relations' (Bettelheim, p. 456). Naturally
it is the expression 'above all' which requires criticism. The
transformation of ideological and political relations is indeed a
necessity which I have no intention at all of questioning, though
the order of the adjectives 'ideological' and then 'political'
does not seem fortuitous to me and is highly debatable, for in
1922 what mattered 'above all', according to Lenin, was to
ensure the development of the forces of production. When he
criticised the slogan of 'democratic production', which was put
forward by Bukharin, Lenin remarked: 'Industry is indispensable, democracy is not . . .' and he had previously made his
point of view quite clear: 'Democracy is a category proper
only to the political sphere.' (Speech by Lenin on 3rd December
1920, *C.W.*, Vol. 32, p. 26.)

I accept no responsibility for this formulation, which
seems far too narrow to me, but this quotation does underline
how important industrial production was for Lenin.

The 'awful catastrophe' in the economic field was to have
dramatic social consequences for the future of the Soviet
experiment. We have studied them as far as population figures
were concerned, and what has been said about the winter
famine of 1921–2 gives some idea of the poverty of the people
just after the end of the Civil War, but the war caused fundamental changes in the position of the social classes. The most
serious change was the disappearance of the proletariat. Lenin
recognised this honestly in his speech on 17th October 1921 (to
the 2nd Congress of the Political Education Departments): 'an
industrial proletariat, which in our country, owing to the war

and to the desperate poverty and ruin has become "declassed", i.e. dislodged from its class groove and has ceased to exist as a proletariat. .... Since large-scale capitalist industry has been destroyed, since the factories are at a standstill, the proletariat has disappeared. It has sometimes figured in statistics, but it has not been held together economically' (*C.W.*, Vol. 33, pp. 65–6).

There were about three and a half million workers in major industry in 1913 (a small number for a population of 174 million). In 1922 there were only 1,118,000 left. There were still proletarians in the ranks of the Red Army, the Party and in State organs (Soviets, People's Commissariats, the Cheka), but as a class the proletariat had all but disappeared. A large number of workers had died during the Civil War in which they had played a very active part.

The various strata of the urban bourgeoisie had undergone the same fate. Together with the nobility, it constituted the majority of those emigrating. The industrialists and financiers, followed by the merchants, had left the country 'en masse'. The socialisation of companies had led to the almost total disappearance of the Russian capitalists who had existed before the Revolution.

The loss had been particularly heavy in the intellectual field. Soviet Russia had been emptied of its grey matter. There were hardly any engineers, doctors or teachers left. Nine tenths of them had emigrated. The nobility had lost both its property and its appointments. All those who had not died in the Revolution and the Civil War had gone abroad.

The peasantry had undergone major changes. As a result of the decree nationalising land belonging to landowners and to the Orthodox Church, this land had been shared out among the peasants, who now owned it and whose sons would inherit it.

In fact, in 1922 Soviet Russia was a peasant-dominated country. Of course, there were richer peasants, the *kulaks* (from a Russian word meaning fist), and very poor peasants, the *biednaks* (24 per cent in 1925), and even agricultural labourers who owned no land, the *batraks*, but the majority of them were middle peasants, the *seredniaks* (64·7 per cent).[3] The Russian situation must be taken into account when interpreting this expression, for these middle peasants were really, according to our standards, poor peasants with little more than a horse and a few hectares of land. As a result of the depopulation of the towns (Petrograd had 2,415,000 inhabitants in 1916 and 740,000 in 1920, Moscow 1,753,000 in 1916 and 1,120,000 in 1920), the influence of the countryside in the life of the nation was even greater than before the war. Therefore, the overall picture of society changed completely between 1913 and 1921. The proletariat and the intelligentsia, like the foreign and Russian capitalists, had vanished. What remained was the middle peasantry, flanked by very poor and very rich peasants, 'officered' by workers and intellectuals who constituted the backbone of the Communist Party and the administrative organs of the country.

The Civil War had not only ruined the economy and turned society upside down, it had created a new state. This socialist state had taken on an appearance which would have astonished anyone who had tried to imagine it on the eve of the Revolution. History cannot be written in advance and even the most fertile imagination scarcely allows one to predict the future. The Soviet state replaced the Tsarist state. No doubt, the Revolution did smash the latter, did break it as Marx had recommended and Lenin understood.[4] The taking of power was preceded by the disintegration of the Tsarist institutions and of the ideological props of the state. The October Revolution had smashed this worm-eaten heap and, in the first few months of Soviet rule, had completed the process of disintegration. But, as the proverb says 'chassez le naturel, il revient au galop' (i.e. deeply rooted traditions, etc., are not easily eradicated). Lenin became aware of this just after the Civil War, immediately before his illness and death. 'Something analagous happened here to what we were told in our history lessons when we were children: sometimes one nation conquers another, the nation which conquers is the conqueror and the nation that is vanquished is the conquered nation. If the conquering nation is more cultured than the vanquished nation, the former imposes its culture on the latter; but if the opposite is the case, the vanquished nation imposes its culture upon the conquerors. Has something like this not happened in the capital of the R.S.F.S.R.?'[5] (*C.W.*, Vol. 33, p. 288).

It was in this way that Greek civilisation conquered the

Roman soul – Graecia capta ferum victorem cepit ('Greece conquered, conquered her ferocious conqueror', Horace, *Epistle* 11, 156) – and that in 1922 the Tsarist state reappeared in the new Soviet state. Bureaucracy dominated the socialist state. The Party programme clearly defined the situation when it characterised the Soviet state as 'a workers' state with a bureaucratic twist to it' (Lenin, *C.W.*, Vol. 32, p. 24), and the articles written by Lenin during the last two years of his active life bear witness to his anguish at this 'survival from the past'.[6] This bureaucratic twist manifested itself in the inability to solve the concrete economic problems, in the existence of a body of civil servants acting in isolation from the masses and enjoying high living standards, and in the mass return of Tsarist civil servants (in the hundreds of thousands). As Lenin stressed in preparatory notes for a speech to the 10th Congress of the Soviets in December 1922 (one of the last things he wrote): 'The State machine in general: bad beyond description; lower than the bourgeois level of culture' (*C.W.*, Vol. 36, p. 588).

The influence of the past weighed heavily on the fate of the Revolution and the future of socialism. Several sources can be identified. First of all, cultural backwardness. In 1920, the majority of the population was still illiterate.

Able to read and write (per 1,000 inhabitants)

	Women	Men	Average
In 1897	131	318	224
In 1920	244	420	332

Thus, almost 70 per cent of the population was illiterate. These figures need to be commented on. In fact, the people concerned were those who had learnt to read and write a little. In the majority of cases, they had forgotten these rudiments. As they did not use their skills, the real percentage of illiteracy is much higher than the figures given by the Soviet Central Statistics Office (based on a 1920 census, published in 1922). The rate of illiteracy was higher among women than among men, higher in the country than in the towns, higher in those regions which had been colonies until the Revolution (Central

Asia, the Caucasus, Siberia) than in Russia.[7] Thus the rate of
illiteracy was higher in Soviet Russia than in France in 1789,
when the average figure was 65 per cent. There were a mere
635,591 pupils in secondary schools in 1914 (591,645 in 1922),
of which only 14,575 were in the country. As for Higher
Education, it was even less well distributed: of a total of
127,000 students (only 36,000 of these at university), 37·6 per
cent were of aristocratic origin, 11·5 per cent came from the
families of top civil servants, 24·2 per cent were children of
merchants and intellectuals, 7·7 per cent from priests' families
and 14·6 per cent from Cossack and peasant families. The
fame of 19th-century Russian literature and the quality of
Russian music must not be allowed to hide the fact that, as
far as intellectual life was concerned, 'the night was darker in
the Russia of 1917 than in France in 1789', as Aulard, holder
of the Sorbonne chair in the History of the French Revolution,
admitted in his *L'Histoire des Soviets* published in 1922.

This cultural backwardness was not simply a question of
education, the *moujiks* of the former Russian Empire lacked
culture. They were superstitious, under the influence of the
Orthodox priests, and they lived in poverty, worshipping icons,
the holy images of Christ, the Virgin Mary and of the Saints,
which were to be found in every peasant's hut. Their favourite
pastime was drinking vodka, which was distilled from potatoes
and consumed in formidable quantities (in 1914 the tax on
alcohol provided a quarter of state revenue). This picture is
generally accurate, though certain details may need changing.

As the French sociologist Georges Friedman noted in a
book published in 1938,[8] the 'powers of darkness' dominated
Holy Russia. Judged by many of its features – most of its
characteristics in fact – Russia was still in the Middle Ages,
and this appears even truer if one studies the consciousness,
mentality and ideology of its inhabitants. Today, you would
have to go to the poor countries of Africa, Latin America or
the Far East to understand this cultural backwardness and to
grasp under precisely what conditions socialism had to be
built. The Tsarist state was distinguished by despotism,
arbitrary exercise of power and autocracy, and the 1905
Revolution had scarcely changed the situation. Basic rights
such as freedom of speech, freedom of the press, the right to

hold meetings and form organisations were practically non-existent. There were neither representative institutions nor elections by universal suffrage. The Duma was nothing more than a consultative assembly elected according to a complex system which favoured the landowners at the expense of the moujiks and, above all, of the workers. So, neither the institutions nor the culture were democratic, and there was no opportunity for democratic behaviour. Like literature and the theatre, the press was gagged and the political police (the Okhrana) was all powerful.

The Tsar was still an Oriental potentate surrounded by nobles and bureaucrats belonging to the different ranks of the Tsarist bureaucracy. (The 'chins' made up the fourteen classes of civil servants. The first eight military 'chins' were largely reserved for the nobility). Individual freedom did not exist, for the police could arrest whoever they liked whenever they liked. You needed a passport to travel within the Empire and a large number of visas to go abroad. The Civil Service was inefficient and corrupted by the practice of accepting bribes (*vsiatka*). The Tsar was honoured like a god and worshipped like one, at least until the tragic Bloody Sunday (22 January 1905), when he had given the order to fire on the defenceless crowd which was bringing a list of its demands to the Winter Palace. Thus, he was at the head of an omnipresent state more like the early Greek kingdoms and the Byzantine Empire than modern, early 20th-century states. Such was the heritage from the past. It was possible to abolish it *de facto* by passing laws, but not to uproot it from men's consciousness. It could be destroyed by force, but could not immediately be removed from the human spirit nor from everyday behaviour. This is the galling fact the Bolsheviks ascertained in 1922. To this were added the consequences of the Revolution and Civil War.

Immediately after the fall of Tsarism on 15th March 1917 and until July 1917, real political liberty existed. After the bloody demonstrations of 17 July, the Provisional Government under Kerensky took repressive measures against the Bolshevik Party on the pretext of high treason: the Party's headquarters were occupied, its papers were banned and its leaders arrested (Kamenev, Trotsky and dozens more). Lenin only saved himself by running away. In Kerensky's shadow, a counter-revolutionary military dictatorship was taking shape, but General Kornilov's attempted *coup d'état* failed because of the opposition of his own soldiers who had been won over by the Bolsheviks. The October Revolution must be seen in this precise historical context. If it had not been undertaken and carried through, Russia would have been bowed under the yoke of a military dictatorship; numerous historical examples teach us that it is hard to get rid of such a regime.

No sooner had power been taken in Petrograd than counter-revolutionary forces had to be faced militarily, and economic administrative sabotage combated. Thus, the young Soviet state started down the path of repression, but it did so slowly and hesitantly. Theoretically speaking, the Bolsheviks had long been aware of this necessity. The role played by violence in history was no secret for either Marx or for Engels who had made precise, lucid studies of it.[9]

The historical experience of socialism since its beginnings confirmed these studies, and we know with what care Lenin, following Marx, had studied the history of the 1871 Paris Commune, which proved to be too kindly and was drowned in the blood of tens of thousands of Parisian workers because it had been too slow to take the necessary measures against its enemies. From this point of view, there was the positive example of the French Revolution with the Terror of 1793–4, and the negative example of the Commune of 1871 which showed the need to wield revolutionary power in precise historical circumstances. With gathering momentum, the latter led to the Red Terror. It would be intellectually somewhat dishonest to study it in isolation from the historical environment which gave birth to it. However, this is what many authors have done, for example Robert Conquest in *The Great Terror*, or, in a literary form, A. Solzhenitsyn in *The Gulag Archipelago*.[10] On 8th November 1917, against Lenin's advice, the 2nd Congress of the Soviets abolished the death penalty, but on the same day it was decided to subject the press to 'workers' censorship' in order to prevent the bourgeoisie from misrepresenting what was happening. On 30th November, all the non-Bolshevik papers in Petrograd were suspended, the Committee for the Safety of the Fatherland and the Revolution was dissolved, then the same fate befell the Petrograd Duma which had given birth to it. On 18th December, the Cadet Party (K.D., that is to say Constitutional-Democratic) was banned, but the White Terror had already begun. In Moscow, Reds and Whites had engaged in violent combat for a week from the 7th to the 16th November 1917. Several hundred Red soldiers were shut inside the Kremlin and, for no good military reason, massacred by the Whites. The Bolsheviks refused to take mass repressive measures (to resort to terror). The few acts of cruelty which did occur were the result of individual initiatives. On 3rd December 1917, General Dukhonin, Commander in Chief of the Army, was killed by a crowd at his headquarters. There were also some executions in Petrograd in November and December, but they were not instigated by the Bolshevik leaders who protected former ministers under Kerensky against popular fury. When the internal situation got worse, anarchy reigned and the Civil War broke out, repression became more severe. As Trotsky declared: 'We are not entering the Kingdom of Socialism wearing kid gloves and walking on a polished parquet floor' ('*Œuvres*', Vol. 3, Book 2, p. 202).

Cadet and right-wing Socialist-Revolutionary leaders were arrested in Petrograd and Moscow. On 23rd December, the Petrograd Revolutionary Tribunal started work. On 20th December 1917, a secret decree (the text was published in *Pravda* on 18th September 1927) from the Sovnarkom – the Council of People's Commissars – set up the Extraordinary All-Russian Commission (the Vecheka according to the Russian initials), whose job it was to 'combat counter-revolution and sabotage'. It originated in the Revolutionary Military Committee which had prepared and actually conducted the October Revolution. This Commission, which was presided over by Dzerzhinsky, an experienced revolutionary (of Polish origin), was composed of eight members. Local commissions was set up on the same model.

By January 1918, the situation in Russia was already dreadful. A White army, of so-called volunteers, was massing on the Don. In the Ukraine as well as in Finland, Reds and Whites were locked in violent combat. German troops were threatening to occupy Petrograd and march on Moscow. Supplies were short everywhere. This is when Lenin wrote an article entitled 'How to Organise Competition', which

Solzhenitsyn uses in *The Gulag Archipelago* to try to prove that
Stalinism can be traced back to Lenin.[11] In the article (written
between the 7th and 10th January 1918, but only published in
Pravda on 20th January 1929), Lenin stresses the role to be
played by workers and peasants in the field of production and
in the organisation of accounting and control which 'can only
be exercised by the people'. He declares 'war to the death
against the rich and their hangers-on, the bourgeois intellectuals; (. . .) war on the rogues, the idlers and the rowdies', and
he adds that 'thousands of practical forms and methods of
accounting and controlling the rich, the rogues and the idlers
must be devised and put to a practical test by the communes
themselves, by small units in town and country. Variety is a
guarantee of effectiveness here, a pledge of success in achieving
the single common aim – to clean the land of Russia of all
vermin, of fleas – the rogues, of bugs – the rich, and so on and
so forth. In one place half a score of rich, a dozen rogues, half
a dozen workers who shirk their work . . . will be put in prison.'

I hope that the reader will excuse this long quotation, but
it is clear that on the basis of this text it would be hard to
explain the Stalin Terror, which was directed against the
people. Lenin's text dates from January 1918 and is explained
by the historical context. E. H. Carr agrees about the establishment of the Cheka. 'At the critical moment of a hard fought
struggle, the establishment of these organs can hardly be
regarded as unusual',[12] and later: 'The development of the
Cheka was a gradual and largely unpremeditated process.'
During the spring and early summer of 1918, the staff of the
Cheka grew, but it was still limited and its powers still modest.
The Czech rising[13] made the situation worse, whilst the
Japanese seized Vladivostock and the British and French
landed at Murmansk and Arkhangelsk.

In July 1918, the left-wing Socialist-Revolutionaries
(members of the Sovnarkom from December 1917 to April
1918, and still associated with the Bolsheviks on the Central
Executive Committee of the Soviets, the V.T.S.I.K.) unsuccessfully attempted a military putsch in Moscow, Petrograd and a
few other towns. On 30th August 1918, in an attempt on his
life made by a right-wing Socialist-Revolutionary (Fanny
Kaplan), Lenin was hit by two bullets and only just escaped

death. On the same day in Petrograd, Uritsky, the leader of the Petrograd Cheka, was assassinated by a right-wing Socialist-Revolutionary student (already in June 1918 a Bolshevik leader in Petrograd, Volodarsky, had suffered the same fate). Until then, the number of executions had remained small. The Royal Family had been executed on 17th July 1918 at Ekaterinburg as Czech troops approached the town. However, there had been no mass executions. On 23rd July, a decree against speculation provided for stiff penalties (up to ten years' hard labour) for all those speculating in foodstuffs. The attempted murder of Lenin opened the bloody floodgates of popular anger. Terror was immediately institutionalised. On 2nd September, the Central Executive Committee of the Soviets declared: 'The Workers' and Peasants' Government will reply to the White Terror of the enemies of the workers and peasants by a mass Red Terror directed against the bourgeoisie and its agents.' A Revolutionary War Council chaired by Trotsky was formed the same day. On 3rd September, the People's Commissar for the Interior issued a proclamation: 'There has been enough kindness and enough negligence. All right-wing Socialist-Revolutionaries known to the local Soviets must be arrested at once. We will take large numbers of hostages from among the bourgeoisie and officers. If the Whites put up the slightest resistance or are in any way active, we will respond not with discussion but with mass shootings.'

These words can only be understood if we put them back into their historical context. The Revolution was in danger. Allied with the Whites, the Czechs were threatening the nerve centres of the country. From all sides, foreign powers were throwing themselves upon Russia so that they could be in at the kill.[14] On 7th September 1918, the Leningrad Cheka announced the execution of 512 people. So, there were thousands of executions and tens of thousands of arrests. It was immediately after the Duke of Brunswick issued his manifesto and the revolutionary army suffered its first defeats in September 1792 that the French Revolution felt it necessary to adopt terror measures against the nobility and accomplices of foreign powers, and that the September massacres took place. The White Terror grew too. Tens of thousands of captured Red soldiers were shot by the White armies and the foreign interventionists. After all, the Imperialist powers were responsible for the First World War which had resulted in a bloodbath without historical precedent. More than ten million dead and tens of millions of wounded! Compared with that hecatomb, the several tens of thousands of victims of the Red Terror were insignificant. It is not our intention to write the story of the Terror, but to understand its origins and to study its consequences for the future. So let us be absolutely frank about it. If the Bolsheviks had not acted in this way, the Soviet Revolution would have been defeated, and today it would, like the Paris Commune, be a mere memory buried in men's minds. Of course, that does not justify the abuses it brought in its train, but, basically, the Revolution had a simple choice – either act like that or perish. And, above all, it must be seen that the Terror was aimed at the enemies of the people, against those responsible for the war and famine, against the speculators and Whites. Thus, neither its aims nor its consequences are comparable to those of the Stalin Terror. Besides, it is not enough to content oneself with smug descriptions of Red atrocities, as does Solzhenitsyn, while the Whites behaved cruelly and pitilessly throughout the Civil War years. The crimes committed by the armies of Kornilov, Denikin, Wrangel, Petliura, Yudenich and Kolchak must be counted in hundreds of thousands: Communists tortured and killed as in Kazan and Samara, mass murders of workers as in Maikop (in the Caucasus), villages burnt as was Lejuka near the Don, where Kornilov's soldiers killed 507 people, and no one mentions the pogroms which took place in the White-controlled Ukraine and cost 100,000 lives (as reported by the Red Cross to the League of Nations). For, in the eyes of the White Generals, the Jews were both instigators and leaders of the Revolution.

We seek to excuse nothing, merely to put things into perspective. For all these events took place in an historical environment quite different from that of the Stalin phenomenon.

1921 saw the setting up of a certain number of institutions, structures and mechanisms which were to outlive the needs and circumstances which had given rise to them. This is particularly true of the political police. Because of events, the Vecheka had become more and more important. It arrested, tried and executed suspects without any external supervision. Prisoners were sentenced in their absence. The Vecheka kept an eye on the press, books, the journeys people made, public places, that is to say everything. It had a big staff (hundreds of thousands of people) and discretionary powers. Its role could not fail to cause some concern among the Bolsheviks themselves. At the 9th All-Russian Congress of the Soviets at the end of December 1921, Lenin gave a lengthy explanation of his views on the subject. 'Before concluding, I want to apply this lesson once more – that our faults are sometimes the continuation of our merits – to one of our institutions, namely to the Cheka.' And, after recalling the plotting of the internal and external enemies of the Revolution, he added: 'You know the only way in which we could reply to them was by merciless, swift and instant repression with the sympathy and support of the workers and peasants.' . . . 'As long as there are exploiters in the world, who have no desire to hand over their landowner and capitalist rights to the workers on a platter, the power of the working people cannot survive without such an institution. We are keenly aware of this, we also know that a man's merits may become his vices, and we know that the prevailing conditions insistently demand that the work of this organisation be limited to the purely political sphere, that it concentrate its efforts on tasks in which it is aided by the situation and the circumstances.' Later, he pointed out: 'But at the same time we say categorically that it is essential to reform the Cheka, define its function and powers and limit its work to political problems' (*C.W.*, Vol. 33, pp. 175–6). So it is clear that for the Bolshevik leaders this was an important question. 'The situation makes it absolutely necessary to restrict its activities, to reform the commission, to define its functions and sphere of action.' We are merely quoting Lenin's own words. The conclusion to his speech was quite unambiguous: '(it is imperative) to put forward the firm slogan of greater revolutionary legality' (*C.W.*, Vol. 33, p. 176).

Then the Congress voted on a resolution proposed by Smirnov and adopted it unanimously. 'Congress considers that the present strengthening of Soviet power both internally and externally makes it possible to concentrate the activity of the Cheka and its agencies, reserving for judicial bodies the fight against those who break the laws of the Soviet Republics. Accordingly, the Congress of the Soviets calls upon the Presidium of the V.T.S.I.K. to revise as quickly as possible the statutes of the Cheka and its agencies, with the aim of reorganising, of limiting their sphere of action and of reinforcing the principles of revolutionary legality.' Contrary to what Carr says, this was not a tactical manœuvre but a principled decision, which encountered serious difficulties in its application. On the 18th February 1922, the Cheka was disbanded and its powers transferred to the People's Commissariat of the Interior, which set up a state political administration (the G.P.U. according to the Russian initials). Anyone arrested had either to be released or brought to trial within two months, unless the Presidium of the V.T.S.I.K. judged this inappropriate.

To sum up, the Civil War saw the creation of a powerful political police whose role worried Soviet leaders. Were the measures taken in 1922 sufficient to combat this danger of the existence of a state within the state? What part was this political police to play in the birth of the Stalin phenomenon? The consequences of the Civil War were even more serious.

Theoretically, the October Revolution had established the 'dictatorship of the proletariat' and the Civil War had strengthened it. The expression 'dictatorship of the proletariat' was invented by Marx and expresses a theoretical concept of great importance. It contrasted the dictatorship of the bourgeoisie which existed in capitalist society with 'a political transition period in which the state can be nothing but the revolutionary dictatorship of the proletariat' (Marx, *Critique of the Gotha Programme*, 1875). It was to last for the period between capitalist and communist society, that is to say for the period of socialist society. Yet Marx had no specific political forms in mind. In *The State and Revolution*, Lenin stressed two complementary ideas: on the one hand, the essential necessity of the dictatorship of the proletariat, and on the other hand, the variety of political forms this 'dictatorship' could assume. After all, what Marx, like Lenin, was concerned with was describing the class content of the state, since, in their eyes, every state was by definition an instrument by which one class dominated another (or all others). By 1922, the Revolution and the Civil War had created a new state which secured the 'dictatorship of the proletariat'. Yet, the situation was certainly strange. Indeed, Lenin admitted that the proletariat had vanished (but not proletarians, large numbers of whom were working in the Soviets and in Party organisations, or were wearing the uniform of the Red Army or the Cheka). Because of the disappearance of the proletariat, the 'dictatorship of the proletariat' could only express an abstract concept. Under such conditions, it is not surprising that the dictatorship of the Bolshevik Party should have become identified, *de facto* if not *de jure*, with that of the proletariat.

The fact that only one party existed in 1922 was linked to the history of the Civil War. As far as the right-wing parties were concerned, the situation had quickly been clarified as a result of the immediate, direct and active part they played in the counter-revolution. As we have seen, the K.D. Party was disbanded and its leaders either sent to prison or prosecuted and its papers banned (some of them were still published in Moscow during Summer 1918, for example *Svoboda Rossii*).

For the other parties, the situation was more complex. After the October Revolution, the Bolshevik leaders had a lively debate before rejecting the idea of a socialist 'bloc' which would have included Socialist-Revolutionaries, Bolsheviks and Mensheviks. The Socialist-Revolutionaries had split into two parties. From the very beginning of the Revolution, the right adopted a counter-revolutionary stance, whilst the left rallied to the Revolution. Thus, from December 1917 to April 1918, the left-wing Socialist-Revolutionaries took part in the Council of People's Commissars, from which they resigned in protest against the signing of the Brest-Litovsk treaty. However, they remained members of the Central Executive Committee of the Soviets until July 1918, when they took part in a military uprising against the Bolsheviks.

By 14th June 1918, the Mensheviks had been eliminated from the Central Executive Committee of the Soviets, and immediately after the July 1918 putsch it was the turn of the left-wing Socialist-Revolutionaries. However, the parties were not disbanded and papers continued to appear. In October 1918, the Mensheviks held a conference at Petrograd, during

which they recognised the historical necessity of the October
Revolution and condemned foreign intervention, whilst calling
for an end to 'economic and political terror'. A fraction of
left-wing Socialist-Revolutionaries adopted a similar attitude.
In November 1919, the V.T.S.I.K. decided to reinstate the
Mensheviks, apart from those groups which had allied themselves with the Whites or foreign interventionists, then in
February 1919 the left-wing Socialist-Revolutionaries were
reinstated subject to the same conditions. In 1920, there was
still a Menshevik Party office in Moscow, and Menshevik
meetings were held in May 1920. In 1920, there were still a
relatively large number of Mensheviks and left-wing Socialist-
Revolutionaries who were members of Soviets. Well-known
Menshevik leaders, for example Dan and Martov, even sat in
the 7th and 8th Congresses of the Soviets in 1919 and 1920.

It was only after March 1921 and the Kronstadt uprising
that the activities of the Mensheviks and left-wing Socialist-
Revolutionaries were banned. It seems that the Bolshevik
leaders hesitated at the end of 1920 and at the beginning of
1921 as to what attitude they should adopt to the Mensheviks
and Socialist-Revolutionaries.

Kronstadt was St. Petersburg's naval port. The sailors
had played a big part in the October uprising. In 1921,
elements hostile to the Bolsheviks, turning to their advantage
the desperate economic situation of the country, launched
strikes in the towns and uprisings in the countryside. Because
there was such poverty, they gained a degree of popular
support. In Kronstadt, the situation rapidly grew worse, a
'Military Revolutionary Committee' was set up and adopted
a manifesto incorporating Menshevik, Socialist-Revolutionary
and anarchist policies. The Bolsheviks decided to nip this
revolt in the bud, for it threatened to spread. After violent
battles, the Red Army under the command of Trotsky and the
young General Tukhachevsky managed to defeat the rebellion.
The attitude of the Bolsheviks in 1921–2 can largely be
explained by the fact that they were afraid of being outflanked
by popular movements which had been taken over by enemies
of the Soviet state, but which were all the more dangerous
because of the tragic poverty in Russia,

The Kronstadt uprising tipped the balance towards

repression. Thus, in 1922, the Bolshevik Party found itself in a monopoly position. As it was the only party, power was concentrated in its hands. As early as 1919, Lenin recognised this. 'Yes, the dictatorship of one party' was his reply to those who criticised it. At the 10th Congress in 1921, he specified 'the dictatorship of the proletariat would not work except through the Communist Party' (*C.W.*, Vol. 32, p. 199). The 12th Party Congress in 1923 declared that 'the dictatorship of the proletariat can only be ensured in the form of the dictatorship of its leading vanguard, that is to say of the Communist Party'. Formally speaking, there was still a distinction between the Party and the state, and as far as the institutions were concerned, there were different structures which enjoyed a certain autonomy (which varied with the time, place and people involved). But in fact the Party was the kernel of the state because all institutions were subordinate to it.

The parts played by the Soviets had gradually diminished since 1917. The requirements of the Civil War explain why discussion had given way to disciplined acceptance of decisions. Bit by bit, the Soviets became bodies for struggle and administration rather than debating clubs. In the Red Army, the re-establishment of strict discipline was witnessed; without this it could never have beaten the Whites. The all-powerful and everpresent Cheka seemed to confound both plotters and critics. On this subject we have precious testimony, that of Lenin himself. In a text written at the beginning of 1919 but published in *Pravda* in 1926, he criticised an article written by Latsis (one of the leaders of the Cheka, according to him 'one of the best Communists, an experienced Communist'). Latsis's article had appeared in *The Red Terror*, the paper published by the Cheka in Kazan. Intending to say that Red Terror is the violent crushing of any exploiters who try to re-establish their domination, he wrote instead on page 2 of the first number of his magazine: 'Don't search the records for evidence of whether his revolt against the Soviet was an armed or only a verbal one' (*C.W.*, Vol. 38, p. 389). According to Lenin, to write in such a way was to 'make nonsensical statements'. As a result of the Civil War, this tendency was often widespread. The Soviets were drained of their democratic sap. Gradually, the Socialist-Revolutionaries, first the right then the left wing, then the

Mensheviks had been totally eliminated from them. This was
the case after Kronstadt. This change in the role of the Soviets
was no doubt not equally great everywhere, but what mattered
was the overall trend.

For to bring into question the right to free speech is to
prevent democracy from functioning. It had never existed in
Russia before the Revolution, and the latter had not, despite
the experiment lasting a few months in 1917, managed to
create it, because of the attitude of the Whites, of the Russian
bourgeoisie and foreign Imperialism, which launched a
merciless civil war to defeat the Revolution.

According to the constitution of the Russian Socialist
Federal Soviet Republic, which had been approved by a vote
on the 10th July 1918 and which remained in effect until 1936,
the different levels of Soviets constituted the essential organs of
the state, a 'new kind of state' modelled on the Paris Commune.
Theoretically, supreme power was vested in the All-Russian
Congress of Soviets, and, when it was not in session, in the
hundred-man Central Executive Committee elected by the
Congress (the V.T.S.I.K.). These bodies were more or less
parliaments. The state was really run by the Council of
People's Commissars (Sovnarkom) appointed by the V.T.S.I.K.
However, the right to vote was far from universal, for numerous
categories of people were excluded: traders, middlemen,
churchmen and all those who did not live from their work
(article 65). If we consider the practical details of the electoral
system, we find that the constitution favoured the urban
proletariat at the expense of the peasantry. For the All-
Russian Congress of Soviets was made up of representatives of
town Soviets (one member per 25,000 inhabitants) and rural
Soviets (one member per 125,000). So there was inequality,
which was only made worse by the way in which voting was
organised in provincial, regional, district and local Soviets.
Besides, voting was not carried out in secret. As for basic
liberties, only the workers and poor peasants enjoyed these,
and they decided, according to the circumstances and the
individuals involved, how they could be used. Thus, freedom
of speech and the right to meet and form associations did not
really exist. The Bolsheviks did not claim that this was political
democracy.

Their critique of bourgeois democracy was not new, and besides it was completely in line with Marx's ideas on the subject. Bourgeois democracy was formal in character. Though workers were right to use bourgeois democracy, they should be under no illusions as to 'the dishonesty, falseness and hypocrisy' of which it was the expression. Lenin was not wrong to show its limitations and to fight against the Socialist parties which had accepted it. Was he not, however, led – because of the circumstances and of his own historical experience (that of Russia) – to underestimate the importance of the phenomenon of democracy? If we read a note written in 1920, 'Contribution to the History of Dictatorship' (which takes up 1905–6 texts), this seems to be the case (*C.W.*, Vol. 31, pp. 340ff.). He did not see, or did not see clearly enough the extent to which the dictatorship – that is to say 'an authority unrestricted by any laws . . .' – can constitute a danger for the workers themselves, even if it is based on mass support and represents the majority of the workers. Does it not mean that it is possible for one man (or a group of men) to exercise unlimited authority and to misuse it? In other words, the dictatorship of the proletariat in the form which emerged in Russia during the Revolution and the Civil War contained the seeds of the Stalin phenomenon. It was not inevitable, but it was a possibility, for the necessary conditions had been created as soon as the mechanisms, structures and traditions of democratic control no longer existed.

To turn the Party itself, whose actual role we have already studied, in 1922 it was in a complex situation. Its numbers had grown rapidly until 1921. There were about 24,000 Bolsheviks in February 1917, when the bourgeois democratic revolution forced Nicholas II to abdicate, and 240,000 in August 1917. By 1920, the figure was 611,978 Communists, and 730,000 in 1921. The 10th Congress (March 1921) decided there should be a purge, and by January 1922 there were only 515,000 members left. The growth in membership was the result of the recruitment of young people who had taken part in the Revolution and Civil War, and turned to the Party out of idealism, but also of careerists who joined the Party out of self-interest (because it was in power). The 1921 purge had been decided in order to eliminate the latter. The dictatorship, which was inevitable in 1921, threatened to turn against the very people who had established it unless it was transformed in a democratic way. It was at one and the same time necessary and dangerous.

In 1922, the 'Old Bolsheviks' (members in February 1917) were only 2–3 per cent of the Party's membership (2 per cent according to Zinoviev). The practical experience of the new Bolsheviks was no doubt considerable, but the same could not be said of their training in theory, which events had not promoted. In terms of quality, the Party was very young, 90 per cent of the members were less than 40 years old, more than half less than 30, and it was very male-dominated (only 7.5 per cent women). Though in early 1923 45 per cent of the members were workers, 26 per cent peasants and 29 per cent office workers and intellectuals, the distribution in local or work-place organisations, or 'cells', reflected the social changes we have already dealt with. Only 18 per cent of the members belonged to factory cells, 30 per cent to peasant cells, 24 per cent to military cells and 19 per cent to office cells. In a letter to Molotov dated 26th March 1922, Lenin noted this: 'Judged by the bulk of its present membership our Party is not proletarian enough' (*C.W.*, Vol. 33, p. 256), and he drew the following conclusion: 'If we do not close our eyes to reality, we must admit that at the present time the proletarian policy of the Party is not determined by the character of its membership, but by the enormous, individual prestige enjoyed by the small group which might be called the Old Guard of the Party' (*C.W.*, Vol. 33, p. 257). Up until the Revolution, the Bolshevik Party had existed underground, even if it had sometimes managed to use what legal possibilities there were after the 1905 Revolution. Most of its militants had known imprisonment, deportation to Siberia and exile, and these conditions had scarcely prepared the Party for democratic life. Next came the Revolution and the Civil War, which were no more favourable from that point of view. Democracy blossoms in times of peace and withers in troubled times.

There was no lack of impassioned debate within the leading bodies (for example when the October Revolution was being prepared and immediately after it, when the Brest-Litovsk Treaty was signed and just after the end of the Civil

War, about the N.E.P. and the role of the trade unions), but
the actual decision-making was restricted to a certain number
of leaders. During the war, because of the requirements of the
time and the need for efficiency, discipline and military
authority naturally replaced public debate. One of the reasons
for the Bolsheviks' successes was their ability to centralise, to
take decisions and to carry them out. They modelled themselves
on the Jacobins in 1793. The decisions taken at the 10th and
11th Congresses of the Russian C.P., as well as at the 11th
Party Conference, confirmed this orientation. For example, in
order to be elected to the Central Committee it was necessary
to have been a member of the Party before the February
Revolution. Thus, leading positions were open to only 2 per
cent of the Party membership, that is to say about 10,000
people. Equally, to be elected secretary of a cell you had to
have taken part in the Civil War, and candidates for regional
secretaryships had to have joined the Party before the October
Revolution. The text of the resolution adopted at the December
1922 11th National Conference of the Russian Communist
Party and ratified by the 11th Congress is very precise.[15] 'It is
important that Party organisations pay very special attention
to Provincial and District Secretaryships, and that comrades
who were members of the Party before the October 1917
Revolution should be chosen as Secretaries of Provincial
Committees, and comrades who have been in the Party for at
least three years as Secretaries of District Committees. It is the
wish of Conference that the election of Provincial or District
Secretaries should require ratification by the Party's highest
authorities.'

Likewise, trade union elections were to take place under
Party supervision. 'Conference thinks it necessary that the
Presidents and Secretaries of Trade Union Central Committees
chosen by Communist factions should have been Party
members before the October Revolution and the Secretaries of
Provincial Trade Union Committees should have been Party
members for at least three years.'

It is true that real debate did go on in the leading bodies,
but the 10th Congress had been induced to abolish factions, a
decision to be explained by the very real danger of a split in the
Party. To counterbalance this measure, the Congress decided

to publish a discussion sheet specifically intended to stimulate debate within the Party, without however reconstituting factions, which would have been or already were parties within the Party. Democratic centralism implies both centralism and democracy. An excess of democracy would have undermined the Party and led to its defeat. An excess of centralism was in danger of killing democracy and leading to the Stalin phenomenon.

Such was the historical environment in which socialism developed in the Soviet Union.[16] In November 1922, Lenin asked himself the following dramatic question: 'We have been alone for five years; there is as yet no revolution in any other countries; war and hunger; shall we perish?' (*C.W.*, Vol. 36, p. 585). The Socialist Revolution had been defeated in every country in Europe for a variety of reasons; in one case because the bourgeoisie had preserved sufficient strength (in Germany), in another because foreign intervention had made it possible to destroy the revolution (in Hungary). History does not proceed mathematically. People and circumstances play an essential role. In some ways, the Revolution had a better chance of prevailing in Germany because of the well-developed productive forces, the large working class and the cultural progress of the masses. The Bolsheviks could have suffered military defeat at the hands of Denikin or Kolchak, and the Spartakists could have won in 1919. So there is no such thing as historical inevitability – yet it is only too convenient to write history as if events had necessarily to take place as they in fact did. A given historical situation can give rise to several alternative developments, and it is here that the interaction of circumstances and the role of individuals, of the masses and of personalities assume their full importance. In 1922, the Soviet Union existed and had to move forward, it had emerged drained of its life blood from so many ordeals onto a new path, that of Socialism. It had to be built under the most difficult conditions possible, with a people in rags and without education, exhausted by eight years of war and surrounded by hostile states.

The Stalin phenomenon can only be explained and understood if we start from this historical context.

NOTES

1. Lenin made a vigorous attack on this utopian policy in 1921 (*Collected Works*, Vol. 33, p. 69).
2. This is the name given to the new Soviet policy just after the Civil War. Its basis was an end to requisitions and free trade within the country.
3. Lenin (*C.W.*, Vol. 32, p. 295): 'the middle peasants have become the predominant element in the rural areas'.
4. Lenin, *The State and Revolution* (*C.W.*, Vol. 25, p. 491): 'Revolution consists in the proletariat destroying the "administrative apparatus" and the whole state machine, replacing it by a new one, made up of the armed workers.'
5. R.S.F.S.R. – the Russian Socialist Federal Soviet Republic.
6. For example, the last articles published in *Pravda* in 1923: 'Pages from a Diary', 'On Co-operation', 'Our Revolution', 'How we should Reorganise the Workers' and Peasants' Inspection', 'Better Fewer but Better' (*C.W.*, Vol. 33).
7. *L'Edification Culturelle en U.R.S.S.* – Moscow, 1958.
8. *De la Santie Russie à l'U.R.S.S.*
9. For example, Engels on *The Role of Force in History*.
10. Let it be quite clear that our critique of Solzhenitsyn's ideas does not concern his talents as a writer and does not justify repressive measures. Ideas should only be fought with ideas.
11. *The Gulag Archipelago* Vol. 1, p. 27; Lenin, *C.W.*, Vol. 26, p. 404.
12. E. H. Carr, *The Bolshevik Revolution*, Vol. 1, p. 159.
13. They were former Czech and Slovak prisoners who had fought in the Austrian ranks; they were freed at the time of the Revolution, and 30,000 took up arms against the Soviets.
14. This is not the place to tell the story of foreign intervention, but it is worth remembering the very real role played by British and French spies in the preparation of the July putsch and the August outrages. (See Bruce-Lockhart's *Memoirs of a British Agent*.) The activities of Sidney Reilly and those of the French General L. de Lavergne are mentioned in numerous works and by many witnesses.
15. As in the *Stenographic Report* of the 11th Congress, from p. 554 on.
16. The Union of Soviet Socialist Republics was founded on 30th December 1922, when the R.S.F.S.R. (Russia), and the Ukrainian, Byelorussian and Transcaucasian Soviet Socialist Republics merged.

2 The Birth of the Stalin Phenomenon

The Bolsheviks, who had power firmly in their hands at the end of the Civil War, faced formidable problems. First of all they had to carry through national reconstruction without foreign aid. This was the aim of the N.E.P. The latter was both a necessity because of the circumstances, and a long-term policy meant to create the socialist economy which did not exist in 1922. Lenin had admitted they had made a mistake in 1918 by attempting to proceed directly to communist production and distribution (*C.W.*, Vol. 33, p. 62). In these circumstances, the N.E.P. meant that in the country requisitioning was replaced by taxation, and to a large extent implied 'transition to the reestablishment of capitalism' (*C.W.*, Vol. 33, p. 66). Free internal trade was restored. Small-scale industry (up to 21 workers) was reborn. Inheritance was re-established to some extent (up to 10,000 gold-roubles). The N.E.P. was a transitional economy, and under the aegis of the socialist state different modes of production, notably state capitalism, co-existed. The Soviet leaders went as far as deciding in principle to grant concessions to foreign capitalists (these would have been valid for 30 years). This policy involved a grave danger, namely that capitalism might defeat socialism in the economy and in society, but the socialist state kept control of transport and large-scale industry, and maintained its monopoly of foreign trade and credit.

Starting from the realisation that the middle peasant predominated in the rural economy, thus in the whole Soviet economy, the Soviet leaders decided to base their policy on giving the peasantry material incentives to develop production. According to Lenin, it would take decades, 'generations', to build a real socialist economy. The N.E.P. encouraged a certain rebirth of capitalism. In the country it strengthened the rich peasants, the kulaks. It enriched minor industrialists, tradespeople and middlemen, those who were known as the

'Nepmen'. At the same time it encouraged the development of the forces of production. Agricultural output increased and industry made progress, though to a lesser extent. The population grew at the same rate as before the war. To sum up, the N.E.P. was a policy for economic reconstruction which bore fruit and made a very necessary economic revival possible.

At the same time relations with foreign powers improved a little. The U.S.S.R. signed trade agreements with many capitalist states which followed the example of Great Britain (which signed a trade agreement with the U.S.S.R. on 16th March 1922). It was recognised by many powers (by France in 1924, but not until 1932 by the United States). It took part again in international conferences after the one held in Genoa in 1922, exploited the contradictions between the capitalist states (signing of the Rapallo Treaty with Germany in 1922), supported and helped anti-imperialist movements (for example, Mustapha Kemal's Turkey). In short, as Trotsky said, this was the start of a 'long period of peaceful coexistence and serious co-operation with the bourgeois countries'.

Nevertheless, the latter continued to set up a *cordon sanitaire* around the U.S.S.R., that is to say a circle of anti-Communist states intended to prevent the 'rotten odour of Bolshevism' from spreading through Europe (Poland, Hungary, Romania, Bulgaria). They continued to refuse real economic aid and to prepare for the overthrow of the new regime. From this point of view the policy of granting concessions tells us a lot. Very few capitalist firms tried their luck, and what we in fact observe is a real boycott of the Soviet market. Autarky was imposed on the Soviet Union by this boycott.

Though economic policy was fundamentally changed from 1921 on, the same could not be said of the exercise of dictatorship by the Bolsheviks which tended to be strengthened, precisely because of the greater liberalism in the economic field and the dangers which it entailed. From this point of view, the importance of the Kronstadt events cannot be overestimated. The strengthening of Party discipline which followed the 10th and 11th Congresses saw the disappearance of the so-called 'Workers' Opposition' faction led by Shliapnikov and Alexandra Kollontai which had been forcefully condemned by all the Bolshevik leaders. For example, it was Trotsky who

made the speech for the prosecution at the 11th Congress and
before the Communist International. Again it was Trotsky who,
on 16th May 1922, wrote in defence of the single party and
repressive measures in *Pravda*. 'These repressive measures do
not achieve their aim when an anachronistic government and
regime direct them against new and progressive historical
forces. But, in the hands of a historically progressive government, they can be very effective means of sweeping from the
arena outdated forces which have outlived their time.' As
Lenin noted at about the same time, 'power has been won and
consolidated in the hands of a single party, the party of the
proletariat which does not even have unreliable fellow
travellers at its side'.

The Bolshevik Party found itself exercising power alone
and became the only party. The absence of even dubious allies
made its task both easier and more difficult; easier as far as its
immediate effectiveness was concerned, more difficult as to the
development of democracy in the future. Thus there was a
contradiction between the military victory of the Red Army
and the problems the regime had with the masses. On the one
hand, the N.E.P. was to win the support of the peasantry. On
the other, dictatorship and repression was to do the rest. There
was no other alternative, apart from giving up power. That was
obviously out of the question and no one proposed it. Under
such conditions, one can understand to what extent any
conflict within the 'thin leading stratum' threatened to
endanger the Soviet regime.

Too often, people think that in 1922 the Soviet regime was
strong because it had triumphed on the battlefield. In fact, it
was never weaker than at precisely this moment when it
appeared strong. Lenin's illness, his withdrawal from political
activity, then his death were to make the situation even more
alarming.[1] It is not good enough to attempt to explain the
Stalin phenomenon by the premature death of Lenin. One all
too often reads, 'Oh, if only Lenin had not died!' But it is true
to say that Lenin's death at the age of 54 is not without
significance among the conditions which gave rise to the
Stalin phenomenon. Lenin's role in the events of the
Revolution and the Civil War was considerable. He did not
create events out of the blue, but forced destiny by his clear-

sightedness, his realism and his obstinacy. It is important to avoid the common mistake of idealising him. Once stripped of the mystical halo with which he is surrounded he is all the greater. He was a man of relentless energy, a statesman who allowed nothing to get in his way when the fate of the Revolution was in the balance. Until then, all revolutions had been defeated because they had not been carried through to their conclusion. Lenin had understood that 'one should not spare dictatorial methods in order to speed up the implantation of Western ways in old, barbaric Russia, nor flinch at using barbaric methods to fight barbarism'. We often make the mistake of judging this period, this country and this revolution on the basis of our own historical experience and our own criteria. Nothing could be more incorrect. Even the French Revolution of 1789 would not be sufficient to give a parallel of these events. Moreover, despite local and colonial wars, and despite the Cold War, since 1945 the world has been mostly at peace and France, for example, has known internal peace despite some moments of serious tension. This was not the case in Russia in 1917. War was raging, involving tens of millions of men in unprecedented suffering. To poverty was added destruction caused by the war, a pitiless, total war which affected the civilian population.

However, Lenin clearly directed his rigour against the bourgeoisie, limiting it to particular cases and individuals, and not against the people. When the October Revolution was being prepared, and just before the Brest–Litovsk treaty was signed he had been in the minority in his own party, and this was to be the case on several other occasions, for example in 1921 when the debate on the trade unions started. He enjoyed polemics and did not hesitate to express brutally frank opinions of others, but in debate he never replaced the confrontation of ideas with repression, and he never held a grudge for very long against those who criticised him.

Despite his violent arguments with Trotsky from 1902 to 1914, he managed to work with him daily from 1917 to 1923 because he was aware of his great qualities and thought it preferable to harness them to the Revolution. He fought against Kamenev and Zinoviev who had opposed the October Revolution, but he went on working with them in the Party

leadership. He was violently critical of Bukharin for having
become a 'left-wing Communist' when the Brest–Litovsk
treaty was signed, but he continued to respect him and went
on working with him. He had great authority among the
Bolsheviks, whom he had led to victory, among a large proportion
of the people, with the workers and small peasants who saw in
him a man who was true to his ideas and fought for their
interests. During his last year in inactivity, he perceived with
sharp realism the dangers which threatened the Soviet regime.
Some emanated from its enemies who, thanks to the N.E.P.,
could hope for a peaceful restoration of capitalism, others
were the result of Bolshevik policy itself, in conjunction with
the situation which existed at that time. This is why it is useful
to follow Lenin's own thoughts on the problem, for his writings
of 1921–2 enlighten us as to the origins, birth and development
of the Stalin phenomenon. His concern sprang in the first
place from the dimensions assumed by the bureaucracy, which
was a resurgence of Tsarism, encouraged by the conditions
under which power was exercised. Lenin was under no illusion
about the difficulties involved in building socialism. It would
be a long and difficult undertaking. The state machine had
been overrun by former Tsarist civil servants, and there was a
tendency for practices current in the Tsarist state to reappear.
for example bribery, and red-tape resulting in a total lack of
efficiency. This situation was the result of cultural backwardness and the fact that, despite the purge carried out after the
10th Congress, the Party was ideologically and politically
weak. This was not just a matter of education. Of course it was
important to reduce illiteracy, but it was necessary to go much
further, to achieve what Lenin called a 'cultural revolution',
that is to say the transformation of mental habits and behaviour,
the most difficult task of all, much more difficult and much
slower than political success or military victory. 'Barbarism',
as manifested in customs or in mentality, had to be destroyed.

 This idea of 'Russian barbarism' recurs like a 'leitmotif' in
everything Lenin wrote towards the end of his life, even when
he was analysing revolutionary processes outside Russia. The
great, highly developed capitalist countries of the West could
proceed to socialism in a civilised manner, he declared on

several occasions, but Russia was different. It was easier for the proletariat to take power there, but harder to build socialism; history was to provide a tragic illustration of the truth of this statement.[2]

In an article entitled 'On Co-operation', Lenin gave a forceful demonstration[3] of the need to involve the population in the 'co-operative system'. He says the peasant still trades 'in an Asiatic manner' (*C.W.*, Vol. 33, p. 470), 'but to be a good trader one must trade in the European manner. They are a whole epoch behind in that.' According to Lenin, since 1917 the 'emphasis' had shifted to educational work. This implied that they should 'reorganise our machinery of state, which is utterly useless' and start 'educational work among the peasantry'. He even specifies that 'the organisation of the entire peasantry in co-operative societies presupposes ... a cultural revolution'. Lenin's reply to the opponents of the Revolution who claimed 'that we were rash in undertaking to implant socialism in an insufficiently cultured country' was that 'the political and social revolution preceded the cultural revolution which nevertheless now confronts us', but 'it presents immense difficulties of a purely cultural (for we are illiterate) and material character (for to be cultured we must achieve a certain development of the material means of production, must have a certain material base)' (*C.W.*, Vol. 33, p. 475). This is Lenin's real 'testament': learn from the West, use state capitalism, develop co-operation, combat bureaucracy, in order to do that carry out a real cultural revolution, encourage production, all of this on the basis of a socialist state and with patience, 'for this will take ten ... twenty years'; even so did he not underestimate the magnitude of the international problems? This is a far cry from the Maoist theses on the 'cultural revolution' which tend to reject Western models of culture, consumption and organisation and finally introduce the idea of moral reform. That is not to say that in Lenin's eyes the latter was unnecessary, but it was one element in the process of change in human behaviour which socialism makes possible.

Lenin was aware of the fact that 'the past ... although it has been overthrown, has not yet been overcome' (*C.W.*, 'Better Fewer but Better', Vol. 33, p. 478), and he noted: 'In

all spheres of social, economic and political relationships we
are "frightfully" revolutionary. But as regards precedence, the
observance of the forms and rites of office management, our
"revolutionariness" often gives way to the mustiest routine.
On more than one occasion, we have witnessed the very interesting phenomenon of a great leap forward in social life being
accompanied by amazing timidity when the slightest changes
are proposed' (*C.W.*, Vol. 33, p. 497).

What Lenin no doubt did not see clearly enough, since he
lacked sufficient historical experience, was the connection to
be made between the extent of the bureaucratic phenomenon
and the Soviet political system as it operated in 1922 with the
single Party, the role of the Cheka (later of the G.P.U.) and
the Red Army, the declining part played by the Soviets and
the inadequate development of democratic life at all levels
within Party and State. In 1922 these different factors existed
independently of each other. Sometimes they came together,
but they did not coincide. The Stalinist phenomenon was to
emerge as a result of their coming together.

Lenin was also worried by the danger of a split within the
'narrow leading stratum' of Party and State. It is at this
moment that Stalin comes on the scene; we have not mentioned
him before because the important yet secondary role he
played until 1922 did not require mention.

Joseph Vissarionovich Djugashvili, who was born in 1879
of Georgian origin, came from a poor family (his parents had
remained serfs until 1861.) After attending a school run by the
Orthodox Church, he entered the Tbilisi (Tiflis in Persian)
orthodox seminary at the age of fifteen. It was a centre of anti-
Russian Georgian nationalist and liberal ferment. Young
Djugashvili published poetry in the nationalist magazine *Iberya*
under the pen-name Soselo. He read lots of French, English
and Russian novels, and books on economics, sociology and
politics. At the age of 19 he joined a clandestine moderate
socialist group, the 'Messame Dassy' (the 3rd group). As a
result of his activities in the seminary he was expelled, on the
pretext that he did not attend examinations. A report by the
principal of the seminary refers to 29th September 898: 'At
nine o'clock in the morning, a group of students was gathered
in the dining room around Joseph Djugashvili who was

reading to them from books forbidden by the seminary authorities', and a few weeks later another report says: 'Djugashvili is generally disrespectful and rude to those in authority.' He found himself unemployed, gave private lessons and for a few months held a lowly post at the Tbilisi observatory. In 1901, he had to go underground as a result of his political activity. From then on, his life merged with that of the Russian Social-democratic Labour Party. As early as 1901, when he was the editor of an underground paper *Brdzola* ('Struggle'), he supported the ideas which Lenin spelt out in *Iskra*. Between 1901 and 1917, he was to undergo several periods of imprisonment and deportation to Siberia. As a professional revolutionary, he proved himself to be both dedicated and competent as a journalist, propagandist and Bolshevik organiser. Many lies have been written about his political activity: it has even been suggested that he was an agent of the Okhrana (the Tsarist political police).[4] In the present state of our knowledge such an accusation is quite groundless. In fact, he was an experienced militant who for many years played an important role in the Caucasus, in Georgia and in Azerbaijan (at Baku). He played an active part in the 1905 Revolution and subsequently led the Bolshevik Combat Brigades which organised 'expropriations', that is to say armed bank raids intended to provide money for the Bolsheviks' fighting fund.

He began to emerge from the Caucasus, taking part in the 1905 National Conference of the Party at Tammerfors in Finland, then in the Stockholm Congress in 1906 and in the London one in 1907. In 1912, he was co-opted to the Central Committee of the Bolshevik Party[5] and given the job of organising the Party in Russia and publishing a legal paper, *Pravda*.

In the same year, Lenin asked him to join him in Cracow (a Polish town then under Austrian occupation) to work on the problem of the nationalities, and then sent him to represent the Party in Vienna. Altogether, he spent six months abroad. So Stalin's experience just before the Revolution was rich in all sorts of tasks, that much can be ascertained. No doubt he did not live abroad as long as Lenin, Trotsky, Bukharin, Zinoviev and Kamenev, but he did travel in Europe. Lenin's regard for

him is expressed in a letter to Gorky in which he mentions 'the
marvellous Georgian' who was preparing a book which was
published as 'The National Question and Social-Democracy'.
He was arrested a few weeks after his return to Russia and was
deported to Northern Siberia; he had been denounced by
Malinovsky, an Okhrana agent who had infiltrated the
Bolshevik Party and become a member of the Central
Committee. He stayed there until Tsarism was overthrown in
1917. In fact we do not know a great deal about Djugashvili's
real life during this whole period. He was modest and
determined, and as a result of his dedication and efficiency he
had reached the top of the Party hierarchy, but his very
self-effacement meant that he did not make much of an
impression on those who worked with him. The only thing that
deserves pointing out is the rather flamboyant quality of the
pseudonyms he chose. Apart from names in common usage, for
example Ivanovich, for many years he also felt impelled to take
as a pseudonym the name Koba (the Indomitable) who was a
legendary hero of mediaeval Georgia, and in 1913 the name
Stalin (Steel) under which he was to enter history on a par
with Alexander, Julius Caesar and Napoleon. The choice of
such pseudonyms speaks volumes about the secret thoughts of
this taciturn man who sometimes worried his fellow deportees.
'He's a nice chap, but in daily life his behaviour is slightly
individualistic', Sverdlov, the future president of the Central
Executive Committee of the Soviets, wrote in March 1914 from
Kureika where he had been deported with Stalin. In May 1914
he added: 'Nevertheless, a man is exposed and his weak points
are revealed, this is the saddest aspect of the conditions of exile
and imprisonment. At the moment my comrade and I live in
separate apartments and we rarely see each other.'[6] Stalin
had married Catherine Svanidze when still very young, and
had been a widower since 1905; his little boy was brought up
by his grandparents. His personal life seems to have been very
empty. He had no friends and no wife. He remained alone
during the long years as a deportee in Northern Siberia. He
spent his time reading; one would like to know what books he
read, but there is a total lack of information on this subject. All
we know is that he tried unsuccessfully to learn Esperanto, and
the only languages he knew were Georgian and Russian.

Compared to the other leaders of the Revolution, he does not seem to have been very highly cultivated. His tastes were simple. He was not particularly keen on food, but he liked vodka. Neither money nor women really interested him. The only things he cared passionately about were the Revolution and power. The former was to bring him the latter. However, his life manifested characteristics which were to prove crucial in the future. Unlike the other leaders of the Revolution, he came from a humble background and knew the people and its way of reacting. His roots were deep in the very recent past when serfdom still existed. As the French historian A. Leroy-Beaulieu stressed: 'For the mass of the people the Middle Ages still exist', and Djugashvili knew that, not just in theory but concretely in the socio-cultural milieu in which he had grown up. Having been a theology student until the age of nineteen, he had retained from his seminary days a secular version of the Orthodox traditon, stripped of its mystical and religious attributes, and this too brought him close to the people. His style, which was similar to that of the Orthodox liturgy, was to be simple, accessible to the most backward of moujiks.

When he was called before a draft board in late 1916, he was exempted from military service because of a slight weakness in his left arm. When Tsarism fell, life was to change for Stalin. He was thirty-eight. The ordeal of life in Siberia had made him even thinner than before. He was lean and fairly short (1·67 m.), his face was pitted with smallpox scars, and his appearance not very prepossessing.

But in 1917 the Revolution was on the march, Tsarism was overthrown. Stalin was released and returned from Siberia to Petrograd with trainloads of deportees who were enthusiastically applauded all the way. On 27th March he arrived in Petrograd, at the same time as Kamenev but long before all the historically recognised leaders of the Revolution. He played an important part, but did not occupy the leading position in the story of this period, in contrast to what was later asserted by a number of hagiographers who were to represent him as Lenin's best and closest disciple. As soon as he got back, he and Kamenev took over *Pravda*, and he took a centralist line in the debate on the future of the Revolution, going as far as to accept the opening of negotiations on socialist unity with the Mensheviks, and proposing a policy of critical neutrality towards the Provisional Government. It was this 'conciliatory' attitude which Lenin was to denounce as soon as he arrived in Petrograd on 16th April. Stalin retreated and from then on he was a consistent supporter of Lenin. In May, he was elected to the nine-man Central Committee which ran the Party. In July and August 1917 he found himself at the head of the Party leadership, because many of the leaders had been arrested and Lenin had gone underground. When Lenin proposed to the Central Committee that an uprising be prepared, Stalin, together with Sverdlov and Trotsky, was one of his firmest supporters, whilst Zinoviev and Kamenev opposed the idea. On 2nd November (20 October) he was elected to the Politbureau, the establishment of which Dzerzhinsky (the future head of the Cheka) proposed, together with Lenin, Zinoviev, Kamenev, Trotsky, Sokolnikov and Bubnov.[7] He belonged to the Revolutionary Military Committee of the Petrograd Soviet, but played a subordinate role compared to Trotsky. He was to recognise the decisive role played by Trotsky in an article published in *Pravda* on the occasion of the first anniversary of October 1917. 'All the practical work concerning the organisation of the uprising was carried out under the leadership of Comrade Trotsky, the President of the Saint Petersburg Soviet. It can be stated without doubt that the Party is indebted mainly to Comrade Trotsky for the rapidity with which the garrison sided with the Soviet and for the efficient way in which the work of the Revolutionary Military Committee was organised.'

After the Revolution, he became People's Commissar for Nationalities, an important post, but not one of the most important. However, because of his support of Lenin in the difficult debate which followed the uprising, he was elected to the four-man Executive which had the task of leading the Party (with Lenin, Sverdlov and Trotsky), as well as to the restricted Council of People's Commissars (with Lenin and Trotsky). In the whole period from November 1917 to the end of the Civil War Stalin's role was considerable, though discreet. In photographs taken at the time – of meetings of the Central Committee or of the Council of People's Commissars – he is so self-effacing that he is hardly recognisable as a slim figure with a huge moustache, sitting modestly in the shadow of the better-known leaders.

It is not our purpose to write a biography of Stalin, nor to discuss his and Trotsky's relative merits during the Civil War. So we shall be content to recall that Stalin's role was important (and probably greater than appears at first sight).[8] But he suffered from the fame of Trotsky who, as People's Commissar for War since 1918, was responsible for victory and gained the resultant glory. In the eyes of the public Trotsky appeared to be the Number Two in the regime. On official photographs, Lenin and Trotsky were to be seen on an equal footing, below Kalinin, the President of the Executive Committee of the Soviets. Throughout this period, Stalin was learning how to control people. He acted cunningly when necessary, for example leaving meetings of the Commissions of the Commissariat for Nationalities when asked to give a delicate opinion, but did not hesitate to make massive use of terror when it was necessary and possible, as for example at Tsaritsyn (the future Stalingrad).

His reply to Lenin, who was worried about the danger of a left-wing Socialist-Revolutionary uprising in Tsaritsyn, is a model of its kind: 'As for the hysterics, rest assured that our hand will not tremble: our enemies will be treated as enemies.' At the same time, he was capable of retreating when the situation was not in his favour, for example when he faced Trotsky in the debate on the conduct of military operations. He was a master tactician, rather than a strategist, who was asserting himself in the field. In March 1919, he was elected as a full member of the reconstituted Politbureau (with Lenin, Trotsky, Kemenev and Krestinsky, whilst Zinoviev and Bukharin were candidate members). Although he was not well known outside the leading circles of the Party, his power grew greater and greater. As a member of the Politbureau and People's Commissar for Nationalities as well as for the Workers' and Peasants' Inspection from 1921 on (the *Rabkrin*), Stalin had in his hands authority which reached into every corridor of power.

In so far as he revealed his ideas by expressing them in public, they do not appear to have differed from those of the majority of the Bolshevik leaders. Perhaps he was less susceptible to Western influence. As a Caucasian in charge of the problem of nationalities, he looked eastwards. Two articles which he published after the October Revolution bore the following significant titles: 'Do not forget the East' and '*Ex Oriente Lux*' (Light from the East). During the debate on signing the Brest–Litovsk treaty, he was put in his place in no uncertain terms by Lenin (whom he generally supported) for doubting the revolutionary potential of the proletariat in the developed Western capitalist countries. However, this did not really make any clear distinction between him and the other Bolshevik leaders.

So what is the source of the concern expressed by Lenin in his notes of the 23rd and 25th December 1922 and of 4th January 1923, and in a series of texts written in late 1922 and early 1923? In our view there are two causes, which are linked. On the one hand, Lenin was afraid that the conflict between Trotsky and Stalin might lead to a split in the Party, civil war and the demise of the Revolution ('I think relations between them make up the greater part of the danger of a split', *C.W.*, Vol. 36, p. 594). And this seemed all the more dangerous to him because of the existence in the Party of elements favourable to the creation of several parties. On the other hand, he was worried about Stalin's growing power and the way in which he was using it. On 3rd April 1922, at a meeting of the Party's Central Committee at the end of the 11th Congress, Stalin was proposed by Kamenev and elected General Secretary of the Party. The post had existed since 1918; Sverdlov had been the first incumbent until his death in March 1919, followed by Krestinsky and, in 1921, by Molotov. Originally, the post was administrative rather than political, but with the accumulation of tasks by the Party and the growth in the role it played, the job of General Secretary became very important, first of all because he was in charge of the cadres and all the activity of the Party machine, a machine which became weightier and weightier. Stalin was also a member of the Orgbureau (the committee responsible for allocating staff). When Lenin fell ill, the General Secretary's role became even greater. He was the only one of the Party's leaders to be a member of the Politbureau, the Orgbureau, the Secretariat and head of two People's Commissariats. Thus Lenin's remark

'Comrade Stalin has unlimited power concentrated in his hands' (*C.W.*, Vol. 36, p. 594) becomes more comprehensible. Lenin was noting an actual position which seemed disturbing to him. 'I am not sure whether he will always be capable of using that authority with sufficient caution' (*C.W.*, Vol. 36, pp. 594–5). On what facts did he base this statement which became a certainty a few days later: 'Stalin is too rude' (4th January 1923)? – and which led him to propose 'to think about a way of removing Stalin from that post'? – apparently a difficult task. He was concerned about the day-to-day work of Stalin, who was in charge of two People's Commissariats, those for Nationalities and Workers' and Peasants' Inspection.

As far as the question of the nationalities was concerned, Lenin had first of all criticised Stalin for his overall plan, which had led him to put forward a constitution under which the non-Russian Soviet Republics would have become a part of the Russian Socialist Federal Soviet Republic (the R.S.F.S.R.). In the end, Lenin intervened and this enabled the U.S.S.R. to be founded at the end of 1922. Then Lenin was violently critical of the attitude adopted by the Bolshevik leaders in Georgia: Dzerzhinsky (the leader of the Cheka), Orjonikidze and Stalin were concerned. Not without reason, Lenin criticised them for behaving in a brutal, nationalistic manner. The Bolshevik leaders in Georgia were abused and even manhandled by the Central Committee delegates for opposing the establishment of a Transcaucasian Soviet Socialist Republic and calling for the continued existence of the Georgian S.S.R. Lenin thundered against 'the onslaught of that really Russian man, the Great-Russian chauvinist, in substance a rascal and a tyrant, such as the typical Russian bureaucrat is', and he added: 'I think that Stalin's haste, his infatuation with pure administration, together with his spite against the notorious "nationalist-socialism" played a fatal role here' (*C.W.*, Vol. 36, p. 606). He characterised Stalin's policy as basically 'Great-Russian chauvinist.' It is true that Stalin was Georgian in origin, but, as Lenin pointed out, 'people . . . who have become Russified overdo this Russian frame of mind'. Stalin became more Russian than the Russians because centralisation was a political necessity, just as Napoleon, a Corsican, had 'overdone the French frame of mind' when

developing centralisation at the end of the French Revolution.[9]
Lenin's choice of words is so blunt that it is worth recalling.
'The Georgian, who is neglectful of this aspect of the question,
or who carelessly flings about accusations of "nationalist-
socialism" (whereas he himself is a real and true "nationalist-
socialist", and even a vulgar Great-Russian bully), violates, in
substance, the interests of proletarian class solidarity . . .'
(*C.W.*, Vol. 36, p. 608). Lenin saw the real danger that Stalin's
activity constituted and the real character of this danger, hence
his warning.

Lenin was no gentler as far as the problems of the Workers'
and Peasants' Inspection were concerned. In an article written
on 23rd January 1923 (and published in *Pravda* on 26th
January), he described the Soviet state machine as 'a survival
from the past . . . a most typical relic of our former state
machine' (*C.W.*, Vol. 33, p. 481), and as an example of this
decrepitude of the state machine he took the Workers' and
Peasants' Inspection, of which Stalin had been in charge
since 1921:

'Let us say frankly that the People's Commissariat of the
Workers' and Peasants' Inspection does not at present enjoy
the slightest authority. Everybody knows that no other institutions are worse organised than those of out Workers' and
Peasants' Inspection, and that under present conditions nothing
can be expected from this People's Commissariat' (*C.W.*,
Vol. 33, p. 490). 'We have bureaucrats in our Party institutions
as well as in the Soviet institutions' (*C.W.*, Vol. 33, p. 495).

At the same time, he suggested that the activities of the
Central Committee, the Politbureau and the Secretariat should
be reformed. These criticisms were even more violent in the
article 'Better Fewer but Better' which was written a few days
later. In short, Lenin's criticism of Stalin was radical. He has
'unlimited power', 'he is rude', 'his haste plays a fatal role',
'his policy is Great-Russian chauvinist', 'he has stepped into
the shoes of the former (Tsarist) state machine: he is a
bureaucrat'.

Incidents of a personal nature involving Lenin's wife,
Krupskaya, and Stalin made the situation even worse. The
problem was not on the level of personal relations between
leaders. Contrary to what is often said, these faults were neither

circumstantial nor minor. They were long-term, serious and had more than just personal implications. So Lenin effected a reconciliation with Trotsky. After forcefully opposing Trotsky's theses on the militarisation of labour and the integration of the trade unions as part of the State (at the 10th Congress),[10] he began to agree with him on many points, though he still criticised his refusal to accept the Vice-presidency of the Council. Repeatedly, he publicly praised him, something he rarely did. In *Pravda* on 8th March 1922, he declared, in reference to the Genoa Conference, that 'From the point of view of practical tasks, and not that of a game of diplomatic leapfrog, therefore, Comrade Trotsky has defined the position more correctly than anybody else' (*C.W.*, Vol. 33, p. 217). On 12th March 1922, he began an article published in the magazine *Under the Banner of Marxism* as follows: 'Comrade Trotsky has already said everything necessary, and said it very well, about the general purposes of *Pod Znamenem Marksizma* in issue No. 1–2 of that journal' (*C.W.*, Vol. 33, p. 227). At the 3rd and 4th Congresses of the Communist International, Lenin and Trotsky struggled together against leftist elements for the development of the united front. On 13th December 1922, Lenin asked Trotsky to defend 'our common position on the monopoly of foreign trade'.[11] After he had criticised Trotsky's proposal to give legislative powers to the Gosplan (the planning commission) on 27th December 1922, he admitted that 'in this respect I think we can and must accede to the wishes of Comrade Trotsky' (*C.W.*, Vol. 36, p. 599). In his remarks about the leadership, he declared about Trotsky: 'He is personally perhaps the most capable man in the present Central Committee',[12] at the same time criticising 'his excessive self-assurance and excessive preoccupation with the administrative side of the work' (*C.W.*, Vol. 36, p. 595); and on 5th March 1923 he asked Trotsky to take on the responsibility for defending the Georgian affair before the Party Central Committee. 'This case is now under "persecution" by Stalin and Dzerzhinsky, and I cannot rely on their impartiality. Quite to the contrary. I would feel at ease if you agreed to undertake its defence' (*C.W.*, Vol. 45, p. 607).

We are quoting these important texts because it seems indispensable for us to know them if we are to understand how the 'Stalin phenomenon' came into existence, and not to glorify Trotsky or to depreciate Stalin. What matters is the nature of the problems raised by Lenin, not the individuals involved. Besides, in 1921 Trotsky proposed a militaristic and bureaucratic policy which, to say the very least, would have made no contribution to correcting the faults in the Soviet machine. Lenin realised they were dangerous, without necessarily seeing all their possible consequences.

'Bureaucratic distortion' and great-Russian nationalist policies could only be combated by a widening of democracy, for which there was no basis in the Russia of 1923, all the more so because it threatened Soviet power itself, as the Kronstadt events suggested. From this point of view, we must not forget that in 1923 the Soviet Union was a country where neither freedom of speech, nor the freedom to hold meetings and belong to associations nor free elections existed, where power was in the hands of a single Party and, within that Party in the hands of a small group of men (a few thousand at most), and where the political police remained all-powerful, where neither democratic traditions nor institutions existed, because of the very conditions under which the Revolution triumphed. Already we have established that a certain number of the characteristics of the Soviet form of socialism come from the historical circumstances and not from socialism itself.

The Smolensk Archives illustrate this fact. When they were found at the time of the German invasion in 1941, the 500 dossiers were sent to Germany. The Americans acquired them in 1945 and took them to Washington, where they are to be found in the military section of the Federal Military Archives. They were used by the American historian Fainsod (who recently died) in a book published in 1958, *Smolensk under Soviet Rule* (Harvard Press, 1958), but have never been published as a whole. In 1922, the Smolensk region had 2,500,000 inhabitants. The Party had 128 members who had joined prior to the 1917 fall of Tsarism and 366 who had joined in 1917. In 1919 membership reached 2,566 (12,000 according to the regional authorities, but these figures turned out to be false). In 1921, when the purge took place, membership figures reached 10,657. There were only 7,245 at the end of 1921, 5,929 at the end of 1923 and 5,655 on 1st April 1924.

Out of a total of 5,416 full or candidate members of the Party, 370 lived in towns, 1,712 in country areas, that is to say that there were 16 Communists per 10,000 people of working age, or approximately one Party member for every ten villages and as the population of the province was 90 per cent rural, the extreme weakness of the Party in country areas is all the more obvious (Fainsod, pp. 35–6).

So, in an area in the West – though a very rural one – in 1924 the Party was still only a drop of water in the Russian sea, and from this stemmed the difficulties in building socialism and the emergence of the Stalin phenomenon. This period cannot be compared to the time when Lenin was alive, though many writers try to do so. The Red Terror, which was directed against the Whites and their political and social supporters, was fathered by the White Terror.

The Red Terror can be compared neither qualitatively nor quantitatively to Stalinist mass repression. Yet, Stalin made his presence felt under Lenin and against him. The historian would be foolish not to see this link, for he would be condemned to explaining the Stalin phenomenon solely in terms of Stalin's personality. A caricature of what he might say would read: 'There was a very good man called Lenin, then came a very bad man called Stalin. . . .' The link between the beginning of the twenties and the mid thirties certainly exists, and it lies in the continuity of political institutions, of phenomena relating to consciousness, and of human behaviour, which were the fruit of the tradition and circumstances which constitute the soil in which the most poisonous blooms of Stalinism were to grow. In 1923 this soil already existed to some extent, which is why Lenin tried to reduce it. That does not mean that this phenomenon was necessary, historically necessary, that is to say inevitable, but that it was a possibility. For all that, should the Bolsheviks have given up power, as is suggested insistently nowadays? As Trotsky was to say, 'the skein of history unrolled backwards'. The Socialist Revolution had triumphed in a poor and culturally backward country and not in a highly developed capitalist country. The U.S.S.R. was the only socialist state and had either to move ahead or commit hara-kiri. She chose to move ahead. It was a historic choice which was not in much doubt.

From 1923 to 1928, the N.E.P. experiment went on and this was a relatively stable period both internally and internationally. At the same time, the trends we noted in the preceding years developed, and Stalin's authority grew. The N.E.P. made economic reconstruction possible. By 1926 agricultural production reached 90 per cent of the pre-war level, and, though industrial production progressed more slowly, by the same year it had still reached the 1913 figures. To realise how rapid this rate of progress was, we need to remember the economic state of the U.S.S.R. in 1922. Though France had suffered much less destruction than the Soviet Union, she was only to achieve the 1913 production figures in 1926. So, the Soviet economic revival, taking war damage into account, was twice as rapid as that of France. The N.E.P. had fulfilled the hopes of those who promoted it. On the basis of a market economy, incentives for workers and peasants, free-trade and small-scale capitalist firms, rapid development of productive forces had been witnessed, while the socialist state maintained control of finance, large-scale industry and transport as well as foreign trade.

In social terms, the N.E.P. had had the expected effects. The proletariat had re-emerged when large-scale industry had been reborn. However, it remained less numerous than in 1913, and, above all, it was a new proletariat rural in origin, to which a growing number of wage-earners had to be added. The N.E.P. had also helped capitalism. In the country, the kulaks had got rich, employed labour, lent money to the poor peasants, increased cultivable acreage by getting round the provisions of the rural code in various ways and, finally, played an increased role in the commercialisation of agricultural and livestock produce, because the output of the rich peasants was higher than that of the middle ones. The number of middle peasants had increased, but the number of landless peasants had also risen, and their situation, like that of the poor peasants, had become rather worse. The *kolkhozi* (collective farms) and the *sovkhozi* (State farms) only covered a small percentage of the land under cultivation (18,000 scarcely covered 3 per cent). In the towns, unemployment was rife (700,000 unemployed in 1924; 1,400,000 in 1928). Merchants and small industrialists had grown rich. The 'Nepmen' were doing very well out of the N.E.P. 'Who will win?' Lenin asked himself in 1921. In 1928 it was not at all clear that socialism had triumphed. No doubt it had precious advantages, but its future was still in doubt, all the more so because economic growth seemed uncertain. As early as 1927, a worrying slow-down in key sectors of the economy was to be observed. The conditions under which the economic development had taken place, requiring, as they did, recourse to state capitalism and small-scale private capitalism, had made it appear all the more necessary to the Bolsheviks that they should maintain their dictatorship, and particularly that of the narrow leading stratum which Lenin mentioned in his letter to Molotov. It is very significant that not one of the Party leaders – despite the disagreements they may have had in the 1923–7 period – questioned the political institutions set up in 1922. The limited number of decisions taken then with the aim of developing democracy or creating better conditions for its growth – the restriction of the G.P.U.'s political powers, the publication of a document for inner Party discussion – were not carried out because of the development of institutions and practices which solidified, became ossified, and were perfected precisely where democracy seemed inadequate to ensure Bolshevik hegemony, which by then had become completely identified with that of the proletariat. The papers from the Smolensk Archives, the validity of which is scarcely in question according to Fainsod, show that although there were decisive debates within the leadership, these had little impact in the provinces, even within the Party.[13] This was perhaps less true in some areas, but the general trend seemed to be for a certain apathy. In so far as one can ascertain the state of public opinion, the impression gained is that there was a deep desire for internal and external peace. The people had suffered badly from 1914 to 1922 and wanted neither external adventures nor internal disorder.

The public mood was in favour of work, the improvement of living conditions, progress in the field of education and a certain rapprochement between Soviet power and the middle peasants, this is pointed out by all those who witnessed the period. Under such conditions, it was natural for the Bolshevik militants to wonder about the future of the revolution in the U.S.S.R. and in the world. The debates within the Bolshevik leadership in the years 1923–7 concerned these problems, but they were rendered more complicated by the situation, by personal issues and by the absence of real democracy, without which no real debate was possible.

When it met in April 1923 in the absence of Lenin, who was to play no further part in politics, the 12th Congress reflected the hesitations within the Party. According to a confidential remark Krupskaya made to Kamenev, Lenin had decided to destroy Stalin politically. Circumstances did not allow him to carry out this intention, and nobody else was capable of doing so in 1923, doubtless because Stalin already held 'unlimited power'. Trotsky did not have sufficient authority within the Party leadership. His past – the role he had played before the war – turned against him a good number of members of the Bolshevik Old Guard. As People's Commissar for War, he could perhaps have tried to use the Red Army to subdue Stalin. It cannot be assumed that the Army would have followed him, and Trotsky, who was aware of the danger of a split in the Party, probably never even considered such a course. He was accused of wanting to be the Bonaparte of the Soviet Revolution, but he had no wish to play such a role. Moreover, they underestimated Stalin to far too great an extent to be able to analyse the situation seriously. Trotsky was sometimes a good strategist. He was a great writer and a good orator, but he was never anything but a mediocre tactician, more at ease in crisis situations than at times of relative peace. He was capable of greatness in troubled waters, in calm waters he was always mediocre. As for Zinoviev and Kamenev, they allied themselves with Stalin, forming what was known as the triumvirate or the *Troïka* (three horse carriage). At the beginning of the Consulate in France after the 18th Brumaire, there were three Consuls, but who, apart from specialists, remembers Cambacérès and Lebrun, whilst everyone knows about Napoleon Bonaparte? Zinoviev and Kamenev were mediocre strategists and unskilful tacticians, they saw Trotsky as a new Bonaparte who had to be kept away from supreme power. Too late, they understood that history never repeats itself and that Stalin was a potential dictator of a new type.

All the leaders were too well aware of the Party's weakness

to start a crisis which might well have been fatal. After Lenin's death, the contents of his 'Testament' were conveyed to the Central Committee and to the Presidium of the 13th Congress (in May 1924), but it was decided not to mention it at the Congress itself. Stalin made an apology for the problems in Georgia, spoke of energetically combating bureaucracy, and promised to be more polite and less brutal, as a result of which he stayed in his post and used his powers to control the Party machine by means of the skilful removal and judicious appointment of functionaries, something made possible by applying the decisions of the 11th Congress. An opposition group had taken shape earlier within the Party leadership, and in October 1923 forty-six leading members appealed to the Central Committee for more rapid industrialisation and greater inner Party democracy.[14] Trotsky did not sign this letter, but he certainly did not disown it.

The Central Committee decided to reprimand the signatories of the letter for being guilty of re-forming a faction, which had been forbidden since the 10th Congress. However, it admitted that more democracy was needed within the Party (in an article by Zinoviev in *Pravda* on 7th November 1923). The forty-six gained some support in Moscow, in army and university cells. The Central Committee reacted vigorously. Antonov-Ovseenko, the Red Army Political Commissar, was dismissed, and the Central Committee of the Komsomol (Young Communist League) was disbanded. The opposition accepted defeat. Given the situation of the U.S.S.R. and of the Party in the country, they had little room for manœuvre. Still facing the threat of foreign aggression, the Soviet Union was still fragile, and the Party's position within the country was in many ways precarious. The Bolsheviks were counting on the results of the N.E.P. and of their policy favouring the peasantry. This is what Bukharin expressed with his customary verve in 1925: 'Get rich, develop your farms and you need have no fear of coercion.' This advice, inspired by that given to the French bourgeoisie by Guizot at the time of the July Monarchy, was naturally criticised by the left opposition and approved of by Ustrialov, a former member of the Kolchak government who intended to use the N.E.P. to restore capitalism in Russia. Bukharin withdrew 'this shocking formulation of a correct proposition', but the debate which it had provoked showed just how difficult the situation was.

The Bolsheviks were also relying on progress in the field of culture, and this was real. Illiteracy was on the decline. At the end of 1926, half the population could read and write, though the ratio was lower among women and the non-Russian peoples in the Union. Secondary and vocational education, as well as the number of students, was growing. *Rabfaks* (workers' universities) and work schools allowed the accelerated training of the technicians the U.S.S.R. needed so badly.

At the same time the Bolsheviks were taking over traditional methods of government, like the cult of the leader. First of all it was Lenin. By the end of the Civil War his portrait was to be found everywhere. Lenin tried to check this phenomenon, but he did not really succeed. After his death, it assumed huge proportions. His body was embalmed and placed in a wooden mausoleum in Red Square opposite the Kremlin where the crowd could go and gaze at it. In *The Communist International*, Gorky explained quite clearly that 'Lenin is becoming a legendary figure and it is a good thing. I say that it is good, for most people have an absolute need to believe, in order to be able to begin to act. It would take too long to wait for them to begin to think and understand, and meanwhile the evil genius of capitalism would stifle them increasingly fast with poverty, alchoholism and exhaustion' (No. 12, 20th July 1920).

It was in vain that Lenin had proposed criticism of this theory. Justifying the exhibition of Lenin's body in the mausoleum, Zinoviev himself spoke of a 'pilgrimage'. Towns and factories were named after leaders while they were still alive. Thus in 1923 there was a town called Trotsk in honour of Trotsky (Gatchina, a town of 16,000 people 46 km. from Petrograd); in 1924 Elizabethgrad became Zinovievsk and on 10th April 1925 Tsaritsyn assumed the name of Stalingrad. This was making use both of Tsarist tradition and Orthodox ritual. The class content of these methods of government was radically different, but the method was still the same, though it had been secularised, socialised so to speak. It involved some danger, as the future was to prove. Stalin had realised how he could take advantage of this orientation, and his training was to help him do so. The speech he made at Lenin's funeral is a model of its kind, for in style and form it reproduces the Orthodox Litany: 'Departing from us, Comrade Lenin enjoined us to hold high and guard the purity of the great title of member of the Party. We vow to you, Comrade Lenin, that we shall follow your behest with honour.' There was the same rigmarole about five other subjects – the dictatorship of the proletariat, the unity of the workers and peasants, the union of the Soviet Republics and faithfulness to the principles of the Communist International. 'Departing from us, Comrade Lenin . . . enjoined us . . . we swear, Comrade Lenin, that we shall follow your behest with honour.' So the cult of the leader, quasi-religious ritual, even going as far as to change the Party into a secular church – 'We Communists are people of a special mould. We are made of a special stuff', said Stalin in his speech at Lenin's funeral – were quite consciously decided upon and put into effect by the whole of the Party, including every shade of opinion. This typical characteristic of the Stalin phenomenon shows to how great an extent it arose from Russian history and not from socialism.

It is not our intention here to go into the details of the arguments and conflicts involving a certain number of the leading comrades, the Party leadership and the Party as a whole. We shall only refer to the essentials, those things directly concerning the birth of the Stalin phenomenon. As early as 1925, Stalin spelled out the idea that it was necessary to 'build socialism in one country'. At that time nobody was asserting that the victory of socialism in one country could be final, but it was both necessary and possible to give this as a clear aim for the people and the Party. The opposition, in 1923 or in 1925–6, was greatly at fault not to grasp the necessity of this slogan, which the rural masses could understand because it implied the renunciation of offensive revolutionary war and adventurism. A great deal has been written about this, and a number of writers have asserted that this slogan was inherently national-istic and ran counter to the views of Marx and Lenin. This is a good example of the 'theological' approach which consists in reading the 'sacred texts' and applying them mechanically to situations which are new compared to the period when they were written. The socialist revolution had failed elsewhere and

there was nothing to indicate that it was likely to succeed any-
where in the near future. Thus the only possible way forward
was to build socialism in one country. Of course the U.S.S.R.
was still playing a revolutionary role by itself making progress
and by helping the international labour movement, but its
first duty was to build socialism within its own frontiers. A
delicate balance was to be maintained between these two
complementary areas of policy, and the fact that this was not
always achieved does not in any sense prove that the decision
taken in 1925 was incorrect.

As the report he made on industrialisation to the 12th
Congress and what he did at the head of the various committees
of the Supreme Council for the National Economy show, Trotsky
accepted the practical consequences of this fact, which was
unavoidable in the circumstances, but he refused to make any
theoretical statement about it. He envisaged future competition
between the Soviet Union and the United States in which
'Americanised Bolshevism will defeat and crush imperialist
Americanism' (*Europe and America*,[15] Berlin, 1926, p. 49). Not
without reason, his refusal to accept socialism in one country
can be presented as the result of the theory of 'permanent
revolution' which he had developed before the Revolution,
and which he had not given up.

At the international level, there was no alternative to
peaceful coexistence; Trotsky himself recognised this in a
conversation with the American Senator King which was
published in *Izvestia* on 30th September 1923. 'We do not
intervene in foreign civil wars. It's quite clear, we could only
intervene if we declared war on Poland. But we do not want
war. We make no secret of our sympathy with the German
working class in its heroic struggle for freedom. To speak more
clearly and more frankly, I say that if we could give victory to
the German Revolution without running the risk of getting
involved in war, we would do everything in our power. But we
do not want war. War would harm the German Revolution.
Only a revolution which succeeds on the basis of its own
strength can survive, above all when a great country is
concerned.'

Trotsky, then Kamenev, Zinoviev and all the opposition,
thought it politic to make the question of 'Socialism in one

country' one of their main arguments. It was easy for Stalin and Bukharin to reply that they should be consistent and learn from past events and from the real situation as it then existed. The slogan 'Socialism in one country' reassured the peasantry and public opinion, and gave everyone a clear view of the way forward. On the other hand, to reject it was to cause disquiet.

In the social and economic field, three problems were at the centre of the debate, those of industrialisation, planning and the struggle against the kulaks. The opposition put forward the view that Russia must be industrialised very rapidly, a course which required rigorous planning and 'primitive socialist accumulation', that is to say requisitions which, given the state of the country, could only come from the rural population and the artisans.

Preobrazhensky formulated his ideas clearly in a series of articles which appeared from 1921 on, and which were published as *Novaia Ekonomika* in 1926. In an article written in 1924 about 'the fundamental law of socialist accumulation', he compared it to 'primitive capitalist accumulation'. The latter was achieved thanks to the capital derived from the exploitation of the small pre-capitalist producers and the colonies, with the addition of taxes and state loans. Well, it was not possible for socialism to exploit colonies. All that remained was 'the exploitation of small-scale industry, the expropriation of the surplus produced by the countryside and artisans'. 'The idea that a socialist economy can grow by its own efforts without using the resources of the petty bourgeoisie, including the peasant economy, is a reactionary idea, petty bourgeois utopianism.' This analysis is all the more interesting because Stalin was eventually to adopt it – without actually saying so – in a Central Committee report on 9th July 1928 to justify the new policy which he was proposing to the Party. In 1923–4 such an analysis seemed likely to compromise the alliance (*Smytchka*) between workers and peasants on which the N.E.P. was based. This is why Preobrazhensky's ideas, which had been taken up by Trotsky and the opposition, were combated and rejected. After Trotsky's report to the 12th Congress, Krasin (People's Commissar for Foreign Trade) asked him a question which history was to make particularly striking: 'Had Trotsky taken into account all the consequences of this

analysis of primitive socialist accumulation?' Trotsky's reply
was awkward, and there was good reason for this, because in
order to achieve it quickly and brutally the Terror would have
to be turned against the peasantry – this was precisely what
was to happen in 1929–30. In fact primitive socialist accumulation was a necessity for the Soviet Union in 1923, taking into
account the economic state of the country at the time. However, it could only be slow – unless it was to be at the expense
of the peasantry (and not only the kulaks), which is what
Lenin had feared and forcefully criticised in the last things he
wrote, and which Bukharin was to take up in this 1928–9
works. It was going to take 'decades' to build socialism.

Let us at once note the fact that this situation bears no
relation to that of the great developed countries in the 1970s.
Primitive socialist accumulation will not be necessary there,
for primitive capitalist accumulation was achieved more than a
century ago. Now, the Stalin phenomenon largely arose from
the conditions under which primitive socialist accumulation
was carried through by Stalin, that is to say from the haste
with which industrialisation and collectivisation of the land
was carried out, and from the Terror, first of all directed
against the peasantry then against the Party itself, which
resulted from it. The objective basis for the Stalin phenomenon
does not in any way exist in contemporary France, for example,
where the level of the productive forces is already high. It is
precisely here that we are aware of the extent to which this
phenomenon was the result not of socialism but of the conditions
under which it developed in a very precise historical situation,
that of the Soviet Union and of the 1920–30 period, conditions
which should be compared with other different ones, for
example those appertaining in France and in the 1970s.

To sum up, it was a phenomenon restricted in terms of
time and place, and not a historical necessity universally true
of socialism, whether past, present or future. The struggle
against the kulaks was linked with industrialisation and
planning. Nobody questioned the need to combat the kulaks,
not even Bukharin. But the problem was how to do this
without compromising the 'alliance' of the peasants and
workers, and within the bounds of the N.E.P. It was this
problem which gave rise to debate and conflict. The opposition

called for harsher measures against the kulaks (particularly in the field of taxation). The Party hesitated for several years and then rejected these calls. However, after a very precise report from Molotov, the 15th Congress in 1927 eventually decided to take steps against the kulaks, whilst, at the same time, taking the decision to speed up industrialisation and to set up the first five year plan. Molotov had pointed out that the middle peasants and kulaks should not be confused. Collective farming would develop slowly and only on the basis that it would be freely undertaken. Exactly the opposite was to happen.

The third major problem raised in the debate which took place in the 1923-7 period was that of democracy. Within the Party, the opposition called for democracy, though this was in some senses an inconsistent position since they had denied it to others, notably the 'Workers' Opposition', in the recent past. This is why they decided to retreat. The question of the banning of factions was a delicate one. To allow factions was to tempt the devil, that is to say to create conditions which might lead to a split in the Party. Inner Party discussion was to go on freely, but without the different opinions crystallising into factions, thus creating structures likely to generate powerlessness and disunity. The margin between the two was narrow, all the more so because Stalin's practical policies to say the very least did not tend to widen democracy. As General Secretary of the Party, he used his position to establish his authority even more solidly by eliminating opposition members – and potential opposition members – from the centres of decision-making, by having them given posts abroad or on the fringes of the Soviet Union. Most of the Bolshevik leaders supported Stalin whom they considered as the most modest and capable of their number to lead the Party in this difficult period. Most of them were to die at his command in the 1930s, but there was no way of predicting this then. We who know what fate awaited them must not forget this.

As early as Summer 1923, Zinoviev took the initiative of calling a secret meeting in a cellar in Kislovodsk, one of the most beautiful spa towns in the Caucasus, with the aim of restricting Stalin's power by turning the Secretariat into a political body. Bukharin, Voroshilov and several other leading figures took part in this meeting which envisaged the setting up of a Secretariat comprising Stalin, Trotsky and Zinoviev (or Kamenev and Bukharin). Stalin was informed of this by Orjonikidze and foiled the manœuvre. In 1925 the Party had 25,000 full-time workers, of whom 767 were attached to the Central Committee headquarters. The Central Committee Department for the Assignment of Cadres (the *Uchraspred*) was in control of appointing leaders. For example, 12,277 appointments were made between the 13th and 14th Party Congresses. In 1924, the Organisation and Cadre Assignment Departments merged to form the *Orgraspred*. Gradually the opposition – which moreover had a fluctuating membership – lost all means of expression and positions of responsibility. Its strongholds – the Red Army with Trotsky, the universities, the Leningrad Party organisation with Zinoviev and the Moscow organisation with Kamenev – were purged. In January 1925, Trotsky lost his post as People's Commissar for War, but not his membership of the Politbureau. Until December 1925, whilst dissociating themselves to some extent from Stalin, Zinoviev and Kamenev continued to oppose Trotsky whom they had wanted to remove from the Politbureau in January 1925. It was at the 14th Congress that Kamenev, followed by Zinoviev, began to criticise Stalin. Kamenev lost his post as a full member of the Politbureau, though he remained a substitute, and was replaced in Moscow by Uglanov (later to be shot on Stalin's orders), whilst Zinoviev was removed from the Party leadership in Leningrad and replaced by Kirov. The opposition was isolated within the Party and in the country, and could only count on the support of a few thousand Communists. Despite the decisions taken at the 10th Congress, they tried to organise a faction. Stalin was able to wrap himself in the banner of Party unity and of Socialism in One Country and to finish them off.

In October 1925, Trotsky was removed from the Politbureau and Zinoviev lost his job as President of the Communist International. After attempts to organise separate demonstrations on the occasion of the 10th anniversay of the October Revolution, Trotsky, Kamenev, Smilga, Radek, Piatakov, Lashevich and Rakovsky were expelled from the Party. Yoffe committed suicide as a protest against the expulsion of Trotsky.[16] A page had been turned in the history of the Soviet Communist Party. The power and authority of Stalin had grown thanks to these events, and in many respects its political and ideological basis was pretty firmly laid.

Democracy within the Party and the country did not emerge strengthened from these events, all the more so because the G.P.U. had come to play a bigger and bigger role in them. It had been formed in February 1922 to restrict the powers of the Cheka, which it replaced, but still had extensive powers. The penal code of the R.S.F.S.R., which was published in May 1922, accepted the principle of 'crimes against the state' by giving (Articles 57, 58, 59) a definition of this concept which was wide enough to include any written or spoken criticism of the Soviet regime or of the way it operated. As early as August 1922, it was decided to allow people to be deported without trial for up to three years for having taken part in counter-revolutionary activity; the decision rested with a 'special commission' of the People's Commissariat for Internal Affairs, in which the G.P.U. played a crucial role.

Gradually, G.P.U. supervision was extended to labour camps, the press, literature, the cinema, the theatre, all public places and even to the Party itself. It was the G.P.U. which in June 1923 had Sultan-Galiev arrested; he was a Tatar Bolshevik who wanted to create a great Tatar Soviet Socialist Republic from the Turkish-Mongol peoples of Central Asia and the Southern Ukraine. It was the G.P.U. which had the leaders of the 1923 strikes and of the underground 'Workers' Truth' and 'Working-class Truth' groups arrested. In October 1923, the Politbureau decided to compel Party members to denounce to the G.P.U. any anti-Party activities which they were aware of. This was a very dangerous path – for, where did anti-Party activities start? – who could decide this? – which opened the way for many excesses, many mistakes and many crimes.

It was the G.P.U. which, in September 1927, raided the press where the opposition was printing its manifesto[17] for the 15th Congress. It 'invented' a White Guard, who had fought under Wrangel, to provide manufactured proof of collusion between the Whites and the opposition. Later Stalin had to admit that this was 'a mistake made by the G.P.U.' At the same time, he conducted a smear campaign against his enemies at home. Thus he declared in 1927 that 'a united front

from Chamberlain to Trotsky' had been formed. In 1923,
Krylenko mentioned for the first time social threats and the
offence of 'threats to society'. In October 1924, the principles
of the criminal law codes of the Soviet Republic stressed the
need for 'measures to defend society' against criminals guilty
of acting against the foundations of the Soviet order. As laid
down in Article 22, anyone identified as 'a threat to society'
could be banned from living in a particular place and deported
from one place to another; this constituted the establishment
of preventive punishment, and was extremely arbitrary – anyone could be declared a threat to society. Krylenko, the Public
Prosecutor of the R.S.F.S.R. (and one of Stalin's future
victims), originated the 'isolators' for 'class enemies'.

In October 1924, a forced labour code was promulgated
by the Executive Committee of the Soviet of the R.S.F.S.R.
According to official figures, which were no doubt lower than
the true figures, there were 185,000 deportees in 1927. A note
from Krassin to Trotsky (which he received on 2nd June 1924
during a meeting of the Central Committee, which was
preserved in the Trotsky archives, and which Carr quotes)[18]
says that the prisoners were used to build railways. So the
G.P.U. (which became the O.G.P.U. after the Soviet
Union was founded – the 'Unified State Political Directorate')
gradually came to be used more against Communists than as a
weapon in the struggle against the direct opponents of Soviet
power. In 1927, this tendency quite clearly existed, but its
consequences were still limited. Nevertheless, it constituted a
potentially serious danger, even more so because the people
recruited into the G.P.U. left much to be desired from a
revolutionary point of view. The Old Bolsheviks (those who had
taken part in the Revolution and the Civil War) had been
replaced by elements of often dubious value.

This situation had not facilitated the fight against manifestations of bureaucracy. The State machine had not been
significantly changed and the number of civil servants had
increased. The osmosis between Party and State had got worse.
In 1928, 38·3 per cent of Party members worked in the Party
or State administrative machines. On the other hand, there
were only 200,000 Communists in the country districts and
only half of them were really peasants. The increase in Party

membership – it rose from 472,000 to 1,304,471 in the 1924–8 period – made it possible to achieve a significant increase in the proportion of members from a working-class background, but as a result there was a qualitative change in the composition of the Party. The importance of the Old Bolsheviks declined. The great majority of the new members were young workers of peasant stock. The Party made every effort to give them a basic training in Marxism. This was the aim of the lectures given by Stalin at the Sverdlov Academy and later published in editions of millions of copies: 'The Fundamentals of Leninism'. Stalin proved to be a talented populariser who managed to present the Bolsheviks' main ideas in a way which was pedagogically sound and made them accessible to many people. At the same time, 'The Fundamentals of Leninism' was a terribly tempting basis for dogmatism if it was treated as a work of theoretical research. During the twenties, the Party managed – within the limitations imposed by its dictatorship – to carry out simultaneously both the mass propaganda required to teach the still uneducated masses a few elementary principles and high level theoretical research.

For example, in philosophy there was the magazine *Under the Banner of Marxism*, in history there was Prokovsky's *History of Russia*; in these fields, as well as in political economy and sociology, Soviet social scientists displayed real ability.

The refusal of the Party to intervene in debates on literature, a degree of freedom for literary creation, as well as in the cinema and theatre, together with the revolutionary upsurge and the facilities given to creative artists allowed the flowering of numerous varied and talented works which are symbolised by the cinema in the 1920s.[19]

Even from this point of view, this period should not be idealised. Non-Communist writers had little chance of expressing themselves and a number of them were still living in exile. The fight against religion was carried on in ways which were, to tell the truth, quite unacceptable, for they threatened freedom of conscience and worship. Marxism, which had become the official state philosophy, was taught more and more dogmatically. Thus, the foundations of Stalinism already existed at the time of the N.E.P., though not its most dramatic consequences and its most vicious forms.

c

Despite some efforts to reactivate the Soviets at the local level, democratic life was poorly developed, and in 1927, had made little progress. In fact the situation had if anything got worse, though the Civil War had been over for five years. It is true that as Trotsky and later Stalin said, the U.S.S.R. was a 'besieged fortress'. The Soviet Union was still isolated, the danger of a war against it still existed and plotting continued, but this did not justify what was happening, and, above all, the continued and increasing lack of democracy within the Party and the country was creating a dangerous situation and the existence of authoritarian structures made the U.S.S.R. vulnerable to a more dictatorial, much bloodier and more personal form of power.

Soon the Stalin phenomenon was to blossom.

NOTES

1. Lenin had his first attack of hemiplegia on 25th May 1922. He resumed work in September, but he had a second attack on 16th December 1922 and a third on 10th March 1923. From then on he was totally paralysed, had to give up all activity and died on 21st January 1924.
2. From a speech to the 7th Congress of the R.C.P. (*C.W.*, Vol. 27, pp. 89–90).
3. It was written on the 4th and 5th January 1923, but not published by *Pravda* until the 26th and 27th May 1923.
4. See *The Secret Story of Stalin's Crimes* by A. Orlov, New York, 1953 (a Soviet fugitive in the U.S.A.) and *Stalin's Great Secret*, by Levine, New York, 1956).
5. It was made up of seven full members and five candidate members.
6. Quoted by Roy Medvedev in *Let History Judge*.
7. Apart from Trotsky (who had been deported), they were all executed on Stalin's orders during the mass repression of the thirties.
8. This is the view held by Deutscher (in *Stalin*, p. 215) who bases it on secret correspondence of the period, which has not been published, but which he was able to consult in the Trotsky archives in Harvard.
9. Corsica had been annexed by France just before Napoleon was born, and there had been a real, anti-French uprising led by Paoli. Though Napoleon was Corsican by origin he still played a decisive role in establishing centralisation as it exists in France.
10. Trotsky had expounded the thesis that 'the militarisation of labour is the indispensable basis for organising our work potential'. He had dismissed the leaders of the railwaymen's union and tried to impose a centralist policy which was criticised by Lenin and by the Party. In the end, Trotsky accepted the Party decisions.

11. Lenin–Trotsky correspondence (in the Trotsky archives).
12. The Russian word 'pojaouli' means 'perhaps' in the precise sense of 'it is possible that . . .'.
13. Fainsod, *Smolensk under Soviet Rule*, p. 38.
14. Among the signatories were: the economist Preobrazhensky, a former Secretary of the Central Committee, Piatakov, Antonov-Ovsenko, Muralov, Bubnov, etc. They all perished during the mass repression of the thirties.
15. It was in this work that Trotsky wrote about the future of Europe. 'In a socialist Europe, we will act as a bridge with Asia' (p. 90).
16. He had been Soviet Ambassador in Berlin in 1918 after taking part in the Brest–Litovsk peace negotiations, then Ambassador in Vienna and Tokyo.
17. The Central Committee had forbidden its publication in line with the decisions on factions taken at the 10th Congress.
18. *Socialism in One Country*, Vol. 2, p. 447.
19. Eisenstein's *Battleship Potemkin* is its most striking product.

3 Problems of Industrialisation and Collectivisation

In 1928, a number of elements of the Stalin phenomenon were already present; some had been there since the Revolution or the Civil War, others had appeared during the N.E.P. period. The traditions (those of old, holy Russia), the institutions (economic, social and political), the historical circumstances and the men (the role of Stalin and the defeat of the opposition) all came together to deepen the soil on which the Stalin phenomenon was to feed. The events of the 1928–34 period were to allow him to make his presence felt in a brilliant though incomplete way, which resulted in the problems of 1934. The decisions about the fight against the kulaks taken at the 15th Party Congress worried the peasantry. A large number of the middle peasants felt these measures were directed against them. In theory, the measures involved increasing taxation of the rich and abolishing taxation of the poor, stepping up aid to collective and state farms, and no longer helping the kulaks. Like Molotov, Rykov, the President of the Council of People's Commissars, had reminded people of the need for caution, but this policy was implemented with great vigour. The 1927 harvest was not very good. The concern we have mentioned, which was encouraged and stimulated by the numerous adversaries of the Soviet regime still present in the country areas and by the kulaks, did the rest. The collections of agricultural produce (*zagotovki*) were poor, in fact they were quite inadequate: 300 million poods were collected at the end of December 1927 (the December 1926 figure was 428 million). The documents from the central archives of the Party which were used by the Soviet historian Konyukhov (in *The Communist Party and the Struggle against Problems in the Supply of Wheat*, Moscow, 1960), show that because of the growing lack of grain at the beginning of 1928 the Party and its leadership were swept by panic. 'A general economic crisis on a national scale' threatened to arise, as the resolution adopted by the April 1928 meeting of the Party Central Committee was to admit. They had a very clear choice; either to retreat in the near future or to push ahead, which meant taking more and more severe measures against the kulaks, but which also implied that the kulaks had been isolated from the whole of the middle peasantry. It was in this area that the deficiencies of the Party, the existence of bureaucracy and the Party's weakness in numerical terms in the country areas was to play an important role. Repressive and administrative measures gradually took precedence over ideological incentives. For a time, the Party was hesitant. In some places it retreated, in others it pushed ahead. At the beginning of 1928, more frequent use was made of article 107 in the penal code: according to this, anyone who tried to speculate could be punished by deportation for three to five years (as well as having his property confiscated). The middle peasants were affected by these measures, this was recognised in a statement from the Council of People's Commissars on 30th June 1928. Bauman, the Party functionary in charge of agricultural affairs, admitted that 'the middle peasant has sided with the kulak and turned against us'. Then there were peasant revolts. The Party called a halt to the policy it had been following (at the July 1928 Central Committee), raised the price of wheat, condemned the abuses and bought wheat abroad.

Meanwhile, Stalin was biding his time. In a speech made to the Central Committee on 9th July 1928, he had taken up Preobrazhensky's thesis of what he called 'internal accumulation'. Since they could not pillage colonies nor have recourse to foreign loans, industrial development could only come from 'internal accumulation'. The peasantry was to pay the price of industrialisation. With this aim in view, 'it (the peasantry) overpays in the relatively high prices for manufactured goods . . . and it is more or less underpaid in the prices for agricultural produce'. Apart from the (direct and indirect) taxes paid by everyone, the peasant is subject to 'a "tribute", . . . a supertax, which we are compelled to levy for the time being'. Stalin took up the 'scissors' image (used by Trotsky at the 12th Congress), that is to say the image of an increase in the price of industrial products and a reduction in the price of agricultural produce, and admitted that 'the scissors' could not

be abolished at once (Stalin, *Collected Works*, Vol. 11, p. 167).
In fact, with characteristic haste and brutality, and often
without even consulting the leading organs of the Party,
Stalin bent his efforts to the adoption of completely new
measures which could be summed up as follows: faster and
faster industrialisation, planning, and collectivisation of the
land – three aspects of a single plan. In order to industrialise
more rapidly, there was a need for total, centralised planning
which would impose the necessary concentration of productive
resources (men, capital and machinery) in certain economic
and geographical sectors. Then it was necessary to transform
the country areas in order to finally remove them from
capitalist influences and to carry through increased levies of
capital, so the collectivisation of farming had to take place.
The Stalin phenomenon was to widen its own initial basis
during the historical process itself, and history begets history
from the actual situation.

It can also be noted that, to a great extent, the Stalin
phenomenon always proceeded from a largely correct analysis,
but which it took to an extreme conclusion as a result of the
means it used to achieve its ends. Who could argue against the
need for industrialisation in 1928? Who would have questioned
the need for planning? Who could have criticised the principle
of collectivisation in a socialist economy and society?

The debate which took place in the Party in 1928–9 was
not democratic. Decisions were imposed upon the Party and
the state, and this was done because it was possible to do it.
Stalin put his opponents in a cruel dilemma: either you support
me, or you are an enemy of the Party, a friend of the kulaks,
against industrialisation of the country and planning, therefore
against socialism. The so-called 'right' opposition was trapped
in this way. It was Bukharin who in 1928 was the quickest to
clearly perceive the policy line that Stalin intended to follow
and its consequences. We are not saying that from 1923 to 1927
Bukharin's way of viewing and implementing the N.E.P. was
always correct. Having got over the 'left-wing Communist'
mistakes he made in 1918, when he opposed the Brest–Litovsk
Treaty, he had had a tendency to lean to the right, but it
appears that Lenin's comradely help allowed him to assimilate
what the latter intended to achieve in the following years.

Doubtless he was not totally right in 1929, but he had grasped a decisive aspect of the problem.

Over-rapid industrialisation, forced collectivisation of the land, and excessively authoritarian centralisation threatened the alliance of workers and peasants, set the middle peasantry against the regime and forced the latter to use terror against the people and against the Party itself. This was all possible because of the absence of democracy and the extent of bureaucratisation. This is why Bukharin and his friends, Rykov (the President of the Council of People's Commissars), Tomsky (the President of the Central Council of the Trade Unions) and Uglanov (Moscow Regional Secretary) had argued against Preobrazhensky's theses on primitive socialist accumulation, which Trotsky supported. In several articles which appeared in *Pravda*, Bukharin summarised his views. The articles concerned are 'An Economist's Notes' (30th September 1928), 'Lenin's Testament' (24th January 1929), which was the text of a speech he made in Moscow on the occasion of the fifth anniversary of Lenin's death and, 'Lenin and the Tasks of Science in Building Socialism' (20th January 1929). Taking as his starting point five articles published by Lenin just before he died ('Pages from a Diary', 'Our Revolution', 'How We Should Reorganise the Workers' and Peasants' Inspection', 'On Co-operation' and 'Better Fewer but Better'), Bukharin rightly showed that what was involved was an overall plan and not scattered remarks, and he added 'the basic theses of comrade Lenin are still profoundly true, and should continue to be the theoretical basis for determining our main tactical line'.[1] However, Bukharin (who was at that time President of the Communist International) made a major mistake when he viewed 'the stabilisation of capitalism as lasting', and from this point of view Stalin's appreciation of the situation was more accurate, for economic crisis was to break out in 1929. The conclusion Stalin drew from this was that there was an increased risk of war against the U.S.S.R., which was all the more justification for industrialisation at 'full steam ahead', and that the revolutionary crisis would come to a head in the developed capitalist countries, which justified putting an end to attempts at reconciliation between Socialists (or Social-Democrats) and Communists, which was advocated by Bukharin. This policy

orientation explains the sectarian positions adopted in the
following years by the Comintern and the Communist Party
of Germany. The fact that the 2nd International and German
Social-democratic Party bore the overwhelming responsibility
for the situation from which Nazism and the Second World
War was to emerge does not in any way exonerate the
Comintern and Stalin. The conclusions which Stalin drew from
his analysis in late 1928 of how capitalism would develop were
false, but his premises were correct. It was still true that, as
Bukharin said, the U.S.S.R. remained very weak. 'In comparison with Europe and America, our level of development is
excessively low, half savage.' In order to develop its industry,
the Soviet Union must not modify 'the alliance of workers and
peasants'. Krupskaya forcefully reminded people of this in an
article which appeared in *Pravda* on 20th January 1929,
'Lenin and the building of kolkhozes': 'To rebuild even the
agricultural base is a long-term job. It is impossible to carry
out a radical reorganisation of agriculture from above.' And
she added that 'it was madness and that there was nothing
stupider than acting in that way'.

So, how was industrialisation to be financed? Bukharin's
reply was: 'Above all by the greatest possible reduction in our
unproductive expenditure, which is in fact huge in our country,
by raising our scores on the quality indicators, firstly productivity'; so there must be 'no issue of notes, no liquidation of
stocks, no excessive taxation of the peasants'. This was a slow
way and Stalin's was fast, but the future was to show that,
historically speaking, the shortest route from one point to
another is not necessarily a straight line, taking into account
the results of this quick way.

Bukharin pointed out that the way he proposed was the
only one 'by which economic development, socialist accumulation, will be a really solid and healthy base, both from an
economic and a class point of view . . . so that the policy of
industrialisation not only does not lead to a break with the
peasants, but on the contrary reinforces the alliance with them'.
Nothing, not the economic crisis, nor the danger of war, nor
the hopes of revoution in Europe, could change the basis of this
policy, for to change it meant struggling against the peasantry
who represented 85 per cent of the population, and starting

down the path leading to mass terror against the people. This, of course, was to be one of the main ingredients of the Stalin phenomenon – and Bukharin pertinently recalled Lenin's remarks about co-operation and the cultural revolution: 'A cultural revolution is necessary to achieve the plan for co-operative work . . . Lenin teaches us that the peasant must be made to follow his own interest and on this basis must be led to socialism through co-operation, and for co-operation to lead to socialism it must be civilised.' And Bukharin pointed out that 'the working class has the job of constantly transforming the peasant class, of re-forming it in its own image, without becoming separated from it'. 'The Red Army which is largely made up of peasants is one of the greatest possible cultural machines for transforming the peasant who will leave its ranks with a new mentality.' The cultural revolution meant the transformation of the peasant mentality, which could only be achieved by educating and setting an example. All these tasks presupposed a reduction in the size of the state machine and an improvement in its work based on 'the real involvement of the effective masses'.[2] In his article on 'Lenin and the Tasks of Science', Bukharin had insisted on the need for the scientific management of the economy, which was so severely lacking, and on the fact that in order to achieve this they would have to learn from the West. In 'An Economist's Notes', he criticised the undertaking of 'superindustrialisation' without reserves – 'a policy which was constantly accompanied by a lack of reserves would be close to adventurism' – and he denounced any attempt 'to use force against the peasantry'.

Stalin could rely on considerable support in his battle with Bukharin. In the Politbureau and the Central Committee he had a majority, provided he did not go too far, which was precisely what he did intend to do. The inadequate development of democracy within the Party and the country was to play an important role in the struggle which was beginning, for the debate – at very best – got under way at the level of the leadership. Then, Stalin, like Bukharin, sought the support of the opposition which the two of them had crushed only a few months before. Bukharin contacted Sokolnikov and then Kamenev. According to Deutscher (*Trotsky*, Vol. 2, p. 440) the minutes of these talks are in the Trotsky Archives. Bukharin expressed his concern about the way in which the regime was developing. The thesis which had been expounded on 9th July 1929, according to which 'as we move forward the resistance of the capitalist elements will increase, class struggle will become increasingly bitter . . .' seemed to him to carry with it the danger of mass repression, of a new Terror. In the manifesto which Bukharin (with Rykov and Tomsky) submitted to the Politbureau in January 1929, he denounced the lack of collective leadership and the fact that 'the Party is not taking part in solving these problems.' 'Everything is done from the top', he added. 'We are opposed to the replacement of collective control by that of one individual whatever authority he may have' (quoted by Rudzutak at the 16th Congress, pp. 201–2 and Orjonikidze, p. 325). According to Kamenev, Bukharin went on: 'Stalin will stop at nothing . . . he will be compelled to drown rebellion in blood . . . he will slay us, he will strangle us . . . the root of the evil is that Party and state are so completely merged . . . he is an unprincipled intriguer who subordinates everything to his lust for power . . . he knows only vengeance and the stab in the back . . . he is the new Gengis Khan' (*Trotsky* by Deutscher, Vol. 2, pp. 441–2).

Leaving aside Stalin's motives – about which there might be debate – history was dramatically to confirm these words. As for Stalin, he, too, repeatedly made overtures to the opposition. He even let it be known that in his view Trotsky had not left 'the field of Bolshevik ideology', and that he, Stalin, was only waiting for an opportunity to bring him back to Moscow[3] (a statement made by Stalin to an Asian Communist, quoted by Deutscher, *op. cit.*, Vol. 2, p. 443). To most of the Trotskyites, Stalin's policy seemed to represent a move to the left. So, according to Preobrazhensky, Piatakov and Radek, they should support Stalin against Bukharin: the latter had foreseen this reaction. He had told Kamenev: 'The things which divide us are less serious than those which divide us from Stalin. What is required above all is the reestablishment of democracy within the Party.' But this was not how the opposition saw things. Only Trotsky refused to support Stalin. As a result, he was expelled from the Soviet Union on 20th January 1929, for he made the re-establishment of inner-party democracy a condition for his support, and Stalin was not in favour of that. At the same time, Trotsky continued to say that 'the Bukharinite right remained his main enemy'.

Meanwhile, events were discrediting the divided opposition even more, reduced as it was to existing as sects, often incoherent in its analyses. For example, Trotsky had denounced the victory of the official Party line as a 'new Thermidor'. Well, Stalin was now talking of crushing the kulaks and the Nepmen, which was quite the opposite of a Thermidor. The debate in the Political Committee and the Central Committee lasted from February 1928 to February 1929. On this date Bukharin was ousted from his posts at the Comintern and *Pravda* and Tomsky from his Soviet Trade-Unions job, but they remained members of the Politbureau, as did Rykov (who was still President of the Council of People's Commissars). In February 1929, the majority of Central Committee members were resolved to move against the kulaks, to impose real planning and to speed up industrialisation. They did not suspect how tragic the consequences of their decisions were to be for the Soviet Union, for the Party and for themselves, since a number of them were to perish tragically in the thirties – four full members of the Politbureau out of nine (Bukharin, Rykov, Tomsky and Rudzutak), and four out of eight candidate members (Kirov, Kossior, Uglanov and Chubar), that is to say eight out of seventeen.

On the basis of the decisions taken in February 1929, the Soviet Union made a radical change in its economic policy, one which went much further than the decisions of the 15th Congress and the Central Committee. The collection of grain in the winter of 1928–9 was pretty bad because of sabotage by the kulaks, speculation and the fears of the middle peasants. So it became necessary to begin rationing agricultural produce. Meeting in April 1929, the 16th Party Conference adopted the first Five Year Plan. It had been drawn up by the offices of the Gosplan where a number of highly qualified economists, often former Mensheviks or Socialist-Revolutionaries[4] (for example Kondratiev, Bazarov and Groman) were to be found, and originally two versions, one optimistic and one pessimistic, were provided for. On the initiative of the Politbureau it was decided to adopt the optimistic one (a 181 per cent increase in industrial production, a 183 per cent increase in the national income). The plan forecast the growth of the co-operative and state sectors in agriculture. In their most elementary form, that of the *tozy* (collectives for working the land in which only part of the land and heavy equipment is pooled, but private ownership continues), the collective farms were to represent 22 million hectares and 4,500,000 households and the state farms 5 million hectares, in total 17·5 per cent of the land sown with wheat in 1933 (43 per cent of the wheat put on the market). Well, despite the decisions of the 16th Conference and the solemn promises made by Stalin and Molotov, an increasingly rapid raising of the targets for industrialisation and collectivisation of the land can be observed in the years 1929 and 1930. The number of collective farms went up as early as mid-1929. At the beginning of November, there were 70,000 of them involving about 2 million households and representing about 7·6 per cent of the land under cultivation. This was a lot more than in 1928 (4 per cent more), but still not so large a figure, especially if we take into account that they were small kolkhozes and that 62·3 per cent of them were *tozy*, and only 30·8 per cent were artels where the ownership of the land was really collective (but in the form of a co-operative) and 6·9 per cent *kommuna*[5] (where all property belongs to the collective). In theory, joining the collective farms was voluntary. The Party leadership endeavoured to create big kolkhozes, and in certain regions high percentages of collectivisation were achieved (19 per cent in the Northern Caucasus and 14 per cent in the Ukraine). Until November the pressures brought to bear by the authorities remained indirect in most cases, and the building of kolkhozes encountered resistance, sometimes armed, from the kulaks.

The following information is to be found in the Smolensk Archives: Western Region O.G.P.U. report for 1929: 'Okrug (district) of Bryansk in the night of the 1st to the 2nd October in the Trubchevsk region, the President of the Khelvevsk village Soviet was seriously wounded by gunfire. . . .' On the previous day, the Selsoviet Secretary had been attacked. In the Okrug of Velikie Louki, at the village of Smorodovnik, in the Tsivelsk region, on 29th August the Selsoviet Secretary was murdered, etc., and these attacks against the supporters of collectivisation ran into thousands in the year 1929. In the

Western region, there were thirty-four terrorist acts in July and August, and forty-seven in October (eighteen of the victims were Selsoviet Presidents and eight Secretaries). In October, 122 people were arrested for these crimes, half of them kulaks, the other half middle or poor peasants.

Though it had reported on the difficulties faced by the kolkhozes, as early as June 1929 the Kolkhozcentr (the central management of the kolkhozes) proposed that the target of 8 million hectares under cultivation by the kolkhozes be reached in 1930. (Between August and November, it was decided in successive instalments to increase these figures to 30 million hectares.) Without waiting for the meeting of the Central Committee, which was to be faced with a *fait accompli*, on 7th November 1929, Stalin published in *Pravda* an article *cum* programme which announced massive and rapid collectivisation: 'The Year of the Great Change'. Let us note in passing that this article was published two weeks after the Wall Street Crash which marked the beginning of the great capitalist economic crisis of 1929. Stalin thought that during 1929 they had witnessed a decisive change because industry had progressed as never before. This was not true. Real but not decisive progress had been made, taking into account that it was no greater than that of the preceding years. As for 'the radical re-alignment within the peasantry', of which Stalin was so proud, it only existed in his mind, as is clearly emphasised by the collective work edited by Danilov which appeared in the U.S.S.R. in 1963 (*Collected Texts on the History of the Collectivisation of the Land in the Soviet Republics*).[6] From November 1929 on, collectivisation was in fact carried out in an authoritarian and bureaucratic way, using administrative measures and, often, force. In his report to the Central Committee on 15th November 1929, Molotov expressed his satisfaction with the results and proposed that collectivisation should be completed in some regions by the end of 1930. The Central Committee was not so enthusiastic, but it did not dare go back on its decisions, as this would have meant admitting that Bukharin had been right and Stalin wrong. It contented itself with setting up a standing commission to keep the problem under review, which was a way of limiting the damage. Taking his desires for reality, Molotov had declared: 'The countryside is

being turned upside down, in fact it has changed into a boiling
sea', but this agitation was more a result of the will of the
Party than that of the peasants. Not only was the Party taking
on the kulaks, who fought back ferociously, but, as Bukharin
had predicted, they had to fight the middle peasants. As the
months passed, the Party leadership imposed ever more rapid
rates of change. In a speech made on 27th December 1929,
Stalin launched the idea of the 'liquidation of the kulaks as a
class', again facing the Party organisations with a *fait accompli*.
He was relying on the support of the poor peasants and the
landless peasants. The definition of the kulaks was vague and a
lot of middle peasants were put into this category. So, most of
the peasants were forced into the kolkhozes. In the first three
months of 1930, a wave of terror swept across the Soviet
countryside.

Thanks to the Smolensk Archives, we are aware of the
Velikié Luki Okrug case. On 28th January, the local Party
Committee voted in favour of deporting the kulaks. As was the
case throughout Soviet territory, the latter were to be divided
into three categories: 'Those kulaks guilty of counter-
revolutionary activity are to be deported, as well as the richest
ones; as for the others, they will have their property confiscated,
but stay in the Okrug and will be given land to clear.' The
12th February circular from the Party Committee warned of
the danger of taking such measures against the other peasants,
but admitted that it had often been the case. In the following
days, many criminal acts were reported. This was because,
like Mao at a later date during the Cultural Revolution,
Stalin had unleashed forces which he could scarcely control.
Class conflict in the villages was made worse by personal
bitterness. The 'seething agitation in the country' of which
Molotov was proud was creating a desperate situation. Panic-
stricken peasants were killing their stock. Farm work was only
carried out partially and behind schedule. Disorder reigned
everywhere. The middle peasants were being 'dekulaked'.
Whole truckloads of kulaks were deported. Millions of peasants
were forced into the kolkhozes, and then the success of the total
collectivisation plan was proclaimed.

Brigades of workers who had come from the towns and
did not know the country sometimes acted at random. A report

from the O.G.P.U. in the Western Region dated 28th February 1930 noted that the kulaks and middle peasants were having even their clothes taken from them. More and more arrests were taking place on the instigation of all sorts of officials, as an O.G.P.U. report dated 23rd February 1930 stresses. As early as 20th February, the Regional Secretary of the Party, Central Committee member Rumantsyev (who was to be shot in 1938) warned all the Okrug Party Secretaries against the numerous 'deviations' which had recently appeared. Among the peasants arrested by the O.G.P.U., there were no doubt kulaks and they no doubt had an anti-Soviet attitude. But on the basis of fighting the kulaks, a revolution was being carried through in the countryside in a bureacratic and repressive fashion, and could not fail to turn the whole peasantry against the Soviet regime.

Here the Stalin phenomenon appears in all its contradictions. It was produced by class struggle and prosecuted it in such a way that only repression could solve the problems it faced. The latter were real, but required different solutions. The aims were socialist, but the means were not in the interests of socialism. The emergence of socialist collectivised agriculture and the elimination of the kulaks were in themselves positive socialist objectives – but the Soviet Union, and the whole international labour movement too, had to pay a high price for the way in which this 'revolution' was achieved. A socialist economy and society were born from the Soviet Revolution and Stalin's policies – without taking this fact into account one misinterprets the contemporary world. At the same time, totalitarian methods were used. They might seem to have made it possible to go faster, to miss out certain stages – but if one examines their consequences, one realises how harmful these methods were, and the extent of the damage which the Soviet Union is still suffering, indirectly at least. Because of the loss of human life, the material damage and the political and ideological problems they caused, it was the longest path to the building of socialism, and not the short cut it seemed to be.

The difficulty of grasping the contradictions of the Stalin phenomenon has proved an obstacle for many analysts. On the one hand, it was conducive to the building of socialism, a fact denied by many writers. On the other hand, it built it in a way which was often barbaric and despotic, which makes socialism odious to all those people who want neither barbarism nor despotism. Many people either deny that the changes effected were socialist in character, or identify socialism and the Stalinist methods as if the combination was an inevitable necessity whatever the time or place. Yet if we examine these contradictions carefully, we are better able to judge the historical and thus specific character of the Stalin phenomenon, which is the product of a specific time and place.

On 1st March 1930, 14,246,000 peasant farms had 'decided' to join a kolkhoz. On 2nd March 1930, *Pravda* published a long article by Stalin which was intended to halt the rural revolution. Stalin reminded his readers that peasants should join the kolkhozes 'of their own free will', and condemned 'these distortions, this bureaucratic decreeing of a collective farm movement, these unseemly threats against the peasants' (*Problems of Leninism*, p. 329). He argued against 'excesses', for example those committed by people who, in order to organise an artel, started by taking down the church bells. 'Remove the church bells – how r-r-revolutionary indeed!' (*ibid*, p. 331). Faced with a catastrophe, he attempted to restrain the forces which he had unleashed. In a few weeks the number of excesses diminished. On 1st May 1930, there were less than 6 million households in the kolkhozes (5,999,000), that is to say a drop of 8,247,000 compared to 1st March of the same year, which means that at least this number of farmers had been forced into the kolkhozes. This gives some idea of the coercion to which the peasants had been subjected. Despite this, the Party's agricultural policy was not changed over the following months. Pressures became more discreet, but they continued. The number of farms which belonged to kolkhozes increased rapidly:

Kholkhoz households

1st May 1930	5,999,000	
2nd February 1931	8,250,000	
10th July 1931	13,839,000	
1st November 1931	15,000,000	(with 230,000 kolkhozes)
1933	15,258,000	
1934	15,717,000	

– that is to say 71·4 per cent of all peasant households.

Stock-breeding was in a catastrophic situation because the peasants slaughtered vast quantities of stock.

Livestock (in millions of animals)

	1929	1933
Cattle	67·1	38·6
Horses	30·7	16·6
Sheep and goats	146·9	50·6
Pigs	20·3	12·2

Though the 1930 harvest had not been bad, that of 1931 was not good, and that of 1932 was apparently quite catastrophic. The liquidation of the kulaks went on after March 1930.

At Roslav, in the Smolensk region, preparations were begun on 15th February 1931 to deport the kulaks to Siberia: 33 families were deported, but these deportations worried all the peasants, who were afraid of being designated as kulaks. On 27th March 1931, 2,202 people (437 families) were gathered at the Roslav resettlement centre. It is understandable that during the 1932–3 winter the U.S.S.R. was on the verge of an economic catastrophe similar to that of 1922, and that certain regions even underwent famine. This was no doubt far from the 10 million dead of which Lewin speaks (*Russian Peasants and Soviet Power*, 1961), but because of the food problem there was again a shortfall in births and an increased rate of mortality.[7] Finally, strict rationing had to be maintained in the towns for many years.

Despite the circumstances under which they were formed, the kolkhozes became centres for technical training and stimulation which encouraged the cultural revolution in the country areas. The setting up of the M.T.S. (machinery and tractor stations) played a considerable role in the countryside. The model constitution for the kolkhoz, which was adopted in 1930, made the artel its organisational model – each kolkhoz elected its own chairman (but the Party organisation nominated him), and the kolkhoz members were paid according to the 'work-day' system.[8] The principle of collectivisation was not in question, the coercion used – contrary to the very principles of

the Soviet regime – in order to create it was. It was to take
years for Soviet agricultute to get over these problems. As in so
many other fields, in agriculture Stalin had imposed his own
ideas. The rapid development of the forces of production was
to be carried out in a planned way and was to start from heavy
industry. This is what Stalin had called the 'metal line', as
opposed to increasing industrial sectors producing consumer
goods which he called the 'textile line'. But Stalin was not
content with this. In an authoritarian manner, he imposed
targets which there was no chance of achieving.

   Communists like Sabsovich ('The U.S.S.R. in Twenty
Years: the U.S.S.R. in Ten Years') even put forward crazy
ideas which doubtless influenced Stalin and other leaders. It
was Sabsovich's intention to catch up with the United States
by 1936! The target figures for industry at the end of the Five
Year Plan which Stalin had put forward were increased every
month. At the 16th Congress, he put forward the target of
17 million tons of steel and 45 million tons of oil. There was
real progress thanks to the sacrifices made by the workers, to
the higher level of investment which was possible because of
greater exploitation of the peasantry, and thanks to the growth
of socialist emulation and to centralised planning. Industrial
output increased by 19·2 per cent according to Soviet statistics
(no doubt an exaggeration of the true facts), and by 13·3 per
cent according to Jasny, an American historian, Russian in

	Coal	Electricity	Steel	Oil
1928	35·5	5	4·5	11·6
1932	64·4	13·5	4·5	28·6

(In millions of tons, apart from electricity which is in thousand
million kWh.)

origin. Let's settle for an increase of 15–16 per cent per year,
which is not bad. Great iron and steel centres and dams
sprang up in the Urals (Magnitogorsk) and the Ukraine,
canals and major railway lines were built, and new oil and
coal fields were opened up (the Dnieprostroi, the Turksib, the
White Sea Canal etc.). New towns like Kuznetsk were built,
and the population of some old towns increased by leaps and
bounds. The U.S.S.R. became covered in building sites – a

start was made on building 1,500 large new factories, most of
which were brought into service during the second Five Year
Plan. Nevertheless, all this remained far below the targets
fixed by Stalin and his economists.

The figure of 17 million tons of steel was only reached in
1939. Utopianism and wishful thinking always smash themselves against the walls of reality, as do misleading promises
and unattainable targets. Stalin made every effort to hide the
truth by cooking the figures. Apart from some general figures
calculated in a way which was not revealed and thus suspect,
Stalin from now on only released comparative statistics.
Although it was useful in many ways, the centralised planning
system was handled in such a way that it encouraged
bureacracy, which was already considerable. The number of
civil servants increased to a significant and unproductive extent.
Often Party full-time workers and functionaries in the state
machine enjoyed material, political and intellectual advantages which gave them certain privileges compared to other
people. However, since it is contrary to the facts, one may
hardly talk of a new class of 'privileged' bureaucrats, as did
some Trotskyites in the thirties and later.[9] Stalin's authority
grew as the years went by. By 1928, the institutions and
mechanisms which were to give the Stalin phenomenon its
tragic dimension already existed, but they were lacking the
impetus which was to set them off. From 1929 on, Stalin
decided everything without consultation. He tended to present
the leading bodies of the Party with *faits accomplis*, to make them
into organs for registering and carrying out his policies, and
until the end of 1934, that is to say until the assassination of
Kirov, the political history of the U.S.S.R. is nothing but a
long series of attempts, which unfortunately never got off the
ground, to re-establish a collective leadership in the Party by
restricting the powers of the 'Gensek'.[10]

The cult of Stalin had gradually developed across the
Soviet Union, everywhere his photograph could be found
outside and inside public buildings. The press was beginning to
extol his virtues. On the occasion of Stalin's fiftieth birthday
in 1929, the State Publishing House published a selection of
articles by leading Party members. On 21st December 1929,
the whole Soviet press devoted numerous pages to Stalin,

celebrating his birthday with articles of fulsome praise supported by photographs. Millions of copies of a terracotta bust and of photographs of him were distributed. His 'companions in arms' quoted him all the way through their articles and speeches. Most of the left opposition leaders had sided with him in order to combat the kulaks and to help build socialism. Only the exiled Trotsky continued to fight against him, but he was alone and ineffective. The right opposition itself supported him. At the 16th Congress in June/July 1930, whilst the tragedy of collectivisation was going on, there was not a breath of criticism of him.

He was making increasing use of the O.G.P.U. For example, it had kept a watch on Bukharin's activities during the 1928–9 events, it was to direct the 'dekulakisation' and the mass deportation of hundreds of thousands of peasants and, finally, it was to organise the first big Moscow trials, the trials of the 'Wreckers'. In contrast to the 1936–8 trials, the aim was to attack non-Communist experts and to prove the existence of a huge foreign plot intended to 'sabotage' the Soviet economy. Starting from the fact that there had been plots against the Soviet Union, Stalin no doubt intended to explain the economic difficulties as caused by 'foreign Imperialism and the internal enemies of the system'. They existed of course, but the way in which the series of trials from 1928 on was organised foreshadows the ones mounted against the Communist leaders in the 1936–8 period too exactly for one not to be tempted to put them in the same category, all the more so because the same policemen and lawyers were involved. A great deal of testimony shows that there was the same kind of set-up.[11] The first trial, that of the Shakhty engineers, took place in 1928. They were mining engineers who, according to the prosecution, were supposed to have sabotaged coal production in the Donbas area. The same methods of examination as at the great Moscow trials were already used. The O.G.P.U. used physical, psychological and moral torture. This trial initiated a wave of terror against bourgeois experts. In 1930 there was the T.K.P. (Toiling Peasant Party) trial. The main defendants were the eminent economist Kondratiev and a lot of other economists and agronomists who were tried *in camera*. At the end of the year, the public trial of the Industrial Party ('Prompartia') took place, involving eight high ranking scientist-administrators, who were accused of having sabotaged the Soviet economy in conjunction with the White Guards and the French government. The Chairman of the Tribunal was Andrei Vyshinsky and the prosecutor was Krylenko (shot a few years later on Stalin's orders). The charges were based on paragraphs 3, 4 and 6 of the 1926 criminal code of the R.S.F.S.R. In excellent harmony, the defendants declared that they were guilty and gave a mass of detailed information about their acts of sabotage and their international contacts. It is practically certain that these confessions were the result of the pressures and numerous, varied tortures they had undergone, but in many spheres people believed them – particularly in the international Communist movement – because of the insane anti-Sovietism which the capitalist countries displayed. The main defendant, Ramzin, the Director of the Institute of Thermo-Dynamics, made a ringing self-criticism. The only proof provided during this trial was in fact the confessions of the accused. The great Soviet historian Tarle was accused of being the future Foreign Minister of the White government. He was arrested and expelled from the Academy of Sciences, then released a little later. Five of the accused, including Ramzin, were condemned to death but pardoned since they were 'criminals rendered harmless as they admitted and regretted their acts'[12] (*The Industrial Party Trial*, p. 232).

In January 1931, the trial of the Union Bureau of the Mensheviks took place. Among those accused was Groman, one of the directors of the Gosplan – an economist of the highest quality – Sukhanov, a former Menshevik in whose house the decisive meeting of the Bolshevik Central Committee had been held on the eve of the October Revolution, and a large number of economists. All of them confessed not only that they had tried to re-form a Menshevik Party in the U.S.S.R., but also that they had plotted with the 'Industrial Party' and the 'Toiling Peasant Party' which had been the subject of the previous cases. They even declared that they had been in contact with the Communist opposition in the U.S.S.R. As a result of this, Ryazanov, the Director of the Marx-Engels-Lenin Institute was called into question and Stalin was able to take his job away and exile him far from Moscow.

All these trials made many people suspicious of intellectuals, high ranking administrators and experts. Stalin had
drastic reductions made in many areas of state activity and
made every effort to bring the Communist intellectuals themselves to heel. Mass repression hit them as early as 1930, and
from then on all researchers were closely watched by the
authorities. All freedom to undertake research or creative work
was stifled. In the historical field, Yaroslavsky was criticised
for his history of the C.P.S.U., and the main target was
Pokrovsky who was 'guilty' of having discredited Russia's past
by showing the origins of Russian Imperialism.

In 1931, Stalin himself wrote a letter to the magazine
The Proletarian Revolution in which he criticised the direction
taken by historical research, for the magazine had published
an over-flattering article about Rosa Luxemburg. 'I think that
they were induced to take that road by the rotten liberalism
which has spread to some extent among a section of the
Bolsheviks. Some Bolsheviks think that Trotskyism is a faction
of Communism. . . . As a matter of fact, Trotskyism is the
vanguard of the counter-revolutionary bourgeoisie which is
fighting Communism. . . . Trotskyism is the vanguard of the
counter-revolutionary bourgeoisie. That is why a liberal attitude towards Trotskyism . . . is stupidity bordering on crime,
bordering on treason to the working class.'

This text is most revealing and characteristic of the way
in which Stalin argued.[13] The counter-revolutionary bourgeoisie was fighting against the U.S.S.R. which it wanted to
destroy. Stalin often started from correct positions. This is one
of the reasons why he was able for such a long time to deceive
so many people of good will, especially abroad. And Stalin
added: Trotskyism criticises the U.S.S.R. and the C.P.S.U.,
which was only partly true, for in February 1930, Trotsky
wrote: 'The success of the Soviet Union in terms of development is taking on global historical significance. Those Social-
democrats who do not even try to appreciate the speed of
growth which the Soviet economy is proving able to achieve
deserve only scorn. The pace is neither steady nor guaranteed.
But it provides practical proof of the immense potential
inherent in the economic methods adopted by Socialism'
('On Economic Imprudence and its Perils', *Opposition Bulletin*,

No. 9). It is true that, blinded by his own personal feelings, Trotsky had not seen the fundamental contradiction within the Stalin phenomenon. Trotsky had his eyes firmly on the history of the French Revolution, and was still thinking of Thermidor – but he had not grasped the fact that Thermidor was the prolongation of the bourgeois revolution with other forms, other methods and even other men. Bonaparte consolidated the bourgeois revolution, just as Stalin was carrying on the Socialist Revolution. Because they had understood this, not out of careerism or fear, most of Trotsky's companions had adopted the Party policy. So Preobrazhensky, Muralov, Piatakov, Smilga, Sosnovsky, Smirnov, Antonov-Ovsenko and Radek, like Zinoviev, Kamenev and several thousand deportees before them, returned to Moscow and were given important tasks in the Party and State organs.

This did not prevent Stalin continuing his argument: 1. The bourgeoisie wants to destroy the U.S.S.R. 2. Trotsky criticises the U.S.S.R. 3. Trotsky is the spearhead of the bourgeoisie. 4. Those who are too gentle with Trotskyism help Trotsky, so they help the bourgeoisie. . . . Here we see the appearance of the various themes which were to be used in the mass repression from 1935 on, and which Stalin had announced as early as 1928 when he declared: 'The more we advance, the greater will be the resistance of the capitalist elements and the sharper the class struggle' (9th July 1928 speech, *C.W.*, Vol. 11, p. 179).

In philosophy, Stalin criticised the Institute of Red Professors and the magazine *Under the Banner of Marxism*, as well as the work of the philosophers Stern and Deborin. By 1930, he began to intervene indirectly in the field of literature, handing out praise and criticism. He abolished all the independent literary associations which still existed and all the publishing co-operatives. In 1929, he had the Union of Soviet Writers founded in order to supervise literary life better, and in 1932 the latter was given a monopoly of organising writers.

However, it would be wrong to think that Stalin encountered no resistance within the Party and its leadership. Of course his authority was great. Bukharin and Tomsky had not been members of the Politbureau since November 1929

and Rykov's expulsion had only been postponed. At the end
of 1930, Rykov was removed from the Politbureau and
replaced as President of the Council of People's Commissars
by Molotov, but – despite this – the Politbureau and the
Central Committee were far from giving Stalin unrestricted
power. The latter was still not free to act as he wished. Of
course Molotov and Kaganovich were unconditional supporters, but all the other leaders were still a threat to him. A
number of the Party leaders, probably even the majority,[14] no
doubt thought it desirable to remove Stalin from his post, but,
because of the despotic power he had, by then it had become
difficult to do so. Given the state the Party was in, it was
difficult to use democratic procedures and anyway Stalin had
no intention of bowing to them. He held power and was ready
to widen the basis of his dictatorship – this is shown by his
attitude from 1935 on. At the beginning of the Stalinist Terror,
some leading comrades tried to resist it, but Stalin and the
O.G.P.U. were on the lookout and kept themselves informed
about any secret meetings which represented a danger to the
General Secretary. Thus in December 1930, Syrtsov (a
candidate member of the Politbureau and President of the
R.S.F.S.R. Council of People's Commissars) and Lominadze
(a member of the Central Committee and Secretary of the
Transcaucasian Party Committee) were expelled from the
Central Committee for having a private conversation in the
course of which they were supposed to have set up a plot
against Stalin. In breach of the Party rules, the decision was
taken by the Politbureau and the officers of the Control
Commission. The Ryutin case was more serious. He was
Secretary of a Moscow district and a former official of the
Central Committee and really seems to have organised a plot
to eliminate Stalin. In 1932 he set up a secret organisation
whose members included Uglanov, former Moscow Party
Secretary and a member of the Politbureau until 1929. Contact
was apparently made with Zinoviev and Kamenev. Ryutin
drew up a manifesto in which he called for the slowing down of
the industrialisation policy and an end to forced collectivisation,
as well as the re-establishment of collective leadership in the
Party. Ryutin and several other leaders were arrested, expelled
from the Party and exiled from Moscow. The same fate again

befell Zinoviev and Kamenev as well as Smirnov, Preobrazhensky and other leading comrades.

However, Stalin was not allowed to reinforce the Terror
as he wished. Faced with the economic problems which the
Soviet Union was experiencing in 1932, he believed that mass
terror was the only way to save his policy. In 1929, apparently
for the first time, he had managed to have a Bolshevik executed.
The man involved was a strange character called Blumkin, a
former left-wing Socialist-Revolutionary who had taken part in
the assassination of the German Ambassador in Moscow,
Count von Mirbach, in July 1918. Then he had joined the
Bolsheviks and became an agent of the Cheka (later of the
O.G.P.U.). In 1929, he had gone to Constantinople where he
had talked to Trotsky who had given him a message to take
back to the U.S.S.R. Radek denounced him and Blumkin was
arrested and shot. In 1932, Stalin wanted to go further and to
drown any opposition to his power and his policy in blood.
The Politbureau and the Central Committee refused to give
in to terror and the O.G.P.U. itself was hesitant. Later Stalin
admitted this in the famous telegram he sent to the Politbureau on 25th September 1936: 'Yagoda has given definitive
proof that he was incapable of unmasking the Trotskyite–
Zinovievite group. The G.P.U. is four years behind in this
case.' Nikolayevsky, a Menshevik who had emigrated to the
U.S.A. and who was Rykov's brother-in-law, had the opportunity to have long discussions with Bukharin when the latter
came to Paris from February to April 1936. He gave an account
of them in an article published in London in 1938, 'The Letter
of an Old Bolshevik'. According to this source, the truthfulness
of which was officially confirmed on several points on the
occasion of the 20th Congress of the C.P.S.U. and subsequently,
Stalin was in the minority in the Politbureau when he proposed
a great public trial for Ryutin whom he wanted executed.
Kirov and Rudzutak energetically opposed further repressive
measures, this time to be directed against the Bolsheviks.
Ordjonikidze, Kossior and Kalinin supported them, Kuibyshev
and Voroshilov hesitated. Only Molotov and Kaganovich
were in full agreement with Stalin. When it met from 28th
September to 2nd October, 1932, the Central Committee
charged Ryutin and his supporters with wishing to restore

capitalism and with helping the bourgeoisie and the kulaks.

Another 'opposition' group was discovered in January 1933 and its members were arrested. Those involved were Smirnov, Eismont (Commissar for Supplies), Tolmachev (Commissar for Transport) and several high-ranking civil servants in the Commissariat for Agriculture. Rykov, Schmidt and Tomsky, the leaders of the 'right opposition', were charged with 'having encouraged them in their subversive activities'. On 5th November 1932, Nadezhda Alliluyeva, Stalin's second wife, committed suicide in a moment of depression which, according to a lot of witnesses, was caused by her disgust at the methods used by her husband.

In 1932 and at the beginning of 1933, steps were also taken against the leaders of the Communist Parties of the Union Republics: Stalin called them 'bourgeois nationalists' because they opposed his centralising and Russian nationalist policy. So in the Ukraine there was a trial involving an alleged 'Union for the Liberation of the Ukraine'. The real aim of this trial was to attack Skrypnik, a Ukrainian Bolshevik leader who had supported Lenin in the 1921–3 debate on the problems of the nationalities. A large number of people were arrested in the universities and Skrypnik committed suicide in 1933. In Armenia, many leaders, including N. Stepanian, Armenian S.S.R. Commissar for Education, were removed. Similar purges took place in the Central Asian Republics. The terror was already being exercised against a large number of peasants, who were far from all being kulaks. New laws had been added to the arsenal of repression. On 7th August 1932, it was decided that in the future the punishment for looting kolkhoz property would be at least ten years hard labour, and the punishment for simply threatening a collective farmer – to get him to leave the kolkhoze – would be from five to ten years hard labour. The punishment for the illegal slaughtering of stock was two years in prison. As a result, the forced labour camps and zones in Siberia began to fill up with hundreds of thousands of people. Two texts show us the extent of this mass repression directed against the peasants. They are in the Smolensk Archives. One is a letter signed by Molotov and Stalin and dated 8th May 1933, the other a circular from the Central Committee and the Central Control

Commission dated 25th May 1933. One reads, for example: 'The Central Control Commission has been informed that locally massive numbers of people are still being arrested, and that legal repression is being carried out on an extraordinary scale. . . .' It is true that in January 1933 the Central Committee had decided to end repression, not to intensify it. Zinoviev, Kamenev, Preobrazhensky and other leaders again returned from deportation and the repression of the peasants was reduced. Without going so far as to stop the forced collectivisation of the land and without giving up the aim of rapid industrialisation, the Central Committee had decided to retreat a little, faced as it was with a food crisis and public discontent. As was his practice in such cases, Stalin had tagged along and changed direction with such enthusiasm that he seemed to have instigated the change himself.

At the beginning of 1933, he had all the more reason for modesty because the results of his policy were hardly brilliant. Despite the communiqués announcing that the high targets fixed by Stalin had been achieved, the results of the first Five Year Plan seem to have been poor. In agriculture, the food crisis was serious. Abroad, Hitler had just taken power in Germany (30th January 1933). There can be no doubt that this was a field in which Stalin bore a heavy responsibility. From 1928 on, the Comintern, which was under the aegis of the C.P.S.U., concentrated its attacks on the 2nd Socialist International, and in Germany the German Communist Party fought against social-democracy as much as it did against Hitler. It had not grasped the novel and criminal nature of Nazism. Of course, the policies adopted by German social-democracy helped to obscure these new facts. The German Communists could still remember how the German Revolution had been crushed by troops under the command of the Social-Democrat Minister of the Interior, Noske. They remembered the foundation of the Weimar Republic, and the often conservative, anti-Communist policies of the Social-democrats in the twenties. They still read socialist communiqués which put the Communists and the Nazis in the same category, but the German Communist Party and the Comintern were not able to perceive the real danger when they should have done.

Stalin stuck to the formulation he had made in 1924:

'Fascism is a militant organisation of the bourgeoisie based on the effective support of Social-democracy. Objectively, Social-democracy is the moderate wing of Fascism . . . these organisations do not conflict, they are complementary. They are not two poles, they are twins.' On the basis of what happened in France in 1934, in 1935 the Comintern was to issue the only slogan and to endorse the only strategy likely to bar the way to Nazism and the other kinds of Fascism – 'Democracy or Fascism'. The alarming situation of the Soviet economy at the beginning of 1933, and Hitler's victory in Germany led the Communist Party of the U.S.S.R. to somewhat modify its policy in 1933 and 1934. Within the country, the targets for the second Five Year Plan were a lot less ambitious than those for the first five years, and investment was much lower.[15] Of course, nothing basic had really changed. Workers still had to have a work-book (introduced in 1931), and could not leave their factory without permission. Absenteeism and poor work were heavily punished, but at the same time new factories were springing up all over the country and hundreds of thousands of shock workers (the *udarniki*) were sparing no effort to improve the quality of work and thus productivity. As for the kolkhoz members, they gradually got the right to cultivate their own piece of ground and to breed their own stock. Without abandoning the collectivisation which had already been achieved, the Soviet leaders still did not really encourage further collectivisation, and operated existing mechanisms with a new flexibility. The 898 million quintal cereal harvest of 1933 made the country safe from famine. Zinoviev, Kamenev and the other opposition deportees came home from Siberia again. The concentration camps were partially emptied, as is shown in the Central Committee circular of May 1933 and the letter signed by Stalin and Molotov. This did not prevent further arrests of Party and State functionaries. For example, in 1933, 35 clerks at the Ministry of the Interior were arrested and shot. In the foreign policy field, the U.S.S.R. had recently denounced all the economic and military clauses in the Rapallo treaties with Germany.[16] In the name of the U.S.S.R., Litvinov put forward a bold plan for disarmament and asked for membership of the League of Nations, which was granted in September 1934. Even literature seemed freer at the beginning of 1934.

The fundamental institutions which gave rise to the Stalin phenomenon still existed, however, without really having been changed. It was simply that the situation was not conducive to its full flowering, and that, as long as it was not fully grown, it was still possible to destroy it – a fact that Stalin was aware of, so he retreated, bided his time and prepared. The 17th Congress of the C.P.S.U. in January 1934 was marked by this ambiguity, but it was only at the end of the year, when Kirov was assassinated, that the position was to be clarified. Then the Stalin phenomenon was to break forth without any kind of restrictions.

NOTES

1. 'Lenin's Political Testament'.
2. All these quotations are from Bukharin's article 'Lenin's Political Testament'.
3. Trotsky was then in exile at Alma-Ata.
4. The Supreme Council for the National Economy insisted on the adoption of higher targets than those provided for by the Gosplan. The plan adopted at the 16th Conference took these increases into account.
5. In many ways these 'kommuna' were the forerunners of the Chinese popular communes.
6. This point of view has been challenged, though on a scientifically weak basis, by two Soviet writers: Voganov (in *Kommunist* No. 3, 1966 and in 'Problems concerning the History of the C.P.S.U.', February 1968) and Trapeznikov (in 'A Historic Experiment by the C.P.S.U.: the achievement of the Leninist plan for co-operatives', Moscow, 1965).
7. The Soviet population was 165,700,000 in 1933, and 170,500,000 in 1939. The increase should have been 3 million a year, a total of 18 million. But it was only 5 million. The deficit of 13 million was the result of the deficit in the birth rate, the results of the 1933 shortages and the Stalin terror. As things stand, it is difficult to give figures for these various factors.
8. 'Work-day': it was the value of a standard day's work at a particular farming job.
9. The phenomenon of bureaucracy must not be mixed up with the existence of a bureaucratic class – management posts were neither hereditary nor were they held for life. One does not find a group of people who occupy the same position in the process of production and the circulation of capital and there is no social reproduction of groups of leaders.
10. General Secretary. At this time, this was the usual nickname given to Stalin who was General Secretary of the C.P.S.U.

11. In particular that quoted by Roy Medvedev in *Let History Judge*.
12. The confessions of the defendants were all the more credible because the French Government and High Command had an anti-Soviet attitude for many years. In 1919, they intervened at Odessa. From 1919 to 1921, they helped Wrangel, Kolchak and Poland. In 1940, they prepared for a military intervention at Petsamo (in Finland), and an airborne attack on the oil-wells in the Caucasus. Stalin always set up his trials with great political shrewdness designed to make the defendants' confessions credible.
13. We must realise that the Trotskyism of 1931 was not that of 1975, which is distinguished by anti-Sovietism and a dogmatic, backward looking strategy.
14. This is why he had most of them executed during the mass repression of the 1936–8 period.
15. For the second five-year period the planned annual growth rate was to be 16 per cent as compared to 21 per cent during the first five years. Investment was also lower (19·5 per cent of the national income as compared to 24 per cent).
16. From 1922 to 1934, German military bases and even arms factories (Krupp) existed in the Soviet Union. The Germans had used this method of getting round the clauses in the Versailles Treaty which forbade them to have an army of more than 100,000 men. (See G. Castellan's study *Le Réarmement clandestin du 3e Reich*.)

4 The Triumph of Stalinism (1934-1939)

Judging by appearances, that is to say by the official speeches, the 17th Congress of the C.P.S.U. went Stalin's way. All the speakers praised him to the skies. And yet, 1,108 of the 1,966 delegates present when this Congress opened in the Great Hall of the Kremlin on 26th January 1934 were to die on his orders in the ensuing years, and this number included 98 of the 139 Central Committee members elected on the last day. Let us try to imagine this hall with its red draped walls, the portraits that decorated it and the platform that dominated it. On that day history had an appointment with history.

The stenographic report shows that 'Comrade Stalin's entrance was marked with loud applause'. The delegates stood and shouted 'Hurrah' and 'Long live comrade Stalin'. Molotov spoke for a few minutes, then handed over to Khrushchev, a young member of the leadership, Second Secretary of the Moscow region, the same man who, twenty years later, was to put an end to the Stalin cult.

Khrushchev introduced the Presidium. Stalin went to the rostrum and read a long report in which he extolled the results of the first Five Year Plan and sketched in the main outlines for the Second. On the platform were the following: Kirov (assassinated at the end of the year), Ordjonikidze (who was to commit suicide in 1935), Kuibyshev (who died under mysterious circumstances in 1935), Rudzutak (President of the Central Control Commission, who was shot in 1938), Kalinin, the President of the U.S.S.R., Voroshilov the leader of the Red Army, Kossior (shot in 1937), Chubar (shot in 1938), Postyshev (shot in 1938), Eikhe (shot in 1940), Petrovsky (who was to lose his post), Zhdanov and Mikoyan, and Stalin's two loyal companions Kaganovich and Molotov.

In the body of the hall the delegates listened attentively. One could pick out Yagoda, the director of the O.G.P.U. (shot in 1936), his successor Yezhov (shot in 1938), and the latter's

replacement Beria (shot in 1953 as the first act of destalinisation). Nearby were the veteran Bolsheviks who had grown grey
in many years of imprisonment, emigration and deportation,
the companions of Lenin: Zinoviev, Kamenev, Bukharin,
Tomsky, Preobrazhensky, Radek, Rykov and Piatakov. The
youngest delegates observed the old guard with interest and
concern. There was only one absentee, Trotsky who was still in
exile. Seventy years of history had come together there on this
cold day in January 1934. Outside it was freezing hard. In its
mausoleum, Lenin's embalmed body was still protected by a
guard with an already well-established ritual. Dozens of
foreign delegates came: leaders of the Comintern and
secretaries of (often underground) Communist Parties. The
'Congress of the Victors' began. It is impossible not to feel
deep emotion when thinking of the tragic fate of these delegates,
representatives of a whole people and a whole era. They had
already had to face many ordeals, but those were nothing
compared to what the future held in store for them: the
Stalinist Terror, the Second World War, Reconstruction.

The fact that all the former members of the opposition
apart from Trotsky were present at the Congress is characteristic of the real contradictions in the 1934 situation. Even
more significant is the fact that the delegates listened to these
former oppositionists attentively. In his report, Stalin did
indeed forcefully denounce Trotskyism, but he did not attack
those present, some of whom had just returned from their
second spell of deportation. One feels that it really was a
congress of Party unity, and that a compromise had been
adopted to avoid a debate which, from either side, would have
threatened this unity. Oddly enough, Isaac Deutscher scarcely
mentions the 17th Congress, though he was a perceptive
historian on the subject of Trotsky and Stalin. Only Roy
Medvedev devotes a few pages to it in *Let History Judge*.

Besides, the speeches made by the former members of the
opposition, who were all to be exterminated in the 1936–8
period, were not lacking in interest. For example, Bukharin
started by paying homage to Stalin and by a personal *mea
culpa* which would make one smile if it were not tragic. 'The
conditions for the victory of our Party were, firstly, the working
out of a remarkably correct policy line by the Central

Committee and by comrade Stalin, secondly, the brave and diligent carrying out of this line and, thirdly, the pitiless crushing of opposition groupings and of the right opposition as the chief danger, that is to say of the very grouping to which I belonged.' Of Stalin, Bukharin said that he was 'the best representative and the instigator of the Party line who achieved victory in the inner Party struggles by taking Lenin's policy as his guide'. According to Bukharin, Stalin was 'the incarnation of the Party's spirit and will, its leader, its practical and theoretical guide'. Next, Bukharin stressed the technological changes brought about by the achievement of the first Five Year Plan. He gave a very intelligent demonstration of the new role of science in production. Then, with rare forcefulness, he stressed the danger of war from two sources: Fascist Germany and Imperial Japan. He quoted at length from Hitler's *Mein Kampf*, whilst Stalin had contented himself with brief reference in his speech. 'We are far from being enthusiastic about the fascist regime in Germany', Stalin was content to say (*Problems of Leninism*, p. 467), and he described the conflict 'between the old policy, which was reflected in the well-known treaties between the U.S.S.R. and Germany' (the Rapallo treaties), and the 'new' policy, which, in the main, 'recalls the policy of the former German Kaiser . . . and this "new" policy is obviously gaining the upper hand over the old policy. . . .'

And though he criticised the policy of Germanic racial superiority *vis-à-vis* the Slavs (*ibid.*, p. 463), he did not even mention Hitler by name. Starting from the idea that fascism is a sign of the weakness of the bourgeoisie, which was quite true, Stalin underestimated its destructiveness and its novel characteristics. In contrast, Bukharin used quotations to show the danger hanging over the Soviet Union, and he ended his speech as follows: 'This is the bestial face of the class enemy. This is what faces us, and this is what we are going to have to do in the most gigantic battles that history will ever have imposed on us. We know very well that it is our side which is fighting for socialism and that as a result it is the side of those fighting for technology, science, culture and human happiness.' And whilst he praised Stalin, he concluded by stressing the need for unity: 'We will fight, we will go into battle on behalf of humanity. In this struggle, unity, unity and unity whatever

D

the cost is necessary. . . .' According to various testimonies which the Soviets themselves later confirmed (in *The History of the U.S.S.R.*, Moscow, 1964, Vol. 2, pp. 270–1), many members of the Party leadership allegedly wanted to replace Stalin with Kirov. Lenin's testament was still very much present in the minds of most of them. Of course, the testament had not been published in the U.S.S.R.,[1] though the 15th Congress of the C.P.S.U. had decided that it should be – but the text had been printed in the Congress report, which is why many of the delegates to the 17th Congress were familiar with it. Kirov, who was Leningrad Party District Secretary, a candidate member of the Central Committee since the 11th Congress (1922) and a member of the Politbureau, as a candidate since the 15th Congress (1927) and a full member since the 16th Congress (1930), had been a loyal assistant to Stalin until 1933 and had played an important role in the battles against the 'oppositions in the Party'. Kirov did not allow himself to be nominated against Stalin, but when the election for the Central Committee took place his name was only crossed out three times whilst Stalin's was crossed out 270 times. Stalin was to remember all this, but at the beginning of 1934 conciliation was still the best course for him.

The Central Committee election reflected this. Some young comrades were elected: Beria, Zhdanov, Khrushchev, Yezhov (one of Stalin's trusties), Poskrebyshev (Stalin's private secretary) and Bulganin, who were to play an important part during the next thirty years, whilst all the leaders elected at the 15th Congress in 1927 were re-elected. The only member of the 1927 Politbureau not re-elected at the 17th Congress was Uglanov. A certain number of former opposition leaders who had apologised were re-elected to the Central Committee: Pyatakov as a full member, Bukharin, Rykov and Tomsky as candidates. To sum up, Stalin was on probation. Changes in the Party rules put quite as strong an emphasis on internal Party democracy as on discipline. It was laid down that Party Congresses should take place every three years and that the Central Committee should meet every four months. The relationship between the various leading bodies was specified as follows: 'Article 33. – The Central Committee shall appoint the Politbureau to deal with political work, the Orgbureau for the overall management of organisational work and the Secretariat to handle the day to day organisational and executive work.' This meant nothing less than the relegation of the Secretariat (and the General Secretary) to a secondary role. The 17th Congress said that the Party leadership was the Central Committee, and Article 33 specified that it should keep Party organisations informed about its work. Of course, in the actual Soviet situation in 1934, this was wishful thinking, but it showed that Stalin faced real problems. Besides, Kirov, along with Kaganovich and Zhdanov, became a member of the Secretariat and of the Orgbureau together with Stalin, Kaganovich, Kuibyshev, Gamarnik, Yezhov, Kosarev and Zhdanov.

Finally, members of the Central Committee could only be expelled by a meeting of the Central Committee and of the Central Control Commission, to be called by the Plenum, and a two-thirds majority of those present would be required (Article 58), which was far from having been the case up until then and which was not to be in the years ahead. If one considers Stalin's political practice rather than his speeches, none of these measures could have been welcome to him, since they strengthened socialist legality and thus restricted the repression of Communists. Beneath the surface, the year 1934 was distinguished by the conflict between these two approaches, involving not the former opposition and the Party, but the Party and Stalin, a battle Stalin was to win in the end by having recourse to provocation, cunning and terror in order to crush the Party.

The compromise reached at the 17th Congress forced Stalin to change his attitude on various points. He enlisted the help of Gorky and tried to win over the writers by receiving them in person. He appointed Bukharin Editor in Chief of *Izvestia* (the second most important paper in the country after *Pravda*), had a talk with Kamenev and gave him a post as manager of the Academic Publishing House. He gave permission for the first Congress of Soviet Writers, which took place with many foreign writers, including Gide, Malraux and Aragon, present. At this Congress, the representatives of the various literary trends spoke relatively freely, though Zhdanov set utilitarian aims for literature, the writer being defined as 'an engineer of souls'. Bukharin protested against this excessively narrow definition of 'socialist realism' and attacked literary ultra-leftism, whilst Radek criticised the new literature, taking as an example James Joyce, who was defended by others with the support of Bukharin. Gorky, Pasternak and Ehrenburg made contributions attacking dogmatism. The majority of those who took part in this Congress, whatever tendency they belonged to, were to perish in the mass repression of the following years. In the international field, the U.S.S.R., now a member of the League of Nations, made repeated overtures to the capitalist countries in favour of disarmament, collective security and unity against fascism.

On 10th July 1934, the O.G.P.U. was abolished; this was perhaps an attempt to reduce the power of the political police. The People's Commissariat for Internal Affairs was made responsible for the tasks which had until then been the responsibility of the O.G.P.U., which became part of the new commissariat (N.K.V.D.). Thus, central departments were set up within the N.K.V.D.:

> State Security,
> Workers' and Peasants' Militia,
> Defence of the Frontier and the Territory,
> Fire Service,
> Corrective Labour Camps and Labour Colonies (the Gulag),
> Registrar's Office,
> Economic and Administrative Department.

The 'Judicial College' was also abolished. The *Pravda* headline read 'Protection of Revolutionary Order and State Security'.

At the same time, a Special Commission (the *Osoboie Sovieshchanie*: OSSO) attached to the N.K.V.D. was set up; the OSSO 'had the right to apply by administrative methods, exile, deportation and incarceration in corrective labour camps for up to five years and expulsion from Soviet territory.' Thus, what was given with one hand was taken back with the other, and the leadership, composition and powers of the political police remained intact. The Party and the State were incapable of really changing it by legal methods alone: it had become a state within the state and Stalin still controlled it directly through his personal secretariat. Anybody who was a 'danger to society' could be deported for five years. The Special Commission was made up of 'the deputies of the People's Commissar for Internal Affairs, the assistant to the People's Commissar of the R.S.S.F.R., the overall Commander of the Militia, and of the People's Commissar for Internal Affairs of the Republic involved'. The Public Prosecutor of the U.S.S.R. took part in the meetings of the Special Commission and had the right to protest decisions at the Presidium of the Central Executive Committee. The latter provision might have allowed some restriction of the arbitrary power of the Special Commission, but Vishynsky had held the post since 1933![2] The Special Commission constituted an emergency body which took decisions without any supervision and without the internal and external situation of the U.S.S.R. really justifying it. Reading the contents of the law setting up the N.K.V.D., one realises the great extent to which insufficient democracy lies at the origin of the growth and triumph of the Stalin phenomenon. There is nothing vaguer than the definition of a 'dangerous' individual – and who can really decide such a thing? The very principle of a Special Commission was particularly pernicious, implying as it did preventive deportation of 'the individual who was a danger to society', with no possibility of a defence, with no lawyer and no right to know the details of the case against him. The majority of the Party leadership were digging their own graves by accepting these provisions, which were of unparalleled strictness and arbitrariness, even if the Prosecutor's office could intervene and to some extent restrict repression, which anyway was not to happen.

Though he had to display some cunning, Stalin still held some real trump cards: the improved economic situation and food supply reinforced his popularity but it also made the emergency measures and the Terror more surprising. Stalin valued these measures because they were the only way to eliminate his past and future opponents, that is to say the majority of the Communists. At the end of November 1934, the Central Committee met again and confirmed the policy of internal détente and anti-fascist unity abroad. The situation was probably getting somewhat uncomfortable for Stalin who

had reason to fear that his power would be further restricted
in the months ahead. Kirov had given the Politbureau report
to the Central Committee; he was Leningrad Party Secretary
and was to settle in Moscow in early 1935 in order to work in
the Central Committee Secretariat. All the members of the
former opposition groups, including Rakovsky, had returned
to Moscow. Only Trotsky was absent, and for how long was
this likely to last? If there was a war, would it not be necessary
to achieve national unity against the enemy, and how could
they not call on the father of the Red Army, the man who had
won the Civil War? Facing a more or less long-term threat,
Stalin had to act and act quickly.

    Seen from this point of view, it is easier to understand why
Kirov was assassinated. He returned to Leningrad on the
27th November and was assassinated by a certain Nikolayev in
a corridor of the Smolny Institute late on the afternoon of
1st December. The precise circumstances, if not the motives, of
the assassination are now known. Details were given by the
Soviet authorities at the 22nd Congress of the C.P.S.U. (in
1961). Nikolayev was mentally disturbed. After the Civil War,
during which he had fought in the Red Army, he held various
administrative posts, but without success. He was expelled
from the Party in March 1934, he was unemployed and
embittered and an easy prey for any adventure. Was he a paid
killer or a fanatic who was used? We will probably never know.
What is certain, however, is that the case is riddled with
implausibility, especially if we remember that the location is
the Soviet Union at a time when the N.K.V.D. was already
all-powerful. A month before, Nikolayev had been arrested by
Kirov's guards. On him they had found a plan of Kirov's
usual route and a document case into which a loaded gun had
been slipped. Nikolayev was questioned by the second-in-
command of the Leningrad N.K.V.D. Zaporozhets, and freed
on the orders of Yagoda, the People's Commissar for the
Interior. He was arrested a second time on a Leningrad bridge
and again released. These two facts are enough to show
that the N.K.V.D. was involved in the assassination of
Kirov. According to Medvedev (*Let History Judge*), Borisov,
Kirov's chief bodyguard (or 'gorilla' as they are now called),
warned him of the danger, but it was in vain. After the

assassination, Borisov died in a car accident caused by the
N.K.V.D. agents who were taking him to Smolny (Khrushchev,
in the minutes of the 22nd Congress, p. 505). All these agents
were shot some time afterwards. Nikolayev's trial took place in
camera with no lawyers present. On 30th December, Nikolayev
and several other people accused of being his accomplices were
executed. The man in charge of the Leningrad N.K.V.D. and
his deputy were relieved of their posts and tried, and perished
during the mass repression. When he was tried in 1938, Yagoda
admitted that he had instigated the murder but on the orders
of Rykov and Yenukidze. Of course, this final detail is
inaccurate. Who, other than Stalin, gave orders to Yagoda?
There is of course no specific proof, and absolute proof of
Stalin's responsibility will probably never be found, but it may
be noted that the assassination of Kirov was to his advantage in
every sense.

Stalin was rid of the man who, increasingly, seemed to be
a potential successor, being less brutal and more moderate,
and he could attribute responsibility to the Communists he
wanted to eliminate. Thanks to the stir caused in Soviet public
opinion and in the Party by this assassination, he could
eliminate his potential opponents and apply the policy which
he had been demanding in vain for several years. To sum up,
whether Stalin was directly responsible for the assassination of
Kirov,[3] or whether he just took advantage of it, it constituted
a real *coup d'état* against the Party and the Soviet State. On the
very evening of the murder, and without consulting his
colleagues in the Politbureau, Stalin had a decree promulgated
which ordered that trials of terrorists already underway should
be speeded up, that death sentences already pronounced should
be carried out at once, though these trials were not in any way
directly linked to the assassination of Kirov. Thirty-nine
people were executed in Leningrad, twenty-nine in Moscow and
dozens more in the Ukraine. The N.K.V.D. forced Nikolayev to
confess that an underground 'Zinovievite' group in Leningrad
had supposedly ordered him to execute Kirov. The Latvian
Consul in Leningrad was alleged to have put the culprits in
touch with Trotsky. Another underground group had allegedly
decided to have Stalin assassinated too. We now know that
these were total fabrications. It was a case of the thief shouting

'Stop thief!' There are few such gross examples of duplicity and provocation in history.

On 16th December, Kamenev, Zinoviev and several former members of the Party leadership were arrested. The first big trial began on 15th January 1935 in Leningrad. Zinoviev was condemned to ten years in prison, Kamenev to five. Hundreds of arrests took place; all those arrested were Communists and they were all deported for five years as the OSSO (the N.K.V.D. Special Commission) decreed. The Party had been purged in 1933 and 1934, 800,000 people had been expelled in 1933 and 340,000 in 1934. Party membership had fallen a little but remained considerable:

	Members	Probationers	Total
1932	1,769,773	1,347,377	3,117,250
1933	2,203,251	1,351,387	3,555,938
1934	1,827,756	874,252	2,701,008
1935	1,659,104	699,620	2,358,714

The measures taken at the end of 1934 and at the beginning of 1935 only concerned a few thousand Communists, but all were threatened. The December 1934 Central Committee circular 'The Lessons to be Learnt from the Events Linked with the Abominable Murder of Comrade Kirov' called for the purging of members of the former opposition groupings. Lists of suspects were drawn up during meetings and there was a flood of denunciations. In Leningrad there were thousands of arrests. The Politbureau approved all these measures as it was faced with a *fait accompli*, worried about the way in which the situation was developing and had been deceived as to the guilt of the internal opposition. The Central Committee was not even convened. In a few weeks, Stalin had got back on course; but he could not carry things right through, for the majority of the Politbureau were still against executing former Party leaders. For Stalin, the problem was that he intended to establish his own dictatorship on the basis of the Soviet system, stemming from the October Revolution and socialism. So he had to appear to be carrying on Lenin's work and not to be making a violent break with the past. He had to proceed stage by stage, and in such a way that his victims seemed to be the enemies of the Revolution and Soviet power. This was necessary both within the Soviet Union and abroad, and reflected a truth which is perhaps difficult to perceive or admit: in fact, he *was* building socialism, even if his methods were despotic. Of course, one may consider that it would have been both necessary and possible to have acted differently. But for the historian that is unfortunately a purely theoretical question, because things happened as they did and in no other way, and it is in the nature of history that it takes a course which is no doubt strange, but which cannot be altered in any respect from the precise moment that it becomes history. To say this in no way implies approval of the Stalin phenomenon, and this book demonstrates the author's feelings; rather it is an attempt to make an objective analysis, one which will therefore take into account all the contradictory aspects.[4] Most of the historians who have written about this period have concentrated on only one aspect of the phenomenon. Some have stressed its despotic side, others the positive record of socialist construction. In my view, neither group is wrong, but the important thing to grasp is the dialectical connection between the various aspects of the Stalin phenomenon.

At the beginning of 1935, the majority of the Politbureau, with the support of most Party members and public opinion, were still opposed to the Terror, for which they could see no clear need; but the Politbureau was no longer capable of restricting the growth of the Stalin phenomenon. This is why the assassination of Kirov marked a turning point in the political history of the U.S.S.R.

With the support of the N.K.V.D., Stalin now had the Party at his mercy. Only the intervention of the Red Army could possibly have changed the situation. In order for this to happen both the will and the capacity must have been present. The leaders of the Red Army did not wish to intervene, at least up until 1936, and afterwards they were not capable of doing so. The Red Army had maintained the tradition of submitting to the authority of the Party, and this made it difficult for it to intervene in internal Party affairs. The memory of the role of the French Army and of Napoleon in the French Revolution, and the fear of military dictatorship, prevented anyone from using the Army to resolve by force a

political and ideological debate or conflict among the leaders.
The real danger lay elsewhere. In 1975, we know this, but
forty years ago people's attention was on the bitter memory of
18th Brumaire.

Stalin was making every effort to control the Politbureau
and to prevent any opposition to his policy, but he still had
problems. Zinoviev and Kamenev were in prison, but they
had not been executed. The proof that Stalin still had problems
is furnished by the fact that when the Central Committee met
in February 1935, Mikoyan and Chubar were elected as full
members of the Politbureau, and Zhdanov and Eikhe as
candidates. Kuibyshev had died of a heart attack[5] on the
26th January, and he, like Kirov, had to be replaced. But
Chubar and Eikhe had supported Kirov and were executed in
the following period. So the results of the Politbureau elections
respected the balance of power as established at the 17th
Congress.

This did not prevent Stalin from starting a reign of
terror within the Party, as the Smolensk Archives show with
great precision and clarity, though it was in no way comparable
to what was to take place from 1936 on. At the same time, he
forced his potential opponents to retreat in ways which he had
cleverly calculated. Yenukidze had to make a public apology
in *Pravda* on 16th January 1935, and Gorky was attacked
in several articles in the Party paper during January 1935.
In March 1935, Yenukidze lost his post as Secretary of the
Central Executive Committee of the Soviets and in June he
was expelled from the Central Committee. Meanwhile,
Stalin had disbanded two associations which in a way represented the moral conscience of the system. These were the
Society of Veteran Bolsheviks and the Association of Former
Political Prisoners. Now, both of them had signed a petition
opposing the use of the death penalty against former Bolsheviks.
In July 1935, Kamenev was tried in camera and sentenced to
ten years in prison on the pretext that he had organised a plot
against Stalin. Nevertheless, 1935 and 1936 were distinguished
by the fragile balance which had been observed at the 17th
Congress. The Communist Party seemed to be still functioning,
but this was a mere façade. The Central Committee as well as
the leading organs of the Party and all levels of grass roots

organisation sometimes met. A new constitution was being prepared by a commission on which Bukharin and Radek, among others, sat. The draft was published on 12th June 1936 and adopted by the Congress of Soviets at the end of the year. It established political equality for all citizens, which theoretically represented a considerable step forward compared to the 1918 and 1924 Constitutions. Apart from this, the basic civil rights were proclaimed (the right to work, leisure, rest, education and retirement), equality of the nationalities and sexes, freedom of conscience and the inviolability of person, residence and correspondence were recognised. The practice of the other freedoms was still linked 'to the interests of the working class' and had to pass through the medium of the mass organisations and the Party. The latter was characterised as 'the vanguard of the working class' and 'the leading nucleus of all the organisations of the working class'. Despite these limitations, the 1936 Constitution represented, in theory at least, a favourable judicial framework for the blossoming of democracy.

This was all the more credible because the Soviet economy was recording indisputable successes. In the industrial field, the second Five Year Plan was reaping the benefits of the investment and effort made since the beginning of the first. Output of fuel (apart from oil) was increasing rapidly, and that of the iron and steel industry was growing even more spectacularly. For example, steel output grew as follows:

In millions of tons

1932	1933	1934	1935	1936
5·9	6·9	9·69	12·59	16·40

The sector producing consumer goods was not growing at the same speed, but this was because priority had deliberately been given to heavy industry. The second Five Year Plan was completed ahead of target, as had been the first (in 4 years and 3 months). Of course, we must take into account the statistical whims of the period, but the successes were real. Agriculture was also experiencing an indisputable improvement. The output of grain was increasing despite a moderate harvest in 1936. For wheat, the yield per hectare went up from 7 to 9 quintals. Livestock was being replaced and, thanks to the collective farmers' private plots, the production of fruit and vegetables was increasing. Even if it was not as great as Stalin said, this economic progress constituted the actual foundations on which the Stalinist terror was to develop, at variance with this progress, with the constitution and the remarkable cultural advance achieved by peoples previously condemned to ignorance.

Repression went on within the Party and the country as a whole until August 1936, though it was still restricted. The 1935 purge had affected tens of thousands of Communists, and in early 1936 it was decided to hold a card exchange which was to remove several tens of thousands more. What was serious was the way in which these purges were carried out. It was based on denunciations and N.K.V.D. checks and gave the purged Communists little chance of defending themselves. In contrast with the earlier purges, which had eliminated 'careerist elements', now those mainly affected were old Bolsheviks; those expelled experienced difficulties in their daily life and in getting work. The instruments of terror were being set up. The existence of the Special Commission (the OSSO) made it possible to deport anyone for five years simply on the basis of an administrative decision. In 1935, laws which made flight abroad punishable by death were added to the arsenal of repression. Relations of soldiers who had gone abroad faced automatic exile. On 7th April 1935, a decree determined that all penalties, including the death penalty, would be applied to all Soviet citizens over the age of 12. The N.K.V.D. saw an increase in its role. Apart from dealing with internal and external security, it also acquired tasks in the economic field. The principle of 'corrective' labour camps was originally based on the wish to re-educate common-law offenders and counter-revolutionaries by making them work for the community. Until 1929, there were not many camps and the number of inmates was not large. From 1930 on, the number of camps and deportees increased because of the repression of the kulaks and all peasants who objected to collectivisation. A lack of reliable sources makes it quite impossible to give precise figures. We do know that by 1933 about 850,000 kulaks (or people taken to be kulaks) had been deported since 1929, but this is about the only precise figure that we have (in a letter from Molotov to Stalin in May 1933). We also know that from 1930 on, several major construction projects were completed under the control of the O.G.P.U. For example, this was true of the White Sea–Baltic Sea Canal (the Stalin Canal) which employed up to 300,000 people from the forced labour camps that had been set up in the North. The first camps were set up as early as 1923 on the Solovetsky Islands (this was openly admitted in a Soviet book published at the time). Apart from the Smolensk Archives, the sources of our information up until 1953 were accounts or testimony from Soviet deserters, from foreigners who had been deported; after 1953, Soviet publications themselves gave deportees who had been released and rehabilitated the chance to express themselves.

The first major Moscow trial started on 19th August 1936. This date is important because for the first time Stalin was carrying out the plan he had been unable to put into action since 1932: he was expanding the anti-Communist Terror. With quite incredible skill and incomparable daring, he sheltered under the flag of the Revolution and of socialism and forced the historical leaders of the 1917 Revolution to admit their guilt. In a world where the noise of arms was becoming ever louder,[6] where Nazism was blossoming and anti-Sovietism was as strong as ever, he was to manage to make the most absurd inventions of his political police seem credible. The accused were to repeat their confessions at the trials thanks to refined methods of torture[7] (physical torture, the use of drugs, threats to their families, political and ideological pressures). The confessions of the accused made the Terror and mass repression appear justified. The Party leadership and the Comintern were faced with a *fait accompli*. How could people have any doubts about the plot when they heard Zinoviev or Kamenev declare that they were agents of the Gestapo and had plotted the assassination of members of the Politbureau? The worst thing was that Stalin in fact had himself had a certain number of them assassinated, certainly two full members, Chubar and Kossior, and three candidates, Eikhe, Postyshev and Rudzutak. He was perhaps responsible for the death of Kuibyshev, certainly for that of Orjonikidze, and probably for that of Kirov. Thus he made the accused confess to the crimes he himself had committed.

There were two other big trials organised according to
the same scenario. In 1937, Pyatakov, Radek and others were
tried, confessed their guilt and most were executed. In 1938,
it was the turn of Bukharin, Rykov and a few others. Tomsky
had committed suicide in 1936, and Orjonikidze perished in
1937, either committing suicide or being killed by Stalin.
The man in charge of the N.K.V.D., Yagoda, had been
dismissed and sent to prison in 1937, tried and shot in 1938.
He was replaced by Yezhov, who, in his turn, was arrested and
shot in 1939. Almost all of those who had been in the Party
leadership in the 1917–22 period were thus executed, after
they had admitted they were agents of the Gestapo or of the
Japanese Secret Service, but apart from their confessions, no
material proof of their guilt was ever produced.

Despite the rules adopted at the 17th Congress, the leading
organs of the Party were not consulted, and there was a very
good reason for this – the majority were against this policy.
That is why Stalin had them murdered. Let us take the Central
Committee which was elected at the 11th Congress, the last
one that Lenin was present at:

Andreyev	died in 1972
Bukharin[8]	executed in 1938
Dzerzhinsky	died in 1927
Yaroslavsky	disappeared in 1938
Kalininin	died in 1946
Kamenev	executed in 1936
Korotkov	executed in 1937
Kuibyshev	died in 1935
Lenin	died in 1924
Molotov	
Orjonikidze	committed suicide in 1937
Petrovsky	sent to prison for 20 years
Radek	imprisoned in 1937
Rakovsky	executed in 1937
Rudzutak	executed in 1938
Rykov	executed in 1938
Sapronov	executed in 1937
Smirnov A.P.	disappeared in 1938
Sokolnikov	executed in 1938

Stalin	died in 1953
Tomsky	committed suicide in 1936
Chubar	executed in 1938
Trotsky	assassinated in 1940
Voroshilov	died in 1970
Zelensky	executed in 1937
Zinoviev	executed in 1936

So, 16 of the 26 full members were executed, assassinated (or forced to commit suicide) or deported by Stalin; a similar fate befell 6 of the 10 members of the 1922 Politbureau, 8 of the 13 members of the 1924 Politbureau and 9 of the 17 men elected to the Politbureau after the 15th Congress held in 1927.

Of 31 members elected to the Politbureau in the period from 1919 to 1935, 20 perished in tragic circumstances. The same was true at the level of the Central Committee and of Regional, Provincial and Local Secretaries. The public trials in Moscow only involved a tiny minority of Communists. Most of the Communists who were arrested were executed or deported without a public trial, and in most cases with no trial at all. In 1937–8, Yezhov sent Stalin 383 lists of leading comrades who were to be tried by the Military Tribunal, but for whom there was only one possible sentence (death), which, according to Khrushchev (Secret Report to the 20th Congress), had been decided beforehand. Stalin and Molotov ratified these sentences (speech to the 22nd Congress by Sverdiuk, First Vice-President of the Party Control Commission).

This Terror cannot be compared with that of the French Revolution nor of the Civil War, and there are two reasons for this. It was in no way justified by revolutionary motives, and it was incomparably bloodier. During the 1793–4 Terror, about 30,000 people died. As for the Red Terror during the Civil War, even according to the most anti-communist sources, it claimed no more than 150,000 victims. But, in the 1936–8 period, the Stalinist Terror claimed several hundreds of thousands of victims, and here we are referring only to those who were executed and not to those who perished in the forced labour camps. Party functionaries were joined by economists, intellectuals, foreign Communists, many Communists from the Union and Autonomous Republics who were of non-Russian nationality, leaders of the Komsomol and the trade unions. Here we are not concerned to draw up a detailed report on this mass repression. We have seen what happened at the level of the Politbureau and the Central Committee. The same was true of all levels of Soviet life. So this mass repression destroyed the Party.

Under the pressure of the N.K.V.D., the Bolsheviks were denouncing each other. In February 1937, the Central Committee, under pressure from Stalin, was to endorse this policy, which still did not prevent two-thirds of its members being arrested and shot by the N.K.V.D. The majority of the members of the Party leadership at the time of the October Revolution were shot. Most of the men in charge of the Gosplan and a large number of People's Commissars and Ambassadors died in the upheaval. For example, two Vice-Presidents of the Council of People's Commissars, the President of the Council of Commissars of the R.S.S.F.R. and his two Vice-Presidents, numerous People's Commissars of the Union, and many Presidents of the Council of the other Union Republics (including the Ukraine, Azerbaijan, Georgia, Tadzikstan and Armenia), or of the Autonomous Republics were victims of Stalinist repression. The leaders of the Party Central Committees in the Union Republics were decimated (in the Ukraine, Uzbekistan, Tadjikistan, Turkmenistan, Armenia and Georgia among others). The majority of the Komsomol Central Committee suffered the same fate.

Stalin also moved against the Red Army. On 12th June 1937, the Soviet press published news alleging that a military plot had been discovered and its instigators executed. Those involved were Marshal Tukhachevsky, Deputy Commissar for Defence, General Yakar, Commander of the Kiev military region, General Uborevich, Commander of the Byelorussian military region and many other generals. Gamarnik, Chief Political Commissar of the Army, had committed suicide a few days before. The Red Army was quite literally decimated by repression. It lost tens of thousands of good officers, and tens of thousands more were deported. Among the victims, let us point out Marshals Blucher and Yegorov, General Vatsetis, many admirals, and most of the officers in charge of military academies. In all, 3 out of 5 marshals, 13 out of 15 commanders of armies, 57 out of 85 corps commanders and 110 out of 195 divisional commanders perished as victims of Stalinist repression.

Repression was just as strong in the field of culture. Stalin had abolished all the new institutions which had emerged just after the Civil War, like the Sverdlov University even though it was there he had given his lectures which were published as a collection in a book which had become famous: *The Fundamentals of Leninism*. Historians and philosophers, biologists and mathematicians, writers and artists perished in their thousands or spent long years as deportees. For example, this is what happened to Knorin, Director of the Party History Institute, to the philosopher Stern, to the biologist Vavilov, to the writers Mandelstam and Babel and to the theatrical director Meyerhold.

The mass repression also affected the foreign Communists in Moscow. The Swiss Platten and the Pole Ganetsky, former companions of Lenin, were executed. The Polish Communist Party was disbanded in 1938. The same thing happened to the Communist Parties of the Western Ukraine and of Western Byelorussia. Repression struck the leaders of the Communist Parties of Latvia, Estonia and Lithuania (the Baltic Republics were not yet Soviet Republics). Leading members of the Yugoslavian C.P. (including Copic, Secretary of the Central Committee), of the Bulgarian C.P. (including Popov and Tanev who had been with Dimitrov in Leipzig) and of the Chinese, Korean, Iranian and Indian C.P.s also perished. Bela Kun, one of the leaders of the Hungarian Revolution in 1919, was executed. German Communists like Eberlein, Secretary of the Central Committee, who had sought refuge in the U.S.S.R., were also victims of repression.

Let us take an example, that of the Smolensk area, which gives an idea of the mass repression. The whole Party leadership, starting with Rumyantsev, an old Bolshevik who was Secretary of the Obkom and a Central Committee member, was eliminated in June 1937. One thousand Party and Soviet cadres were replaced in a few weeks. Repression spread to the victims' families and to non-Communists. The reasons for it were not always political. The system of denunciations and their volume were such that it was very easy for the denouncer

to become a victim of repression in his turn. In this way
millions of people were deported. We do not know their
numbers; they were high, but it does not seem possible to give
precise figures. The cross-checks carried out by certain Western
writers are often based on fanciful calculations, and from the
Soviet side we only have fragmentary information, published
in a variety of places after the 20th Congress of the C.P.S.U.
They are certainly of the order of several millions. Medvedev
says 5 million people were arrested from 1936 to 1939, and
between 400,000 and 500,000 were, he says, executed. These
are the figures which Naum Jasny (who was strongly anti-
Soviet, however) and Isaac Deutscher adopted. One need do
nothing more than read the speeches made by the Soviet
leaders at the 22nd Congress of the C.P.S.U. in 1961. Shelepin
(who was then President of the Committee for State Security
and who is now President of the Central Council of Trade
Unions) demonstrated that Stalin, Molotov and Kaganovich
were responsible for these executions (stenographic report in
Cahiers du Communisme, pp. 291–2), but it is hard to imagine
that the other members of the Politbureau were not aware of
what was happening: this was true of Zhdanov, Khrushchev
(however, he could hardly say so in 1961 when he was General
Secretary of the C.P.S.U.), Mikoyan and many others.

Spiridonov (a member of the Central Committee and
Party Secretary in Leningrad) declared: 'For four years a
continuous wave of repressive measures broke over men who
had done nothing dishonourable. Many were executed without
proper examination or trial, on the basis of hastily fabricated
cases. The victims of repression were not only these workers
themselves, but also their families, including children . . .'
(*ibid.*, p. 358). D. Lazurkina (Leningrad) added: 'And what
atmosphere was created in 1937? Fear for which we Leninists
were not responsible reigned. People could rely on nothing.
We went as far as slandering each other' (*ibid.*, p. 364). Others
spoke of the purges in Georgia, Armenia and Byelorussia.
There have been few dramas of this kind in history. Let us
think of the hundreds of thousands of Communists suffering in
body and mind, persecuted by the very people who should
have protected them, their own brothers-in-arms, the victims
of a system they had built and of a man whose success they had

ensured. Members of the Politbureau even attributed to the N.K.V.D. all the crimes from which they exonerated Stalin. Eikhe wrote to Stalin: 'The confessions which have been put in my file are not only absurd but they contain slanderous statements about the Central Committee. . . . Now I wish to talk about the basest part of my life and my serious guilt with regard to the Party and yourself' – this was the fact that he had given way under torture, and he concluded: 'I have never betrayed either you or the Party . . .' (27th October 1939).

Thus Zhdanov, who had become Leningrad Party Secretary in 1934, was the only member of the Regional Secretariat left. The 7 members of the Central Committee were executed. Only 9 of the 65 members of the Regional Committee survived. Khrushchev played an important part in the purge in Moscow and the Ukraine (this does not detract from the virtues he was to display in the future), as did Mikoyan in Armenia. Eikhe had made the following bitter statement: 'There is nothing more bitterly distressing than to find oneself in the prisons of a government for which one has always fought' (1st October 1939). Rudzutak said: 'In the N.K.V.D., there is a grouping which has not yet been liquidated, which extorts confessions from the innocent and which artificially manufactures trials. . . . The methods of examination are such that they force people to lie, to slander entirely innocent people apart from those who have already been indicted. . . .'

Bukharin, who had been tortured and forced to lie about himself and about others, wrote a long letter to his wife a few days before he was executed: 'My life is coming to an end, I bow my head beneath the executioner's axe, which is not the axe of the proletariat; the latter owes it to itself to be merciless but also spotless. So I can feel how powerless I am before this infernal machine which, doubtless with the help of mediaeval methods, has acquired colossal power, mass-produces slander and acts with audacity and assurance. If I have on more than one occasion made mistakes about what methods should be used to build socialism, may posterity judge me no more harshly than did Vladimir Ilyich. We were marching towards one single goal for the very first time, and the path had not been marked out. How times change! Then *Pravda* devoted a whole page to discussion; everyone discussed what were the best means and methods, quarrelled and then made up, and everyone was marching in unity. I appeal to you, the future generation of Party leaders, one of your historic tasks will be to conduct a post mortem on the multitude of heinous crimes which is proliferating during the present dreadful period, blazing up like a flame and stifling the Party. I appeal to all Party members.'

The words of the man whom Lenin had called 'the Party's favourite child'[9] have a grave resonance today, and force us to make the mental effort necessary to understand the Stalin phenomenon. By November 1938, it had taken on such dimensions that it made itself felt in every field of economic and social life. Despite Stalinist totalitarianism, the socialist economy had expanded until 1937. The reason for this was its very essence, that is to say the socialisation of the means of production and exchange, the capacity for growth which it possessed quite independent of any political system or method of management. The latter no doubt weighed more or less heavily upon economic growth, and in this sense the Stalin phenomenon played a negative role by checking this upsurge.

By 1938, the Terror had become so intense that it became an obstacle to economic growth itself. The third Five Year Plan, which was only adopted at the 18th Congress in 1939, had in fact been launched in 1938. The change-over to a war economy because of the threats to peace also slowed down economic expansion. More funds had to be committed to the Army,[10] to the armaments industry and to the development of the eastern part of the country, which would be less exposed if there was an invasion. This does not explain why there was no growth in steel output between 1937 and 1939.[11] The disappearance of hundreds of thousands of qualified managerial staff and the resultant disorganisation of production are the only reason for this stagnation.

The realisation of this was no doubt why the terror abated. On 13th November 1938, the Central Committee and the Council of People's Commissars voted in favour of easing repression (this was not made public). On 8th December, it was announced that Yezhov, the man in charge of the N.K.V.D., was leaving his post. Yezhov bore a heavy responsibility for what had happened. The term the 'Sezhovshchina' or the Yezhov period is used to denote this period of terror. It is both true and false. Yagoda, who was in charge of the N.K.V.D. before him, and his successor Beria were just as cruel and despotic. Besides, the N.K.V.D. was only Stalin's secular power, his inquisition, though this inquisition could be more or less arbitrary and despotic. When Yezhov was in charge, it reached the heights of cruelty and horror. So the elimination of Yezhov[12] represented a degree of détente. Several thousand of the N.K.V.D.'s most brutal torturers were in their turn tortured and shot. A few thousand people were released, such as the future Marshals Rokosovsky and Meretskov, the future General Gorbatov, the physicist Landau and Tupolev the plane-builder. The number of fresh arrests fell, they did not however cease. Eikhe was shot in 1940. Many officers who had served in Spain were arrested and shot when they came home. This had happened to Antonov-Ovsenko (who had taken the Winter Palace in 1917). It happened to General Stern, to Gorev and to many others.

These were the conditions under which the 18th Congress of the C.P.S.U. opened in April 1939. Nobody said a word about all those who had perished, though they had been elected to the Central Committee at the previous Congress. Stalin presented the political report and Zhdanov reported on the Party. Storms were piling up over the Soviet Union. In the East, Soviet and Japanese troops were fighting massive battles on Lake Khasan, in the West, the Nazis, who had swallowed up Austria and Czechoslovakia, were threatening to attack the Soviet Union, with the blessing of the French and British who had signed the Munich agreements with Hitler in September 1938. In Spain, the Civil War was ending in victory for Franco. Economically and militarily weaker than Hitlerite Germany, the Soviet Union had been further weakened by the Terror which had struck heavy blows against the Red Army and the economy. Stalin had crushed the Party in order to become its master and to eliminate the past, present and future opponents of his policy and dictatorship. The dictatorship of the proletariat had become identified with that of the Party just after the Civil War. In 1939, it was identified with that of one man. In his report, the latter stated: 'It cannot be said that the purge was not accompanied by grave mistakes. There were unfortunately more mistakes than might have been expected. Undoubtedly, we shall have no further need of resorting to the method of mass purges' (*Problems of Leninism*, p. 625).

Millions of Soviet citizens were still deportees, three members of the Politbureau, Chubar, Eikhe and Postyshev, were still in prison, soon to be shot. Yakovlev was shot during the Congress. Of the 1,827 delegates at the 18th Congress, only 35 had survived from the 17th Congress (about 2 per cent). At the same time, the Soviet economy had undergone an impressive transformation. A new society had been born. Illiteracy had been reduced and among young people had even disappeared. Culture was widely spread among the masses, even among those who had formerly been the most backward. The Stalin phenomenon had appeared and flourished in the soil of socialism, not as a natural consequence of it, but rather as the product of the conditions appertaining at a specific time and place. Since 1917, there had been no lack of ordeals for the first socialist revolution in history to face. The Second World War was to bring other ordeals at least as demanding.

NOTES

1. An American writer, Max Eastman, who was a friend of Trotsky disclosed its contents in 1925 in *Since Lenin Died*.
2. Vyshinsky, a former Menshevik who had joined the Bolsheviks, was the Prosecutor in the big Moscow trials.
3. Stalin who, as we shall see later, was responsible for the murder of several hundreds of thousands of Communists, was not worried about one victim more or less. His lack of scruples and political morality allowed him to use illegal means to keep himself in power and to establish his dictatorship.
4. After Volume 2 of my *Histoire de l'U.R.S.S.* (*Le Socialisme dans un seul pays*, published by Editions Sociales), J. Ozouf, writing in the *Nouvel Observateur* accused me of justifying Stalin's crimes by explaining them.
5. A heart attack so convenient – for he was an opponent of Stalin's 'terrorist' line – that it has been suggested that it was provoked. We cannot really assert that this was the case, apart from the fact that it was a very happy coincidence for Stalin who was rid of a leading comrade who was capable and popular in the Party and whose views were very similar to those of Kirov.

6. The Spanish Civil War started on 16th July 1936, when General Franco, with the help of Hitler and Mussolini, rebelled against the legally established democratic government.

7. We do not think it necessary to dwell on these now well-known methods, for our aim is not to describe in detail the Stalinist Terror, but to give a general view of the Stalin phenomenon and to explain it. In my opinion Artur London's book *On Trial* gives a fairly accurate idea of what took place when the trials were held. Torture was authorised in 1937 (in a telegram sent by Stalin on 1st January 1938, which Krushchev quoted at the 20th Congress of the C.P.S.U.), but it was used long before then.

8. Those whose names are printed in italics died as a result of the Stalinist Terror.

9. 'Bukharin is not only a most valuable and major theorist of the Party; he is also rightly considered the favourite of the whole Party.' (Lenin went on to criticise his theories, *C.W.*, Vol. 36, p. 595.)

10. The military budget represented 3·9 per cent of the Soviet Budget in 1933, 16·1 per cent in 1936 and 25·6 per cent in 1939.

11. In millions of tons – 1937 = 17·7; 1938 = 18·1; 1939 = 17·6.

12. Yezhov was appointed Commissar for Sea and Inland Waterway Transport, disappeared at the end of January and was shot on a date which is not known.

5 The Ordeal of the Second World War

In foreign affairs, the Soviet Union did not experience total success in the 1934–41 period. However, there was no lack of mitigating circumstances. The great democratic capitalist states of the West had not grasped the novel character of Nazism and the threat to civilisation that it represented. Originally, they merely saw it as a sometimes worrying antidote to Communism, but Hitler had soon become as much a threat to the West as to the East. As early as 1933, Litvinov, People's Commissar for Foreign Affairs, had remarked that 'a cannon which can fire towards the East can also fire towards the West'. If a broad anti-Hitler coalition had been built a few years earlier, it would have prevented the Second World War and made it possible to crush Hitlerism before it became dangerous. Though President F. D. Roosevelt was anti-Nazi, the United States was neutral and intended to stay that way. France had had anti-Hitler impulses, hence the signing of the 1935 Franco-Soviet Pact, but had not followed its policy to its logical conclusion. In the end, France had adopted the British policy, which was much more anti-Communist and anti-Soviet than anti-Nazi. This was clearly evident during the Spanish Civil War when the Popular Front Government headed by Léon Blum chose not to intervene in the Civil War (though with pangs of conscience) because this was what England had decided. In conclusion, neither the United States nor Great Britain nor even France made any real effort to conclude an alliance with the Soviet Union against Hitler. Worse still, by signing the Munich Agreements in September 1938, the British and French handed Czechoslovakia to Hitler and then tried to divert the Nazi threat to the East.[1]

Faced with the Hitlerite menace, the Soviet Union tried to isolate Hitler and reach agreement with the West. The British, and to a lesser extent the French, bear the responsibility for a failure which was to have dramatic consequences since it led to the Second World War. However, does this mean that Soviet policy was perfect? That is not our opinion. Its weaknesses stem from Stalin's underestimation of the Nazi threat and its novel character. We have seen that this was the case in 1933, and it went on until 1941. One of the consequences of the policy adopted by the West was to make Stalin more suspicious of the great capitalist countries of the West. Stalin could only underestimate the importance of democratic phenomena and the danger of fascism. It is utterly wrong to lump together Nazism and the Stalin phenomenon, as does the American philosopher Hannah Arendt in her book on *The Origins of Totalitarianism*. Nazism is a political and ideological form of contemporary capitalism. It is built upon capitalist foundations, but took on forms radically different from those which then existed in France, Great Britain and the United States.

On the other hand, the Stalin phenomenon arose from the socialist revolution and flourished in the period of socialist construction. The Stalin phenomenon was and is no more the only form in which socialism can exist than Nazism was and is the necessary political and ideological form in which capitalism must exist. Both were the product of a specific history; of historic circumstances, of the part played by certain individuals, of specific national histories, the one German the other Russian. The goals pursued were totally different, for the very reason that the class content was quite different. Similarities may exist. A concentration camp is a concentration camp, a denunciation is a denunciation, and torture is torture, irrespective of the economic and political form. The Russian and Soviet historical experiment did not proceed via political democracy. By expanding the economy and by educational and cultural development, it no doubt made a contribution to ensuring that democracy would be achieved in the distant future; it built the foundations for its future development, but it did not enable the Soviet leaders to grasp the importance of democratic structures, nor how they are linked to socialism.

Even Lenin, whose approach to this problem was, however, based on a sound theoretical understanding, always underestimated its importance because he started from his own experience in Russia and only assimilated democratic experiences from the outside and through their most negative aspects,

as manifested by the attitude of the 2nd International during
the First World War and later during the socialist revolutions
in Hungary and Germany. This is why Lenin's writings after
the Soviet Revolution contain numerous judgements which
criticise democratic structures and can only visualise revolutionary processes through the distorted and distorting prism of
his own experience, which appeared all the more conclusive to
him because there was no other experience of a victorious
revolution. On the basis of such a view, it was easy to conclude
at that time, followed by the Comintern, that the only road to
Socialism was the Russian one, and the reaction to the 'bankruptcy of the 2nd International' made it all the easier. Of
course, Lenin accepted that the revolution could take different
forms. 'Do not imitate the Russian Revolution slavishly', he
wrote; but he envisaged that they would occur within a pretty
strict model in which violence, force and civil war played a
bigger part than the ballot box or any other democratic
process. The fact that his personal experience determined his
theories is demonstrated by the fact that, after considering the
possibility of a peaceful transition to socialism between April
and July 1917, he hardly mentioned it later, quite simply
because conditions had been transformed in Russia. His
definitive remarks on the role of civil war and force, which can
be found in *The Dictatorship of the Proletariat and the Renegade
Kautsky* or in his *Notes on the History of a Dictatorship*, can be
understood in the light of the great revolutionary crisis which
marked the end of the First World War and followed immediately after it. The imbalance caused by the war was such that
the path of violence and civil war could seem to be the only
one possible in the capitalist countries in the West. A revolutionary crisis with rich potential existed, as the German
Revolution was to show (despite the fact that it failed). The
latter seemed to show just how right the Bolsheviks were, since
it was the absence of a revolutionary party disciplined and
prepared over a long period for the Revolution, and the
opportunism or even anti-communism of German Social
Democracy, which had finally enabled the German bourgeoisie
to defeat the socialist revolution.

In *The Dictatorship of the Proletariat and the Renegade Kautsky*,
Lenin starts from the actual political practice of Kautsky and

the German socialists. There is no doubt that, from a historical point of view, his criticisms are well founded, for the Social-Democrats contributed to the defeat of the German Proletarian Revolution which could have been carried through just after the First World War by means of a violent process similar to what took place in France in 1871 or Russia in 1917. The capitalist state had been weakened and destroyed by the war and defeat. The ground had been prepared for a violent revolution, for an immediate and brutal seizure of power. All Lenin's experience of history led him to assert this: 'Dictatorship is rule based directly on force and unrestricted by any laws.' 'The revolutionary dictatorship of the proletariat is rule won and maintained by the use of violence by the proletariat against the bourgeoisie, rule that is unrestricted by any laws' (*C.W.*, Vol. 28, p. 236).

His criticism of bourgeois democracy is justified, but it led him to underestimate the historical role of democracy itself. It is quite true that there is no such thing as 'pure' democracy, a concept for which he criticised Kautsky, but in a socialist society democracy cannot be restricted to the economic and social spheres. In 1918, and even in 1923, Lenin could not possibly know that, whilst socialism was a period of transition from capitalism to communism, it would last for decades and decades and that the state would take on an ever greater role.

Lenin's 1918 Theses start from a very precise historical situation which has not recurred and will not do so ('history does not offer second helpings'). His criticism of Kautsky was historically well founded in 1918, but the problems to be solved today are radically different. In 1918, Lenin asked the following question in the same work: 'The theoretical question is quite different: Is the dictatorship of the proletariat possible without infringing democracy in relation to the exploiting class?' and he replied:

'(Kautsky) does not talk about the main thing, namely the fact that the proletariat cannot achieve victory *without breaking the resistance* of the bourgeoisie, *without forcibly suppressing its adversaries*, and that, where there is "forcible suppression", where there is no "freedom", *there is, of course, no democracy*' (*C.W.*, Vol. 28, pp. 256-7).[2]

The truth is that the requirements of the Revolution and the Civil War led the Bolsheviks to violate 'democracy'. Eventually, the 'violations of democracy' affected the working class and the Communists themselves. This was a result of the lack of democracy which Rosa Luxemburg had quite rightly brought to light in her analysis of the Russian Revolution.

The replacement of 'democracy for the rich by democracy for the poor' which Lenin talked about in another text written in 1918 (*Of Democracy and Dictatorship*, Vol. 28, p. 371) does not necessarily imply the destruction of democratic structures and institutes, and when they did not exist – as was the case in Russia – it requires that they be created, otherwise there is a risk of despotic power as during the Stalin period. What appeared to be the norm in 1919 was to be revealed as exceptional over the following years, and as a result the overall strategy (originally) adopted by the Communist International proved not to correspond to the facts of the real situation in the capitalist countries. On the other hand, it was to correspond much more closely with the situation in the colonial countries, where the national liberation movement was capable of rushing peoples towards the socialist revolution along paths which were historically different from those of the Russian Revolution, but resembled it in as much as democratic processes played a small part. Besides, the Communist International was affected by what happened in the Soviet Union: because of the 'delay in the revolution in the great capitalist countries', the Soviets had to build 'socialism in one country'. The lack of distinction between the Party and the State in the U.S.S.R., the triumph of bureaucracy and dogmatism which the Stalin phenomenon brought, were to set the Comintern formidable problems. It was based in Moscow and became increasingly associated with Soviet policy because of the influence of the Soviet Party. As the only Party holding power, the Soviet Party had a direct influence on the general line adopted by the Comintern, and for this very reason also influenced that of other Communist parties, since the Comintern was a centralised body whose decisions were binding upon the member parties.

Before its setback in Germany, the Comintern had suffered a resounding defeat in China, where it had extolled collaboration between Chiang Kai-shek's Kuomintang and the Chinese Communist Party. The defeat of the German Communist Party in 1933, and its destruction by Hitler faced the Communist parties and the Comintern with new problems. Stalinist dogmatism prevented a serious discussion about the ways and means of carrying through a socialist revolution against the capitalists who were reorganising to fight the economic crisis and prevent any new one, but it was unable to prevent the Western Communist parties from considering a new policy on the basis of the defeat in Germany. It was to emerge in France and Spain. Initially, it was only a defensive policy designed to achieve anti-fascist unity. This was the aim of the agreement of the French Socialists and Communists in July 1934. However, the alliance gradually widened and, under pressure from the Communist Party and its General Secretary Maurice Thorez, became more positive. The choice between 'democracy or fascism' had led the French Communists to realise the importance of democratic processes both in themselves and as related to socialism. The French 'Front populaire' and the Spanish 'Frente popular' were then to be born. It is true that the French Communists did not at this time take this policy to its logical conclusion. They refused to take part in the Popular Front government, and either did not see or did not dare say to what extent this new orientation changed the basic strategy of the Communist movement, and made it possible to evolve a new conception of the socialist revolution in the developed democratic capitalist countries in the West. The 7th Congress of the Comintern (in 1935) indicated a compromise between these different opinions. In his report, Dimitrov analysed the French example and in strong and correct terms posed the alternatives of 'democracy or fascism'. Soviet coolness was manifested by the most prominent leaders' lack of enthusiasm for attending the Congress – neither Stalin, nor Molotov, nor Kaganovich, nor any member of the Politburueau spoke, although the Congress was being held in Moscow. Stalin's hostility to Hitler was still moderate. This we noted in the context of the 17th Congress. His hostility to any form of political democracy and his distrust of the democratic capitalist states, which was after all justified by the past and present, did not give him any incentive to

realise the nature of the Hitlerite danger, or its reality and
dimensions. This does not mean that the Soviet Union did
not make any effort to conclude an alliance against Hitler.
Although it felt economically and militarily weak, the Soviet
Union made a great deal more effort than the developed
capitalist states, but the question is whether it made enough,
taking into account the danger. In the course of its 7th Congress,
the Comintern gave the Communist parties more latitude,
but that was all. Faced with the danger, would the disbanding
of the Communist International, which was eventually
decided upon in 1943, not have enabled the Communist
parties to evolve more daring policies of national unity quite
independent of the ups and downs of Soviet policy? Besides,
the Stalinist Terror of the 1936–8 period gave the opponents
of alliance with the U.S.S.R. excuses which did not fail to
influence the Socialist parties which were members of the
2nd International, and did not make it any the easier for them
to take part in the anti-fascist alliance. Of course, all this did
not justify the policy of non-intervention in Spain or the signing
of the Munich Agreements, but there can be no doubt that,
if the Soviet Union had at certain times taken more daring,
more spectacular and more unifying initiatives, this would
have put the Westerners in an embarrassing position *vis-à-vis*
their own public opinion.

The fact remains that, because of the Franco-British
attitude, the Soviet Union was forced to sign a pact with
Hitler on the 23rd August 1939. In our opinion, Stalin was not
wrong to sign the German–Soviet Non-aggression Pact. From
his point of view, it was completely justified in order to gain
time to enable the Soviet Union to prepare for an inevitable
conflict, in the absence of an unequivocal agreement with
France and Great Britain, which had been rejected by these
countries. On the other hand, what is more problematic is the
conditions under which this agreement was achieved, and
what followed from it from the point of view of Soviet foreign
policy and the Comintern. The non-aggression pact included
secret clauses which were debatable as a matter of principle
since they made provision for territorial changes affecting
Poland, Romania and the Baltic States (Estonia, Lithuania
and Latvia) and Finland by agreement with Hitler.[3] There can

be no question that certain territories, for example Eastern Poland, had been wrested from Soviet Russia by force just after the Civil War (the Riga Treaty, 1921), and that their inhabitants were Ukrainians and Byelorussians.

In accord with the public clauses of the German–Soviet Treaty of the 23rd August, the Soviet Union remained neutral at the beginning of the Second World War, but Stalin and Molotov declared that France and Britain wanted to destroy the Hitlerite regime 'on the false pretext of fighting for democracy' (Molotov's speech to the Supreme Soviet on 31st October 1939). In December 1939, *Pravda* went as far as to devote three columns to a reprint of a speech Hitler had made in Munich, and, when he replied to telegrams of congratulations on his sixtieth birthday from Hitler and von Ribbentrop, Stalin said: 'The friendship between the peoples of the Soviet Union and Germany, which was cemented in blood, has every reason to remain solid and lasting.' Stalin and Hitler exchanged pleasantries on the occasion of the anniversary of the October Revolution. Economic exchanges grew, and the Soviet Union sent Hitler wheat, oil and large quantities of other raw materials. The Soviet press ceased all criticism of the Hitlerite regime, and, on the other hand, made repeated attacks on the democratic capitalist states. To sign a diplomatic agreement with Hitler was one thing, it was a 'tragedy for the U.S.S.R.' to be forced to do so, but to act in this way was quite another thing. It could hardly help to prepare the Soviet Union to face the Nazis in an inevitable conflict in the near future. For example, this policy led to the war against Finland. Of course, the government of that country was violently anti-Communist, but did that justify a war? The Red Army, which had been weakened by the 1937–8 purges, only managed to defeat the Finnish army after several months' fighting (from 25th November 1939 to 12th March 1940).

Between September 1939 and June 1940, the population of the Soviet Union had increased by a total of 21,385,000 inhabitants, and five new Soviet Republics had been set up (Latvia, Lithuania, Estonia, Moldavia and the Karelo-Finnish Republic). During this period, the Comintern came to follow a political line identical to that of the U.S.S.R. The Communist International asked the Communist parties not only to approve the German–Soviet Pact, but also to combat Anglo-French policy, which was declared solely responsible for the Second World War. It is true that the latter remained equivocal. France and Great Britain, who had entered the war to defend the independence and territorial integrity of Poland, let it be crushed by the Nazis without even launching an offensive. From September 1939 to May 1940, hostilities hung fire on the Western front. This was the period of the 'phoney war'. At this point in time, the French High Command was mainly concerned with organising military operations against the U.S.S.R., in the North in Finland (there was a plan for a landing at Petsamo) and in the South (there was a plan for an airborne attack on Baku).[4] Nevertheless, from September 1939 on, fascism and democracy were at war. The Comintern's line, which had to be followed by all Communist parties, thus forced the French Communist Party to oppose the war, when, despite repressive measures directed at it,[5] the Communist members of Parliament had initially voted for the military budget. If the Comintern had been disbanded in 1933, Communist Parties would have been able to act independently without, however, displaying anti-Sovietism. It would have sufficed for them to show why the Germano–Soviet Pact was a necessity from the Soviet point of view because the Western powers had refused to conclude a military alliance with the U.S.S.R., and at the same time the French Communist Party could have supported the French war effort and fought against the French bourgeoisie which, despite the declaration of war, still wanted to direct its blows against the U.S.S.R. rather than against Hitler, and was really preparing for the great betrayal of Vichy and collaboration.[6]

Thus the Stalin phenomenon was demonstrating, as it had been since the twenties, how harmful it was in the international field. It added to the obscurity of a foreign policy the basis of which even experienced politicians found hard to grasp. It led to serious setbacks for the Comintern both in its practice and in its theory. It is true that Communist parties had been founded or had been 'bolshevised' in many countries, especially in colonial countries. So the activity of the Comintern cannot be reduced to these failures alone, though they were still considerable, particularly in the developed capitalist countries.

The Soviet Union did not take sufficient advantage of the
respite afforded by the German–Soviet Pact to prepare
militarily, politically or economically for war. Industrial output had been stagnant since 1937. The 1940 steel output of
18,300,000 tons was only a little higher than that of 1937.
Soviet statistics published at the time were more optimistic
about the overall increase in industrial output, but they
included the figures for the territories which the U.S.S.R. had
taken over and to some extent embellished the truth. The
armaments industry was in a catastrophic situation. Production
of the old models which were unsuitable for modern war had
been stopped, and new types of planes, tanks and guns had
been brought into service, but mass-production of these
had hardly begun by 1941. Agriculture was still poor. Grain
production was only a little higher than in 1913, and there
was less livestock (except for pigs). The Army was still recover-
ing from the bloody purges of 1937–8, this had been evident
during the war in Finland. Only 7 per cent of the officers had
graduated from a Higher Military Academy. The High
Command included some top class Generals, notably Zhukov
(who had become Commander-in-Chief in February 1941),
but there were also a large number of leaders who were not
highly qualified for the job. This was true of Marshall Voroshilov, Kulik (who commanded the artillery) and Mekhlis
(Chief Commissar for the Army). Since the 18th Party Congress,
efforts had been made to improve the economic and military
situation, but because of the consequences of the Stalinist
Terror, the damage inflicted by which should not be underestimated, they were still a long way behind.

Since July 1940, that is to say since the defeat of the French,
Hitler had been prepared for the invasion of the U.S.S.R. He
was master of the greater part of Europe, and, with the help
of his Romanian, Italian, Hungarian and Finnish allies, he
was concentrating colossal forces along the Eastern frontier.
Stalin was convinced that Hitler would not attack until 1942,
so he was not prepared to take any notice of the numerous
warnings given him by his own secret service (Richard Sorge
in Japan, the Dora network in Switzerland, the Trepper
network and the 'Red Orchestra' in Western Europe) and by
Churchill and Roosevelt. He thought the latter warnings were

E

Anglo-Saxon devices to feed him false information in order to plunge him into war against Hitler earlier. On 14th June 1941 the Tass News Agency denied that there was any cooling in Germano–Soviet relations.

On 22nd June, the German armies attacked along the whole length of the front. The Soviet Army was not in a state of alert, and several hours after the beginning of the invasion the imperturbable Stalin still thought that what was involved was mere border skirmishes of no significance. In history there has rarely been a mistake which provided a more forceful illustration of the danger of absolute power in the hands of one man. Before history, Stalin and his regime bear the heavy responsibility of the Soviet lack of preparation in June 1941 and of the initial defeats. The often-used argument according to which Stalin's work from 1929 to 1939 – forced collectivisation and the Terror – was necessary and made the Soviet Union's victory in the Second World War possible, appears derisory if one takes into account the terrible blows struck against the Soviet economy and the Red Army, the negligence of the Soviet authorities on the eve of the war and during the first few weeks after the invasion, and Stalin's historic mistakes as, once again, his strategic forecasts proved to be totally erroneous.

This is not the place to undertake a detailed history of the U.S.S.R. during the Second World War. We only wish to pick out those elements directly linked to the Stalin phenomenon which allow us to grasp how it made itself felt, to gain a better understanding of its characteristics through a dramatic crisis. The first few weeks of fighting were catastrophic. The majority of Soviet planes were destroyed on the ground within hours of fighting. The German tanks advanced 250 km. in three days. Despite acts of great heroism, which were not sufficient to seal the breaches, the Soviet troops retreated in disorder. By December, the Nazi troops had taken the Baltic Republics, Byelorussia, part of the Ukraine including the Donbas area, the Crimea (apart from Sebastopol), Kiev, Kharkov and Odessa. They were at the gates of Leningrad and 25 km. from Moscow. So the Soviet defeat was of considerable proportions. However, Hitler had not achieved his goals. Despite the siege, Leningrad continued to resist under incredible conditions (without food or fuel) and the Germans had been halted before Moscow. Hitler's plan – to defeat the U.S.S.R. before the winter and to force its capitulation – had failed. The Soviets had lost many battles, but they had won the war.

During the first few days after the invasion, Stalin apparently had a real nervous breakdown. He realised that his policy was a total failure and locked himself in a room in his Kremlin flat. He did not speak to the Soviet people until 3rd July. This speech was measured, firm and friendly and appealed for loyalty to the spirit of Lenin and the Soviet system as well as to the Russian national feelings. From then on, he took control of the nation's affairs. He was President of the State Committee for Defence[7] which centralised all civil and military power, and he later became Generalissimo (Commander in Chief of the Army). It would be inaccurate to portray Stalin exclusively in the guise of a bloody despot. During this ordeal he was also a worthy and courageous leader. On 7th November 1941, with the Germans 25 km. from Moscow, he organised the parade to commemorate the 24th anniversary of the October Revolution. The previous day, he had spoken at the Mayakovsky Metro Station, and on 7th November he again spoke, unperturbed by the storm. He asked the Soviet peoples to resist Hitler and developed the themes of his 3rd July speech. His attitude in November enabled him to symbolise the Soviets' will to resist. This did not prevent him from making serious mistakes in strategy, as for example when he refused in September 1941 to evacuate Kiev, which led to the encircling of thousands of Soviet troops who were taken prisoner by the Nazis.

The war highlighted and probably accentuated the contradictory aspects of the Stalin phenomenon, which have already been mentioned several times. During the ordeals of this period, Stalin was at one with the people. At the same time, the Stalinist system still existed and its consequences were sometimes taken to the extreme. In the pre-war years, centralisation had made it possible to concentrate the available human and capital resources on the economic front. At the same time, it had contributed to the growth of a huge bureaucracy in the field of management of individual enterprises, the relations between central management and the enterprises etc., but this bureaucracy existed on the basis of socialist ownership of the means of production and distribution. There was no longer private ownership of the means of production and distribution, so there were no more capitalists. Thus, there was no private appropriation of surplus value or profit, even if a certain number of bureaucrats could benefit from the situation. This centralisation, based on socialist ownership, was decisive in the economic field during the early months of the war. It made it possible within a few weeks to dismantle 1,523 big factories situated in the West, to transport them to Eastern regions (Siberia, the Ural region, the Volga region), and to get them quickly back into production despite German bombing, the rapidity of the Nazi advance, the severe cold of the Russian winter and the fact that most healthy men had been called up. The bureaucracy did not disappear totally, but, faced with the vital needs of the period, it largely vanished, leaving behind a system which was rational, for capitalist profit had no place in it. Thanks to these measures, and despite a brutal drop in output as a result of the invasion,[8] by 1943 the Soviet armaments industry was able to produce a greater quantity of arms than Nazi Germany (3,000 planes, 2,000 tanks and 10,000 cannons and mortars per month), arms of at least as high quality. The socialist economy thus displayed an absolutely extraordinary facility for adapting and expanding, if we take into account the problems caused by the invasion and the position it was in on the eve of the war.

The same was true of the political and ideological fields. Soviet resistance was exemplary. Here and there there were failures: they were the result of either human weakness and cowardice or of the most negative aspects of the pre-war Stalinist phenomenon. In the occupied territories, there were a few individuals who worked for the Nazis either out of self-interest or because they were afraid. Nevertheless, deliveries to Germany from the Soviet territories only represented a seventh of what the Reich obtained in France. The explanation is very simple. In France, capitalism existed and, for a variety of reasons, a large part of the French bourgeoisie chose economic collaboration with the Germans. One recalls De Gaulle's famous remark to the employers' representatives at the Liberation: 'So here you are! Where were you during the war, gentlemen?' There were also cases of collaboration with Hitler in some non-Russian Republics – for example in the Tatar Autonomous Soviet Socialist Republic (in the Crimea), the Autonomous Republic of the Kalmuks, in that of the Chechen-Ingushi, in the Autonomous Republic of Kabardino-Balkar and in the autonomous region of the Karachay – but the peoples involved were still culturally very backward and had recently been offended by Stalin's russo-centralising policy. The same phenomenon could be found in the Ukraine though on a much smaller scale. Orthodox priests and Uniates (Christians who followed Greek rituals but who owed allegiance to Rome) were also tempted by the demon of collaboration because of pre-war religious persecution. Finally, there was the treason of Vlasov, a Red Army General, Second in Command of the Volkhov Front, who with German help recruited an army mainly from among inmates of Hitler's camps who saw this as a chance of being released. Later, a certain number of them were to rebel against the Nazis and help the Resistance in Europe. In *The Gulag Archipelago*, Solzhenitsyn describes Vlasov's betrayal as 'a phenomenon totally unheard of in all world history: that several hundred thousand young men aged twenty to thirty took up arms against their Fatherland as allies of its most evil enemy' (pp. 261–2). It is rather the opposite which is true. If one compares the situation in the U.S.S.R. with what happened in Europe under Hitler's occupation, the whole difference becomes apparent. Apart from Vlasov, not one high ranking Red Army officer betrayed the Soviet Union, nor were there any national Party leaders and very few regional leaders. We know that this was not the case in France where members of Parliament, former ministers, generals and admirals, etc., collaborated extensively with the Nazis.

What was the reason for the attitude of the Soviet people? How can we explain this resistance and the heroism of tens of millions of people, most remarkably illustrated perhaps by those who fought at Stalingrad and at Leningrad, both soldiers and civilians, heroism on a scale of which there is scarcely an example in history? For some, for example Hélène Carrère d'Encausse, the main reason for such an attitude is the nationalistic reflex, that is to say the Russian national feeling. It is true that Stalin appealed to it well before 1941, even going so far as to rehabilitate a certain number of events and men from old Russia, something about which opinions may differ. From 1941 on, and particularly at the time of the serious crisis of summer 1942, when German troops entered the Caucasus and approached Stalingrad, the Soviet authorities went further in this direction. In the Red Army, epaulets and officers' privileges such as had existed under the Tsar were brought back. Officer cadet schools named after Suvorov, a Tsarist General who had fought against the armies of the French Revolution, were founded. The names of heroes from the past were honoured, for example Alexander Nevsky, Ivan IV (the Terrible) and many other 'great ancestors', as Stalin called them in a speech made on 7th November. At the end of the war against Japan, Stalin was heard to say that victory 'wiped out the shame' of the Russian defeat in 1904 (this was in an imperialist war waged against Japan by the Tsar). A new Soviet national anthem replaced the *Internationale* in 1943. It celebrated the unity of the Soviet peoples 'sealed by great Russia'. Stalin also repeatedly extolled the 'alliance of the Slav peoples' against the Germans, and many articles in the press contained a nationalistic tone which is understandable in the circumstances, but which is worth discussing, though it does not, however, explain Soviet resistance. Nationalism was no less powerful in France, this was made quite clear just after the Second World War when the colonial wars took place. But it did not prevent collapse in July 1940, the Vichy regime, massive collaboration among the leading groups in the country and confusion among a considerable proportion of public opinion. To tell the truth, the Soviets' fight was on two levels; firstly it was a national struggle against the German aggressor, secondly it was a revolutionary struggle to defend socialism. After all, Stalin did not make a single speech without recalling the origins of the state, the Soviet Revolution, the Civil War, the role of Lenin, the role of the Bolshevik Party, etc.

This is what makes it so difficult to analyse the Stalin phenomenon. Starting from certain elements of Stalin's policy since 1929, for example forced collectivisation and the Terror, some historians lose sight of the phenomenon's contradictory characteristics, which we have tried to bring out on several occasions. Being a socialist state, the Soviet system guaranteed extremely rapid economic and cultural growth, which removed previously backward peoples from poverty, superstition and ignorance and made possible a real upsurge in productive forces. As a totalitarian political system, it constituted an obstacle to the rational use of all the potential of the socialist economy. Now, the Stalin phenomenon had these two characteristics. Under the leadership of the Party and Stalin, the Soviet people defended the Soviet system, despite the totalitarianism from which they themselves to a large extent suffered. What was without precedent in history – 'an unheard of phenomenon' as Solzhenitsyn says of Vlasov and his men, but he missed the real 'unheard of phenomenon' in this war – was that millions of Soviet citizens who had been the direct or indirect victims of Stalinist terror played a heroic and self-sacrificing part in the struggle of the Soviet people, this was really extraordinary! A well known case is that of General Gorbatov, who was arrested, tortured and deported to Magadan. In 1940, after Marshal Budyenny had intervened on his behalf, he was released, was given important commands during the war and ended it at the 'Meeting on the Elbe' as commander of the Soviet Army Corps which linked up with the American troops in the spring of 1945.

Any state in previous history which had undergone such ordeals would have been annihilated. This did not happen to the Soviet state because its basis was socialist, quite independent of the existing political institutions or the policy followed by the State and those in power. It is true that had a different policy been adopted, the U.S.S.R. would have been better placed to face Hitler, but one does not exclude the other. It is utopian to think that the most negative aspects of the Stalin phenomenon could disappear on 22nd June 1941. The institutions, the habits and the men remained, and made their presence felt to a varying extent during the war. The latter had a double effect in diametrically opposed directions. It heightened the authoritarian character of the state. Because of the stiffening of the sinews which they demand and the discipline they impose on those fighting, wars have always been favourable to despotism. Democracy is a luxury which can only be afforded in times of peace. Philip of Macedonia, a despot at the head of a centralised kingdom, had no difficulty in defeating Athens, where democracy still predominated. ('People are talking, they are getting agitated, they are not doing anything and Philip is approaching', said Demosthenes.)

In February 1941, the N.K.V.D. had been split into two sections – the N.K.G.B. (State Security) and the N.K.V.D. itself – but this division was not effective until 1943. It continued to exercise its meddling control over every sector of Soviet life. The concentration camps were only emptied of officers who were indispensable for the defence of the country and high-ranking technicians, but they were filled with Poles who had fled to the U.S.S.R. from the Nazi invaders, inhabitants of the Baltic countries and Germans from the Volga region, whose Autonomous Republic had been dissolved on the 18th August 1941 – and all the inhabitants who had been deported (600,000 people). On the pretext that a certain number of cases of treason had been noted, several other autonomous republics were also dissolved and their inhabitants deported. This happened to the Autonomous Republic of the Kalmuks (200,000 inhabitants), the Autonomous Republic of the Chechen-Ingushi (600,000 inhabitants), the Kabardino-Balkar Autonomous Republic (300,000 inhabitants) and the Autonomous Republic of the Crimean Tatars (200,000 inhabitants), as well as the Autonomous Region of the Karachay (100,000 inhabitants). Thus, Stalin was reviving the methods he had used against the kulaks during the 1929–30 operation. His starting point was correct: the fight against betrayal and the need to make sure that the Red Army's rear was secure, but this led him to extreme solutions which were quite out of proportion with the crimes committed, a fact which on the whole made the situation worse. At the same time, there was still rigorous censorship not only of the press, literature and all means of expression, but also of private correspondence. It was in February 1945 that Solzhenitsyn was arrested for having been imprudent enough to suggest in a private letter that Stalin was not the greatest military genius of all time.

The Communist Party played an essential role in the war, which claimed more than two million Communist dead, but, according to Khrushchev, the Central Committee did not hold a single meeting from 1941 to 1945. There were regional and local meetings, but no central meeting. So Stalin was still running the State and the Party in an individual and despotic manner. The only field in which, despite his title of Generalissimo, he had to make way for specialists, was the conduct of military operations. Otherwise, he went on working in the Kremlin, from where he directed the Soviet war effort with the same advisers as before the war: Molotov, Kaganovich, Malenkov and Beria. Zhdanov was in Leningrad and Khrushchev on the Southern front. Voznesensky was in charge of the economy (he had been a candidate member of the Politbureau since 1941) and Zhukov remained Chief of the General Staff throughout the war, though he also took command in key sectors at decisive moments. Mikoyan, Andreyev and Shvernik occupied less responsible posts. As for Voroshilov, his influence gradually declined until he lost his post as a member of the State Committee for Defence in 1944.

As the years went by, Bulganin and Kosygin played a more and more important role. At the same time, paradoxically, the requirements of national unity against Hitler made possible relaxation within the country. Stalin got back into contact with the Orthodox Church and authorised the reopening of dozens of churchs and the legal operation of ecclesiastic institutions. An Orthodox Council was held in 1943. Jews and Muslims also saw an increase in their rights. The setting up of a Jewish Anti-Fascist Committee was authorised, as was that of a Central Muslim Directorate in Tashkent, and anti-religious propaganda was stopped. The League of the Godless was disbanded and its journals banned. Writers were able to publish their works with relatively greater liberty than before the war. However, things did not develop as smoothly as might appear. In the middle of the war, Stalin had two Polish Jewish leaders, Alter and Ehrlich, shot, though he had just released them from prison. However, the overall trend was still towards greater flexibility in relations between the authorities and the various national and religious groups, which were very varied. These were all reasons for hoping that the post-war period would be freer than the pre-war period, Ilya Ehrenburg's memoirs bear witness to this hope. But such hopes rested on a failure to take into account the tragic consequences of the war.

Although the Soviet Union was victorious, it emerged weakened from the Second World War. Of course, Stalin was at the height of his popularity. For tens of thousands of Soviet citizens he was the 'Little Father of the Peoples', the guide who had defeated Hitler. The Red Army took Berlin, liberated many European capitals and was scarcely 500 km. from the French border. For the European peoples themselves, Stalin represented liberation and an end to nightmare which had lasted several years. In fact, the human and material losses of the U.S.S.R. were enormous. All the more so because until the 6th June 1944, that is to say until the Normandy landings, it bore the main burden of the war against Hitler on its shoulders. The 'Second Front' was promised for 1942, then put off until 1943 and only achieved in 1944. Despite the military operations in North Africa and Italy, for a long period the U.S.S.R.'s Western allies were content to make fine statements and to send arms and provisions. Even after June 1944, the greater part of German military strength was to remain concentrated on the Eastern Front. Hitler was to go on fighting in the hope of splitting the Allies. In the West, German towns were surrendered by telephone, whilst in the East the Wehrmacht fought ferociously for every inch of territory. The consequences can be seen: British losses totalled 375,000 dead, American losses 405,000 and French ones 600,000. Though Britain and France sustained serious material damage (but in no way comparable to that of the U.S.S.R.), the United States was totally spared. These are well known facts and do not diminish the virtues and sacrifices of the various countries, but the extent of these facts and figures must be considered. From 1941 to 1945, the U.S.S.R. lost at least 23 million people.[9] To this figure must be added the drop in births caused by the war. The number of civilian and military victims of the siege of Leningrad alone is higher than the total British, French and American losses during the Second World War. Material damage was immense. The richest and most populous part of the Soviet Union had been pillaged by the Nazis: 1,700 towns and 70,00 villages had been destroyed. The fields had been devastated by battles, and the factories and railways had been destroyed. Over an area of hundreds of thousands of square kilometres, the Soviet Union 'was now only ruin and grief'. In

1945, agriculture and the industrial sector producing consumer goods were only at 60 per cent of their 1940 level, and industrial output was barely 70 per cent:

	1940	*1945*
Steel	18·3	12·3
Electricity	48·3	43·2
Coal	165·9	149·3
Oil	31·1	19·3

(These figures are in millions of tons, except for electricity which is in U.S. billions of kWh.)

Once again the U.S.S.R. needed rebuilding. Let us bear in mind the incredible bloodletting it had undergone since 1917, and for which imperialism was mainly responsible (the First World War, the Civil War and the Second World War). The Stalin phenomenon can also be explained in the light of these facts, of this tragic fate and of this incredible animosity towards the first socialist state. Here again, there is no question at all of an attempt to justify or excuse, the aim is to realise the nature of the problems the U.S.S.R. had to solve and of the obstacles it had to overcome. The Soviet population developed as follows:

1913	164·8
1922	152·3
1940	194·1
1950	178·5

(in millions of inhabitants)

It is difficult to calculate, since the territorial limits of the Tsarist Empire in 1913 and the Soviet Union in 1950 were not the same, and there are no Soviet statistics for the years 1933 to 1940 and 1940 to 1949. However, the actual losses can be estimated as follows (in millions of inhabitants):

1913–1921:
First World War, Civil War, Hostilities, Epidemics 13·5
1930–1939: Food crisis, Stalinist Terror 7·0
1941–1945: Second World War 23·0

      43·5

To these figures must be added the shortfall in births caused by
the higher death rate and lower birth rate during the wars
(45 million people). So the population of the Soviet Union was
about 90 million fewer than it ought to have been if wars,
famine and mass repression had not 'mown down before they
were ripe' so many Soviet citizens, often among the best
qualified: cadres of the Party, the State and the economy,
young men and women whose qualities had scarcely started to
develop.[10]

The Soviet Union, which had gained glory but been bled
white, faced the United States, which had emerged richer and
more powerful than ever from the Second World War. They
alone possessed atomic weapons. Their industry represented
half of world industrial output. Soviet national income was
barely a quarter of American national income. Relations
between the partners in the anti-Hitler coalition were not easy;
not only were their economic and social systems diametrically
opposed to each other, but the political systems were radically
different. The delay in opening the Second Front was only
partly offset by the June 1944 landings. It was in vain that
Stalin sought to reassure the Anglo-Saxons by facilitating the
disbanding of the Comintern, he still worried them. In
Teheran and then at Yalta, whilst they agreed to force
Hitler's Germany to surrender unconditionally, the three
Great Powers were only really able to take note of the actual
situations which had emerged directly from the military
operations of the Second World War. The dividing of the post-
war world on a territorial basis as well as on the basis of
economic, social, political and ideological systems, which still
largely exists today in 1975, did not take place at Yalta, but on
the battlefield: 'cujus acies, cujus respublica', the army
determines the type of regime. This was made quite clear in
Greece when Churchill's tanks crushed in a bloodbath the
Greek Resistance fighters who were not prepared to accept
that the Greek authorities who had favoured the Nazis should
stay in power. It is true that Stalin displayed brutality and
even cynicism in his dealings with other states and with the
Communist parties involved. It is true that he could have
protested more vigorously against British policy in Greece, but
basically that would not have made much difference. In 1945,

the U.S.S.R. was poor and weak and the United States rich and powerful, and the U.S.S.R. neither wanted to nor was in a position to launch into a third world war. In his book *Sur la Crise du mouvement communiste*, Fernand Claudin omits this fact when he deals with the situation in France and Italy immediately after the Second World War. These two countries had been liberated by the Anglo-Saxons, and even if their peoples had so wished, which was not the case, they could not afford the luxury of a revolution which the Americans and British would have drowned in blood without the U.S.S.R. being able to intervene, for the very simple reason that it was in no position to do so.

So, far from disappearing at the end of the war, the Stalin phenomenon maintained its position in 1945. Its institutions, habits and personnel emerged strengthened from the war, and the General Secretary's authority and popularity were increased. Victory had not removed the causes which had given birth to the Stalin phenomenon. The conditions which would have allowed its elimination did not yet exist.

NOTES

1. France concluded a non-aggression treaty with Germany when von Ribbentrop, the German Minister for Foreign Affairs, came to Paris on 6th December 1938 (see the correspondence from the French ambassadors in Berlin in the *Livre jaune français*).
2. Italics in the original text.
3. The text of all these agreements is to be found in the Wilhelmstrasse secret archives (Volume 8). Secret minutes of 23rd August 1939 and 28th September 1939.
4. Weygand's *Mémoires*, Vol. 3, pp. 71–8.
5. Communist papers were banned as early as 29th August 1939, and the French Communist Party was proscribed as soon as war was declared.
6. This, for example, is what the French Communist Party did in June 1940, when it put forward measures to save the nation from the invasion, but until 1941 the Comintern line made it hard for it to carry out this new policy.
7. Molotov was Vice-President, and Beria, Voroshilov and Malenkov were members.
8. At the end of 1941, the territory occupied by the Germans represented 40 per cent of the Soviet population. It produced 38 per cent of all grain, 58 per cent of steel, 63 per cent of coal and 60 per cent of aluminium.

9. And no doubt as many as 25 million.
10. We are only giving imprecise figures. They constitute acceptable estimates and convey a trend which enables us to weigh the suffering of the peoples of the U.S.S.R., and the problems posed by this unprecedented loss of blood.

6 After the War: Zenith and Decline of Stalinism

Within the Soviet Union, the situation was not noticeably different from what it had been in the thirties. How could it have been otherwise? Stalin, more popular and omnipresent than ever, was still at the head of the state. At this period, the cult of Stalin reached proportions which remind one of the devotion shown to the Hellenistic kings and the Roman emperors, but with the help of the infinitely greater resources of contemporary science and technology. Not only were tens of millions of copies of photographs of him distributed everywhere – not to have one in one's house was taken as an act of defiance – but tens of thousands of statues and busts of him appeared all over the country. The press, literature, the cinema and the theatre praised him like a living god. A bust of him was set up on top of Elbruz, the highest peak in the Caucasus, and it bore the following inscription: 'To the greatest man of all time.' Factories, kolkhozes and dozens of towns were named after him. The highest peak in the Pamir Mountains also took his name. As Ilya Ehrenburg wrote: 'In the minds of millions of Soviet citizens, Stalin was transformed into a mythical demigod; everyone trembled when they heard his name, and thought that he alone would manage to save the Soviet Union from invasion and ruin.' It was dangerous to criticise him, even in private correspondence. As for removing him from power, that was unthinkable. In his hands he held all the reins of power, and he had an eye to hanging onto them. In order to do so, he relied on the political police. In 1946, the People's Commissariats had become ministries – the N.K.G.B. was now the M.G.B. (State Security), and the N.K.V.D. was the M.V.D. (the Ministry of the Interior) – but the police's prerogatives had not changed and were still exorbitant. All Soviet citizens, including all Party members, all organisations and administrations, all public places, factories, universities, literature, the media, foreigners, the Army and the Post Office were under its daily, despotic supervision. The 'OSSO' (the Special Commission) still existed and could still deport individuals who were 'enemies of the people' without public trial (for ten years since 1938, and for 20 years since 1943).

There should be a study of these essential instruments of terror, but, needless to say, we have little information about them. We know that members of the political police earned high salaries, had considerable privileges and were numerous (certainly over a million people). The M.V.D. was armed with discretionary powers and thus dominated the State and the Party. Under the pretext of combating enemies of the system, it consituted a formidable force, a sort of inquisition which nothing could stop. For most Soviet citizens, Stalin's person was sacred. This was a transposition from the religious to the secular plane, which, in this Godless society, expressed an age-old need for reassurance. Have we not found a similar cult of Mao Tse-tung in Communist China, where he was the 'great helmsman', he whose words enlightened the world? Has it not been observed in many socialist countries and in the non-socialist countries of Africa and Asia? It is a method of government as old as the world, and one which is far from completely obsolete, as too often imagined, in the developed capitalist countries. After all, the Hitler phenomenon occurred in one of the most highly cultured countries in the world, that of Goethe, Marx, Beethoven, Wagner and Nietzsche. We are not saying that the cult of the leader is a good thing, but we must bear in mind its historical reality, and its religious and psychological as well as political bases. The Bolsheviks made use of this fact. By acting in this way, they created the mechanisms to which they themselves fell victim and which socialism was powerless to destroy for many years.

Thanks to these mechanisms, the M.V.D. prospered, and the end of the war did not stop it. All the Soviet prisoners released from Hitler's camps were regarded as suspect and because of this were deported as 'enemies of the people'. The attitude of the police authorities can be explained in two ways: to be taken prisoner was an act of cowardice and deserved punishment, or the fact that they had lived abroad in contact with the Nazis was suspect. Anyway, several million soldiers released from Hitler's camps were deported to the camps run by the Gulag (the Department managing all the camps which was supervised by the M.V.D.). There they found a lot of German prisoners and those who had been deported before or during the war.

The total lack of democratic freedom and the repression made it impossible to attack the M.V.D. The Party itself was only going through the motions. The Central Committee no longer met, and no Party Congress was held from 1939 to 1952, that is to say for thirteen years. Even the Politbureau now only played a modest role. It was replaced by five, six or seven-man commissions which met in the Kremlin together with Stalin. As he grew older, he became more and more suspicious and no longer trusted anybody at all. Any proposals other than those he himself made were rejected and the proposer was often punished, so that his advisers got into the habit of not making any. Voznesensky, Vice-President of the Council, a member of the Politbureau, in charge of the economy, was removed from all his posts at Stalin's behest and without anyone being officially notified. His name simply disappeared from the Soviet press. Some time later, he was arrested and shot without trial.

In order to justify the resumption of the Terror (even though on a smaller scale than before the war), Stalin invoked the Cold War and imperialist plotting. As had been the case concerning the kulaks and the dangers of aggression in 1929–30, or concerning Hitler and Japanese Imperialism in 1937–8, Stalin started from facts which were clearly true. For a large number of Soviet citizens and for foreign Communists, this made his claims credible, especially since the accused still confessed to imaginary crimes. It is true that the prime responsibility for the Cold War rests with imperialism, and firstly with the most powerful imperialist country, that is to say the United States. Its aim was to contain Communism within the territorial limits fixed by the fortunes of war at the end of the Second World War, even to roll it back and to establish its own authority in the whole non-Communist part of the world. In the case of declining imperialist powers which had been weakened by the war, the final spasms of colonialism were added to this. In France and Britain, colonialism threatened to make the Cold War more dangerous. So the United States, the only country to have atomic weapons until 1949, played the role of 'policeman of the world'. With the Truman Doctrine, the Marshall Plan and the Atlantic Treaty, it set up a formidably powerful military bloc, which had its own integrated military organisation – N.A.T.O. Communists were eliminated from West European governments (in France, Italy and Belgium) to which they had belonged since the Liberation, and the United States helped to re-establish a strong German state (the Federal Republic) and a prosperous Japan.

Stalin used the Cold War to justify his policy. The U.S.S.R. had emerged terribly weakened from the war, and only appeared to be economically powerful. In the Red Army (which had become the Soviet Army just after the war), it possessed a formidable force (7 million men in 1945, about 4 million in 1948) which was well equipped with conventional arms, but, precisely because of the exhaustion caused by the war, it had neither the desire nor the capacity to undertake an offensive. The requirements of reconstruction outweighed any other concern, but the situation was difficult. Industry was still mediocre and Soviet agriculture was experiencing great difficulties. Large budgets had to be devoted to education and research; in particular they had to catch up with the United States in the atomic field and to prepare for future developments in space research. Well, an atomic bomb is as expensive (if not more so) in the U.S.S.R. as in the United States. If one takes into account the fact that in 1945 the American national income was four times higher than that of the Soviet Union, the same atomic bomb cost the Soviet citizen four times more than the American citizen. Soviet living standards were very low in 1946. There was no chance of them rising quickly, because in the Soviet situation it was impossible to produce butter, textiles, steel, atomic bombs and space rockets at the same time. We must also add that, because of war damage and catastrophic weather conditions, the 1945–6 harvests were poor:

$$1945 \quad 47,300,000 \text{ tons of grain}$$
$$1946 \quad 39,600,000 \text{ tons of grain}$$

that is to say that the 1946 harvest was 40 per cent of that of 1913 (to feed a much larger population). A policy of honest co-operation with the allies who had defeated Hitler would have made it possible to avoid the Cold War and the armaments race. In February 1945 at Yalta this was still a possibility. The three Great Powers agreed to 'denazify, demilitarise and divide up Germany',[1] commissions for the division and for reparations were even set up. Stalin raised the question of American economic aid – which was quite logical since the U.S.S.R. had been destroyed by Hitler and the United States was rich. Roosevelt did not say no. The Potsdam Conference was more difficult. Hitler had died in his bunker and Germany had capitulated. Truman had replaced Roosevelt, who had died in April, and the United States was testing its first atom bomb in preparation for using it against Japan. There was no longer any question of American economic aid unless accompanied by political strings; this was the case of the 1947 Marshall Plan. The world was to be cut in half, and the U.S.S.R. would have to rely on its own resources to achieve recovery. Even reparations were to be restricted to what the U.S.S.R. levied in its own occupation zone, which was the poorest one.

Stalin's policies in the post-war period are explained by this historical environment and this enables us to understand why and how, on the basis of institutions which had survived, there was a return to a more or less identical policy. Soviet citizens had to make heavy sacrifices and considerable efforts in order to improve the standard of living a little. Because of the war, in 1947 it was much lower than in 1928. Finally, strict discipline was necessary. Thanks to the existing institutions, Stalin imposed these efforts, these sacrifices and this discipline; he justified repression by the Cold War and imperialist plots. It was necessary to protect the Soviet people from any comparison with the West which – in the absence of explanations – would probably be to the detriment of the Soviet system. For this reason, he imposed a stricter ban on contacts with the outside world, on Soviet citizens travelling outside the U.S.S.R., and on foreigners travelling in the Soviet Union. Entry visas for the U.S.S.R. were only given to foreign diplomats and delegates of foreign Communist parties or friendly organisations who had been invited for meetings or study trips. The Soviet press described the life style outside the U.S.S.R. in horrific terms and the political police kept an an extremely strict check on the travels and correspondence of foreigners in the U.S.S.R. At the same time, Stalin used Russian nationalism more openly and more extensively than ever. All the important technical and scientific inventions of the modern period were attributed to Russians. History books continued to glorify the Russian past, including its most dubious aspects. Thus, Tsarist colonial conquests were presented as the great historic opportunity for the peoples conquered by Russian imperialism. Movements which had opposed such conquests were criticised as being 'bourgeois nationalist in inspiration'. The Communist parties of the non-Russian republics again became a target for repression. In Georgia, in the Soviet Baltic Republics (Lithuania, Estonia and Latvia), in the Ukraine, in the Central Asian republics, hundreds of thousands of people were arrested and deported. However, the Russian Communists still did not escape repression. The struggle 'against cosmopolitanism' and the anti-semitic campaigns must be placed in the context of this policy of Russian nationalism.

The struggle against 'cosmopolitanism' made it possible to eliminate all foreign influence. This was a strange fate for a revolution which drew its inspiration from a German who was Jewish in origin, a certain Karl Marx, and many of whose founders had the same origins. Whilst he did quote him occasionally when it was necessary to justify some aspect of his policy, though he did so seldom and with decreasing frequency, Stalin took care not to honour the memory of Marx; in 1953 there was no statue of him in Moscow, whilst there were several tens of thousands of busts of the Generalissimo. This policy caused enormous havoc. The humanities and the natural sciences were gagged. An intellectual iron collar gripped the Soviet Union. In political economy, the theses of Varga, who was making a subtle analysis of the development of capitalism, were condemned and his research was halted. The new methods used by American economists involving the use of mathematics were castigated as bourgeois. The magazines *Problems of History* and *Problems of Philosophy* were criticised for a lack of ideological firmness. Under the control of Zhdanov and then Suslov after 1948, literature, music and art were subjected to more and more strict supervision.[2] Denunciations of Western influences were accompanied by political and ideological demands which became increasingly incompatible with original creation and serious research. The cinema and the theatre did not escape these directives. In biology, Lysenko became the high priest of an anti-scientific 'church' which criticised Mendel's theses which were considered to be idealistic. Quantum theory, the theory of relativity and the resonance theory in chemistry were criticised as bourgeois. Cybernetics and psychoanalysis were wiped off the scientific map. In the eyes of the Soviet authorities, Einstein and Freud became dangerous cosmopolitans. Thus, by contrasting 'bourgeois' science and 'proletarian' science, they helped Marxism to become more ossified and Soviet science to get left behind. The Party pronounced judgement on everything, and its judgement was that of Stalin, 'the great Coryphaeus of science' as a zealous writer had dubbed him. Zhdanov's attacks on 'decadent' music reached the heights of dogmatism and stupidity, for they were directed at Shostakovich, Prokofiev, Muradeli, Khachaturian and Kabalevsky. Zhdanov even went as far as to criticise musicians for over-utilising the sound of the drum or the cymbals. He criticised abstract painting: 'Absolutely crazy; for example, they draw a head on forty legs, one eye looking this way, the other into the distance.' As early as 1946, the Leningrad magazine *Zvezda* was attacked by the Soviet leaders. The nature of these attacks can be gauged from the following extract from Zhdanov's report on a great Leningrad poet, Anna Akhmatova: 'It would be hard to say whether she is a nun or a fallen woman; better perhaps to say she is a bit of each, her desires and her prayers intertwined.' And Zhdanov quotes the following poem to justify his opinion:

> 'But I vow by the garden of angels,
> By the miraculous icon I vow,
> I vow by the child of our passion . . .'

'Such is Akhmatova, with her petty, narrow personal life, her paltry experiences, and her religiously mystical eroticism.'[3]

As for anti-semitism, this developed on the basis of Tsarist traditions which had not totally disappeared from a sector of public opinion. Theoretically, that is to say in law, racism was forbidden by the constitution and punishable by the courts. In practice, things were quite different. Stalin initially attacked

Jewish culture and religious manifestations. He had most of the leaders of the Jewish Anti-Fascist Committee, which had been founded during the war, and a large number of Jewish writers executed. After 1949, he tackled Zionism: following a well-known model, this struggle made it possible to develop anti-semitism by treating Zionism and Judaism as the same. In the course of several big trials held in the People's Democracies, like the Slansky trial (until the trial, he had been General Secretary of the Czechoslovak Communist Party) in which Artur London was also condemned, the accused 'confessed' (by the same methods used at the great Moscow trials), 'that they were working for international Zionism, the agent of American imperialism'. The equation of Zionists and American imperialists and of Jews and Zionists woke up the age-old fiend which was slumbering in the anti-semitic part of public opinion. Thus Stalin found scapegoats to whom he attributed responsibility for the continuing economic problems of the Soviet Union.

On 13th January 1953, the Soviet press announced the discovery of a plot instigated by doctors who were almost all Jewish in origin. Having murdered various well-known people, they were allegedly preparing to assassinate a certain number of Soviet leaders. The 'doctors' plot' carried anti-semitism to a level not previously reached in the Soviet Union, and Stalin went so far as to consider the mass deportation of the two million Soviet Jews who had survived Nazi persecution. Among the utterly staged 'affairs' in the post-war period there was the so-called Leningrad affair: thousands of officials who either came from the Baltic city or were in the local administration were arrested and shot without being tried. Among the victims were a Central Committee Secretary, Kuznetsov, the President of the R.S.F.S.R. Council of Ministers, Rodionov, and the Moscow and Leningrad Party secretaries. The press did not even mention it. Other leaders came to a tragic end. Such was the case of Lozovsky, former President of the Red Trade Union International. Stalin also removed many soldiers whose prestige threatened to eclipse his own. Thus Marshal Zhukov found himself in command of the Odessa military region. Voznesensky, a full member of the Politbureau, vanished and the public was not even informed.

Abroad, the bourgeoisie made use of all these facts and continues to do so. Despite all the precautions taken, this situation could not be concealed outside the Soviet Union, which had diplomatic relations with dozens of countries. Turncoats who had fled to the West described life in the camps and showed how the Soviet political police operated. Foreigners, Poles for example, had to be released in compliance with international treaties. So, imperialism justified its policies on the basis of the Stalin phenomenon and the totalitarian aspects it had taken on. Churchill spoke of the Soviet 'iron curtain,' and violent anti-Soviet campaigns took place fuelling the Cold War. Turncoats from the U.S.S.R. – for example Kravchenko – took part in this campaign. This was of course fair enough, and had a basis in reality, though it only put forward those aspects which were the blackest and least favourable to the U.S.S.R. For many, it was above all an excuse to justify their aggressive policy towards the U.S.S.R., to get the Atlantic Pact and N.A.T.O. accepted and to make people forget the anti-Communist repression in Greece, the atrocities committed by French colonialism in Indochina, Madagascar and Algeria, support for Franco in Spain, Salazar in Portugal, Chiang Kai-shek in Formosa, etc. As for the industrial and cultural progress made by the Soviet Union, it was not considered in good taste to mention it.[4]

The attitude adopted by the international Communist movement, which denied the truth of these facts until the 20th Congress of the C.P.S.U. in 1956, can be explained in this context. The foreign Communist parties claimed that they were lies and bourgeois propaganda. From this point of view, the most significant event was the action brought against the *Lettres françaises*, which called the statements made by Kravchenko in *J'ai choisi la liberté* lies: the revelations which had been made about the Soviet Union since 1930 appeared suspect to Communists, all the more so because the accused in the great Moscow trials had confessed and because imperialist plots were not just an invention of the M.G.B. Now, information mainly filtered through via Soviet turncoats who had fled to the West (Krivitsky, Orlov and Kravchenko), via Trotsky and Trotskyites and via university study centres in the imperialist countries. People could not be unaware of such dreadful provisions as the right of administrative deportation, but they were attributed to the rigours of class war and the attitude of the capitalist states. The Communist parties and their leaders had all been trained by the Comintern. The Communist international had made the unconditional defence of the Soviet Union one of the pillars of its policy. It was one of the twenty-one conditions for membership of the 3rd International. So, the movement had got into the habit of considering everything the Soviet leaders said as gospel truth, and of defending the Soviet Union as a whole. For a long time, the latter was the only socialist state in the world: a 'besieged fortress' which appeared to be the victim of numerous plots and to be weak amid the storm. It was necessary to defend it because Hitler or French, British or Japanese Imperialism threatened it, then because Hitler had attacked it, later because the Americans and British were preparing to do so. It had become impossible to distinguish between Stalin and the Soviet Union, hence the difficult position Tito and the Yugoslavian Communist Party found themselves in in 1948 when Stalin imposed a break.

In 1975, it is easier to arrive at a calm evaluation of these matters. As a young Communist just after the Second World War, I felt I was taking part in a great crusade for socialism at a period when the Cold War was at its height, and the French 4th Republic was getting bogged down in colonial wars, a whole series of scandals and social injustice. My Stalinist ideas were based on a profound belief that until the Second World War the Soviet Union alone had been marking out a new path, and on the preponderant part it had played in the victory over Nazism. Unlike some people, I do not feel that I ruined my youth and sacrificed it for an empty ideal. I have simply learnt, and it was a cruel experience, that, as Romain Rolland wrote to Hermann Hesse on 5th March 1935, ' "philosophes", as they were called in Jean-Jacques' time, no longer count in the eyes of those who are in power. Fortunately the cause they serve is bigger than them.' I do not blame those who retreated with dignity to their own Aventine with the not unjustified feeling that they had been mistaken, they they had been deceived, knowingly by some, unknowingly by others; but it seemed to me that it was possible to take the analysis further and to dissociate Stalinism from socialism, for after all it was only its first avatar created by history in very specific spatio-temporal conditions.

On 5th March 1953, I was in hiding in a small house in the southern suburbs of Paris a few steps away from the Seine.[5] I remember that I cried for a long time when I heard the announcement of Stalin's death on the radio. The people of my generation all bear this wound in their hearts and we must recover from it if we wish to proceed further and higher on a road which, as Marx himself perceived, is no easy one. I of course understand that Stalin is now ancient history for young people, since they were born after his death, but the questions raised by this history remain.

What was profoundly new in comparison with the pre-war period was the existence in Europe and Asia of a certain number of states which were starting to build socialism, though on the basis of very different conditions and following very varied processes. The circumstances of the Second World War and its consequences were such that none of the great developed capitalist countries was part of the socialist area which by 1949 stretched from the Elbe to the Pacific. The Soviet Union, which had become the second most powerful nation on earth (though still far behind the United States) because of victory and the collapse of Germany, proved to be the most powerful of the socialist states. Not only had it been the first to open up the way, but it was largely thanks to it that others had taken the same path. Apart from China, the new socialist states had small populations.

Country	Population	Surface area (in km²)
Albania	1,175,000	28,748
German Democratic Republic	17,313,000	107,173
Bulgaria	7,100,000	110,842
Hungary	9,165,000	93,011
Poland	23,970,000	311,730
Romania	16,000,000	237,384
Czechoslovakia	12,339,000	127,827
Yugoslavia	15,772,000	237,384

Apart from Czechoslovakia (or at least the Western (Czech) part), these were relatively poor countries, essentially agricultural and still only slightly developed from the economic and cultural point of view.

According to a report by the Finance Commission of the American Senate, in 1939 the *per capita* income of these countries was half way between that of Western Europe and that of the countries in the third world (South America, Africa and Asia). The economic characteristics and social structures of these countries were similar to those of the Tsarist Empire in 1917. With the exception of Czechoslovakia, few democratic traditions and structures were to be found there. The case of the German Democratic Republic, which was established in 1949, is of course different, since it was part of the former Reich.

Stalin considered that these countries should be strictly subordinated to the Soviet Union. He intended to impose on them political and economic systems similar to those in the Soviet Union, and to keep a strict check on their foreign policy. As the Yugoslavian crisis shows, he could not conceive of relations as between equals being formed between the new Eastern European states and the Soviet Union. At the end of the Second World War, a powerful movement had brought to power the Yugoslavian Communist Party under the leadership of Tito. The Red Army had helped liberate the country, but its role had not been decisive, for the Popular Liberation Army already controlled nearly the whole country.

As soon as the Cold War started, Communist and Workers' parties[6] met in order to adopt a common strategy; the meeting took place from 22nd to 27th September 1947, at Szklarska Poreba in Poland. Zhdanov, who together with Malenkov represented the C.P.S.U., presented a report in which he showed how the world was divided into two camps, asked the Communists from the various countries not to underestimate their strength and to close ranks behind the Communist Party of the U.S.S.R. in the struggle against imperialism. At this meeting, the Yugoslav Communist Party – with the agreement of the Soviets – criticised the policies of the French and Italian Communist Parties, which they considered opportunist because they had not made use of all the revolutionary potential which existed in France and Italy at the end of the Second World

War. These criticisms did not make sufficient allowances for
for the difference between the situation in the countries of
Eastern Europe and those of Western Europe. In the former,
the liberation had been the work of the Red Army, in the latter
the work of the Anglo-Saxon armies.

After endorsing Zhdanov's report and the Yugoslavs'
criticisms, the conference accepted the principle of setting up
an information office for Communist and Workers' Parties (the
Cominform), which was intended for 'the organisation of
exchanges of experience and the co-ordination of activity on
the basis of mutual agreement'. The aim was not to re-establish
the Comintern, but to some extent to make good the lack of
'lasting and sound relations', as Malenkov put it.

Belgrade was chosen as the headquarters of the Cominform. The very notion of equality between the socialist states
was quickly called into question, for the Yugoslav Communist
Party did not accept this inequality. Stalin had said to
Khrushchev: 'All I have to do is to move my little finger, and
Tito will vanish, he will collapse.' In fact, Stalin wanted to
make an example of Yugoslavia, but the latter was not
impressed.

As early as 18th March 1948, the Soviet leaders decided to
withdraw their military advisers from Yugoslavia. Yugoslavia's
response to the Soviet injunctions was in the negative, and in
June 1948 she was condemned by the Cominform. Stalin
apparently expected to be supported by a large section of the
Yugoslav Communist Party and thought that by making the
affair public he would make Tito submit or resign. In April,
several Yugoslav leaders had already supported the Soviet
line. Stalin accused Tito of bourgeois nationalism and the
Cominform resolution made an unambiguous appeal for 'the
sound forces within the Yugoslav Communist Party to force
the leadership to adopt a new political line'.

However, Stalin's 'little finger' was not sufficient to bring
Yugoslavia to heel. A Soviet-inspired military plot in Belgrade
failed. Direct military intervention was the only option
remaining to Stalin, but, faced with the determination of the
Yugoslavs and the American attitude, he did not dare undertake it. The Yugoslav Communist Party was in a difficult
position. It was the position Trotsky had been in at the end of

the twenties and during the thirties. If they opposed Stalin, did this not mean that they were opposing the U.S.S.R., thus striking a blow against socialism and, objectively, helping imperialism? However, there was a fundamental difference. The Yugoslav Communist Party was in power and Tito was the leader of a state in transition from capitalism to socialism. The United States helped Tito in his struggle against Stalin but Tito refused any anti-Communist conditions and the Yugoslav Communist Party built a socialist economy in its country whilst refusing to set up a new break-away International. Yet they did not have much room for manœuvre.

Though economically isolated in the Balkan Peninsula, Yugoslavia managed to hold out, despite violent incidents which took place for several years along its borders with Bulgaria, Hungary and Czechoslovakia.

Stalin, who was powerless to defeat Tito, exercised stricter control over the other People's Democracies in Europe. In these countries, either the Communist Party became the only party (as was the C.P.S.U.), or the parties which remained only kept a semblance of autonomy. Most of the independent Social-Democratic leaders had to emigrate or were arrested and shot, accused, as was traditional at the time, 'of spying for American Imperialism'. By 1949, the Communist and Workers' Parties had total control of public life. Everywhere the political police, which was controlled by the Soviet M.G.B., played a dominant role, and a special watch was kept on the media, whilst intellectual circles were particularly hard hit by repression. The Communist parties underwent severe repression which was reminiscent of that which had afflicted the C.P.S.U. before rather than after the war.

Thus, big public trials of Communist Party leaders were organised; the latter confessed their crimes after torture sessions similar to those which had taken place in the U.S.S.R. in the years 1937–8. In Hungary, Rajk, the Foreign Minister, was excuted, and Kadar was sent to prison (in 1953, there were 150,000 political prisoners). In Poland, Gomulka was tried and sentenced to life imprisonment. In Bulgaria, Kostov, a Party Secretary, was tried and executed, as was Dzodze in Albania. Czechoslovakia is an interesting case as it was the only country in this part of Europe which was relatively highly developed and had an experienced bourgeois democracy. The Czech Communist Party was powerful (38 per cent of all the votes cast in the whole country in 1945) and, contrary to what is still often said nowadays, the Soviets only intervened indirectly in the process which led to the February 1948 events. Czechoslovakia was not in the British and American armies' occupation zone and the country had been liberated by the Red Army. This was a factor in favour of the development of socialism in that country. However, a counter-revolutionary *coup d'état* nearly took place in 1948; it failed because of popular opposition and not as a result of intervention by the Red Army. The so-called 'Prague coup' was nothing other than the people's riposte to this attempt to reduce Communist influence in Czechoslovakia and to wipe out the gains which had been made at the liberation.

It was afterwards that the Soviet protectorship became hard to bear. Czechoslovakia copied the U.S.S.R.'s methods of political leadership, economic management and planning. The result was particularly catastrophic, for the Czech situation was less favourable than any other to the importing of Soviet methods. Repression struck the Czech Communist Party and the intellectuals. Gustav Husak was sent to prison, and, with the help of advisers from the Soviet Secret Service, a big trial was organised: among others, Slansky, the General Secretary of the Czech Communist Party, had to confess to imaginary crimes. The others included Artur London and E. Loebl, who were to be released a few years later.

As for the German Democratic Republic, it experienced problems as a result of the mass exodus through Berlin, where people could pass freely from the Eastern sector to the Western one.

There were also economic reasons for Soviet pressure on the People's Democracies. For example, joint Soviet–Romanian companies controlled no small part of the Romanian economy (Sovrom-Petrol). Economic relations between the U.S.S.R. and the People's Democracies were often unequal, for the U.S.S.R. purchased their products below the world market price and paid for them in non-convertible roubles. The worsening of the Cold War and the risk of a third world war reinforced these tendencies for inequality and justified them in terms of the requirements of discipline in the 'anti-imperialist camp'. As always, Stalin's policy started from actual facts.

For the reasons we have already mentioned, Stalin had no intention of embarking upon a new world war, but he needed a degree of international tension to justify his internal policy and his attitude to the People's Democracies. American imperialism, which bore the main responsibility for the Cold War, carried out repeated aggressive acts, but in 1949 the Soviet Union tested its first atomic bomb, and in Europe a certain, precarious balance, based on the arms race, became apparent.

The Atlantic Treaty and N.A.T.O. were opposed by the Warsaw Treaty and its military organisation, the German Federal Republic by the German Democratic Republic and the Coal and Steel Pool among the Western European countries by the Comecon (founded in 1949). So the two camps got organised and consolidated their positions.

In this field, as in all the others, the results were contradictory. The Eastern and Balkan parts of Europe were undergoing profound social and economic transformations. The capitalists and great land-owners were losing their hegemony whilst the foundations of socialism were being laid, thus making possible rapid growth of the productive forces and the fight against cultural backwardness. At the same time, as in the U.S.S.R., Stalin's policy was leading to a despotic system, which coincided with tradition in most countries, and a strengthening of the bureaucracy.

Because of the Chinese Revolution, the situation in the Far East was somewhat different. It had followed a historical path which was quite different from the classical models of Marxism–Leninism. The Chinese Communists, who were driven out of the big cities, which were anyway small in number relative to the Chinese population, because of repression, founded a new (essentially rural) republic which was the basic cell for the future People's Republic of China, carried through a programme of land reform which was to serve as a model for the future transformation of the country, whilst the People's Army, the instrument of victory over imperialism, was being forged. This Republic resisted all military pressure, that of the Japanese and that of the Chinese Nationalists of the Kuomintang under Chiang Kai-shek.

Stalin hardly displayed great understanding in relation to the policy of the Chinese Communist Party. He had established good relations with the Chiang Kai-shek government and he intended to keep them: during the war against Japan, he had been in favour of integrating the Communist forces in the Nationalist army. With the unhappy experience of 1927 behind him, Mao Tse-tung categorically refused to put his head into 'the lion's mouth'. Despite the advice of the Soviets who wanted the Chinese Communists to undertake large-scale military operations against the Japanese, he was content to develop guerrilla activity. In April 1941, the U.S.S.R. had signed a non-aggression treaty with the Japanese, but she was afraid that it might be broken, and so insisted that the pressure on the Japanese forces in China should be increased. The 'revolutionary war', a combination of armed struggle and political work, enabled the Chinese Communists to liberate huge zones behind the lines of the Japanese troops and the Kuomintang. When Japan capitulated, the Chinese Communists had at their disposal forces which were considerable, and which had grown during the period of war against Japan. The Soviet Union took part in the end of this war and liberated Manchuria. But Stalin went on dealing with Chiang Kai-shek; this he himself said to the American diplomats Hurley (United States Ambassador in China) on 15th April 1945, and Hopkins (Adviser to the American Government) on 28th May 1945. He and Chiang Kai-shek signed a treaty of friendship and alliance which returned to the Soviet Union the territorial privileges which Tsarist Russia had enjoyed in China. Yet Soviet aid to the Chinese Communists was considerable, for it enabled them to seize pretty large areas in Manchuria and part of the Japanese military equipment, but it remained far below what the Chinese Communists might have hoped for. Stalin tried – but in vain – to get the Chinese Communists to take part in a Government of National Union led by Chiang Kai-shek. The civil war was to last until the end of 1949. Despite American aid, the Chiang Kai-shek regime, which was deeply corrupt, collapsed militarily and politically.

The birth in 1949 of the People's Republic of China created a completely new situation in the Far East. It strengthened the position of the People's Republic of Korea

(North Korea) led by Kim-Il-Sung and facilitated the struggle against French colonialism in Vietnam of the Viet-minh under the leadership of Ho Chi Minh. At the same time the triumph of the Chinese Communists strengthened the anti-imperialist camp. Stalin, who had learnt from his experience with the Yugoslavs, realised that he could not treat Mao in the same way as Tito. As for Mao, he regarded an alliance with the Soviet Union as a necessity – and the attitude of the Western powers who boycotted the new state hardly left him any other choice. The Sino–Soviet Treaty, which was signed in 1950 – and which was valid for thirty years – set up an alliance which was meant to be solid and lasting. The U.S.S.R. obtained the setting up of joint Sino–Soviet concerns in Sin-Kiang as well as for the operation of airlines. In 1952, it was to return the Manchurian railway and the Port Arthur base to the Chinese, it promised to give China funds for economic development and to help from the technical point of view (Soviet specialists were to be sent and Chinese technicians trained). But, the U.S.S.R. was to keep the Dairen base until a peace treaty was signed with Japan. Weeks of talks had been needed to get that far. Nevertheless, the compromise which was initiated in 1950 was to last for some time and even to withstand the ordeals of the Korean War, when China intervened to help the People's Republic of Korea maintain its independence in the face of the Americans.

The real difficulties in relations between the two great Communist states were not really to begin until just after Stalin's death. The two states were doubtless linked by a common ideology, but Marxism had been adapted to China by Mao, just as it had been adapted to Russia by Stalin. The problems which the two states had to solve were noticeably different and the burden of history did more to separate them than bring them together. Sino–Soviet relations appeared to be set fair, but this euphoria sprang from forced optimism rather than from the real situation.

Thus, in 1953, the anti-imperialist camp seemed to be utterly united behind the Soviet Union. Only Yugoslavia had escaped its pull. But there was no lack of tensions behind this apparent unity, and they were to make their presence felt after 1953. Nevertheless, the worst had been avoided, for they had managed to prevent a third world war. At the time of the Berlin crisis and then during the Korean War 'peace had only hung by a thread', but the thread had not parted. As the size of the campaign for signatures to the Stockholm Appeal against the use of atomic weapons, and the activity of the 'peace partisans' demonstrated, the peoples of the world had no intention of again experiencing the horrors of a war which was likely to be even more destructive than the one before.

In this field there were limits, even for Stalinist policies, and they did not overstep them. Occasionally they helped increase international tension by facilitating the schemes of the imperialist countries, and they were used to justify anti-Communism and anti-Sovietism. However, imperialism did not manage to win back the ground lost since the Second World War, and it went on losing ground with the Chinese Revolution, and the growth of national liberation movements in Asia, Africa and Latin America. From every point of view the situation was least satisfactory in the developed capitalist countries.

Despite the return to terror and the increase in bureaucratic phenomena, from 1946 to 1953 the U.S.S.R. experienced considerable industrial and cultural growth, but, on the other hand, agriculture did not really achieve any progress.

In the industrial field, the production of energy sources and that of heavy industry increased during the fourth Five Year Plan and in the first half of the fifth.

	1940	*1945*	*1950*	*1953*
Coal	165·9	149·3	261·1	320·4
Oil	31·1	19·4	37·9	52·8
Electricity	48·3	43·2	91·2	134·8
Steel	18·3	12·3	25·4	38·1
Cotton	3·9	1·6	3·8	5·3
Footwear	211	63	203·4	239·5

Coal
Oil
Steel
Cotton
⎫ in millions of tons

Electricity: in millions of kWh.
Footwear: in millions of pairs

F

The industrial sector producing consumer goods was still at a mediocre level; this was not surprising since investment was directed above all to the nuclear power industry, to armaments, steel, education and major construction projects. In 1953, the U.S.S.R. was still only producing small numbers of television sets, washing machines and electrical domestic appliances. The chemical industry was very backward and no nylon was yet produced. The U.S.S.R. only produced a little more footwear than in 1940, insufficient and poor quality cloth and very few motor vehicles (mainly lorries and buses). This explains why contacts with abroad were banned and the press painted a false picture of life in the West. For many years, because of the initial situation, the hostility of the rest of the world and the Second World War, sacrifices were necessary, but they were largely imposed upon the Soviet people by force and by threats. Instead of persuading people, Stalin preferred to repress them. The bureaucratisation of the state and his lack of faith in the people led him to put more trust in the M.V.D. than in open debate. There was often a lack of day-to-day consumer goods and they were of poor quality. In the towns, the housing crisis was catastrophic. In Moscow, the rule was that several couples lived in one flat. There was nothing surprising about all this. The available funds were set aside for projects which would benefit the community in the long term. Indeed this was in reality a fairly realistic and intelligent policy. However, it still had to be explained so that people could understand it. Improvements could probably have been made here and there, and the bureaucracy probably did slow the growth of the productive forces, but it is characteristic of the Stalin phenomenon that, on the basis of a socialist economy and within a socialist society, it provided bad solutions for genuine problems, that is to say it used force, nationalism and bureaucracy.

In agriculture, on the other hand, the situation was frankly dreadful. The consequences of the war made themselves felt here, but they did not provide the whole explanation.

The 1952 harvest was smaller than that of 1940 – 92,200,000 tons as against 95,600,000 tons – and only slightly better than that of 1913. Compared to 1940, production of cotton, sugar-beet and potatoes had gone up, but that of fruit and vegetables had gone down.

Livestock was still at a very low level, barely higher than that of 1914:

	1914	1953
Cattle	54·1	56·6
Pigs	23	24·3
Sheep	89·7	94·3

(in millions)

Total Soviet agricultural production had only increased very slightly whilst the population was larger – 159,200,000 inhabitants in 1913, 188,000,000 in 1953.

The policy of the bureaucracy had worsened the already difficult situation to which the Second World War had given rise. The level of investment in the agricultural sector had remained low: 7·3 per cent in the fourth Five Year Plan, 9·6 per cent in the Fifth one. The price of farm produce had remained low, whilst that of industrial products had increased.

As Khrushchev admitted in September 1953, the principle of giving the peasants material incentives was seldom respected. Measures were taken to limit the size of the personal plot that the collective farmers had the right to own under the terms of the 1935 kolkhoz regulations. Although they covered less than 4 per cent of the land under cultivation, they represented half the Soviet production of vegetables, fruit, potatoes, milk and meat, and half the livestock.

Archaic cultivation methods were still in use and the application of Lysenko's theories was proving catastrophic. For one year in three (or even in two), a considerable part of the cultivatable land lay fallow. The Ministry departments (the 'Glavki') forced the kolkhozes to grow new crops which were not really suitable for their soil and climate. In the Ukraine, spring wheat was introduced in place of winter wheat. As part of the crop rotation system, it was made obligatory to grow fodder one year, though this kind of crop was often unsuited for the climatic and soil conditions. The system of agricultural planning suffered all the more from bureaucracy because this was an area where planning itself is very hard. Stalin had not visited a collective farm since 1929, yet he still meant to determine agricultural matters just as he did all others. He was said to have found out about farm life by watching a film called 'The Kuban Cossacks', which conveyed a more than optimistic picture of this life.

All these economic problems – and their repercussions in the social field and on the standard of living – led to discussions both within the leadership of the Communist Party and the relevant economic bodies. We do not always know about them in detail, but the main outlines can be grasped. On 19th February 1950, *Pravda* published an article which criticised the 'link' system in the kolkhozes (the 'Zvenos'). They were small working units which *Pravda* criticised as not very rational, and which it proposed to replace by the 'production brigade' system. Then *Pravda* raised the problem of merging kolkhozes, and on 4th March 1951 it even published an article by Khrushchev which advocated the setting up of large urban groupings of agricultural workers, 'agrotowns'; but, on the following day, it pointed out that this article was only meant to stimulate discussion, and the agrotown plan disappeared into thin air. Andreyev, a member of the Politbureau and Secretary of the Central Committee, who had been criticised in the article on the links, had to make a public apology and lost his posts (he kept his titles until the 19th Congress in 1952).

Yet the number of kolkhozes was reduced, falling from 252,000 in 1950 to 76,355 in 1952, which made no immediate improvement to the agricutural situation. According to what Khrushchev said at the 20th Congress, Stalin even considered increasing levies on the countryside and refused to put up the price of agricultural produce.

Stalin made public gigantic plans for the 'transformation of nature'. These involved making the deserts fertile, irrigating the steppes, planting tens of thousands of screens of trees, diverting rivers in Siberia and making big lakes which were designed to change the climate. The Soviet press talked of the 'great building sites of Communism'. Admittedly, this period did see the opening of the Volga–Don Canal, the Yugssib (the Ural–Kuzbass railway) and the first hydro-electric works on the Volga, but, under the conditions prevailing in the Soviet Union in 1952, the plan then published, which was called the Davydov plan after its author, was utterly utopian.

As time went by, and he got older and exercised power in a more and more solitary way, Stalin grew less and less able to run the country with an understanding of the facts of Soviet life. He lived in his dacha at Kuntsevo twenty kilometres south-west of Moscow, and only left it to go to work in his office in the Kremlin; to get there he took a road which was reserved for him – for him alone! – and under constant M.V.D. surveillance. He demanded total obedience from his subordinates. According to Khrushchev, a badly phrased question, a foolish look or a tactless remark were enough to make Stalin get rid of one of his assistants. At the end of his life he became so suspicious that he removed Voroshilov, who was accused of being a British spy, and threatened Molotov and Mikoyan, whilst he had the former's wife and the latter's two children deported. He also had Kaganovich's brother arrested (he was a member of the Central Committee).

As Bulganin remarked when returning by car from Kuntsevo with Khrushchev: 'Sometimes you go to Stalin's house because he has given you a friendly invitation, and when you are sitting opposite him, you do not know whether you will spend the night in your own bed or in prison.'

At the end of his life, Stalin's personality comprised pathological characteristics of which one cannot help but be aware, even if they do not constitute the main cause of the events we are studying. His megalomania was striking. As a result of it, he went so far as to set up busts of himself along the garden paths of his own dacha. People have often said he was a paranoiac, and, to judge by the increasing suspiciousness he displayed towards his most loyal assistants, this was certainly the case.

Nevertheless, Stalin's life style remained very simple. His only real pleasure was in exercising power, a terrible passion which is sometimes more serious than the love of money. This is what made him suspicious of others, for he was afraid that others might act as he had done. He had several bedrooms in his Kuntsevo dacha, and he himself never knew which one he would sleep in that night. This sums up his whole character.

In October 1952, the 19th Congress of the C.P.S.U. was held. Neither the Central Committee nor the Politbureau had met for years. As for the Congress, the last time it had met was in 1939. Stalin ran the Party with the help of commissions made up of six or seven leading comrades who were changed according to his whims. The Party existed at rank-and-file level in the districts, provinces and even Union Republics, though the M.V.D. kept a strict check on the activities of functionaries and Communists in the basic and regional organisations, something which prevented any genuine debate.

Stalin did not speak at the 19th Congress, but on the eve of it he had published a 'theoretical' work: *Economic Problems of Socialism in the U.S.S.R.* In it, he made a superficial study of the economic laws of socialism and predicted another world war among the capitalist countries. This work marked a certain retreat compared to the excesses of the previous years, in as much as Stalin admitted the existence of 'objective laws' in economics; but, though he admitted this fact, he rejected any change in the system of economic management, price calculation and planning.

His political analysis was dominated by his conviction that wars between capitalist countries were inevitable and that Lenin's analysis was still completely valid. As the magazine *Kommunist* stressed in January 1953, according to Stalin, 'as long as capitalism exists in the main capitalist countries, one cannot envisage ending capitalist encirclement'. This provided justification for the Cold War, the Terror and the theory of the stepping up of class struggle as socialism develops in the national or international field. Suslov had clearly stated this at a Cominform meeting in November 1949: 'Historical experience shows that the more desperate the situation imperialist reaction finds itself in, the more it rages and the more military adventures are to be feared from it.'

Malenkov presented the general political report to the 19th Congress, and Khrushchev the proposed new Party rules. The debate was academic. None of the major problems was studied in depth. Stalin made a very short speech which was meant for the foreign Communist parties; in it, he extolled internationalism, peace and the struggle for democracy and national independence. What he said was good and true but was often contradicted by his political practice. The most interesting thing was the make-up of the leading bodies elected by the Congress. The membership of the Central Committee was doubled. There were 236 full and candidate members, of whom 60 per cent had already been members of the Central Committee elected in 1939. Repression had thinned out the ranks of the Party leadership less than during the period between the 17th and 18th Congresses. The Politbureau was replaced by a Presidium with a large membership (25 full members and 11 candidates). It is true that there was to be a functioning Presidium with a membership about which we have no information.

Apart from Andreyev (who was however elected to the Central Committee), all the sitting members were re-elected (with the exception of Kosygin who had been a full member since 1948 and now became a candidate again). Suslov became a full member of the Politbureau and Brezhnev a candidate member. Besides Stalin, the ten-man Secretariat included Malenkov, Khrushchev, Suslov and Brezhnev.

The Party was no longer called Bolshevik. Since 1945, the People's Commissars had become ministers and the Red Army was called the Soviet Army. The new rules laid down that the Central Committee should meet every six months and Congress every four years (instead of every three months and three years).

A new Party programme was to be prepared, and a commission chaired by Stalin was elected for this purpose.

The 19th Congress ended on 14th October 1952. It marked Stalin's zenith; on the first day of Congress, A. Surkov, a well-known writer, described him as the 'great architect of Communism'. The ovations of the Soviet and foreign delegates rose enthusiastically towards him. The minutes record that 'All those present rise. There is a storm of applause which changes into a long ovation: "Long live comrade Stalin!" "Hurrah for comrade Stalin!" "Long live the great guide of the workers of the world, comrade Stalin!" "Hurrah for the great Stalin!" "Long live peace among the nations!"'

On his seventieth birthday in 1949, Stalin had already received hundreds of thousands of presents from all over the world. The Museum of the Revolution in Moscow had been transformed into a museum for Stalin's presents. The French Communist Party had organised a big exhibition in Ivry. Stalin seemed to be identified with the Revolution and with socialism.

On 7th November 1952, there was a big parade organised for the thirty-fifth anniversary of the October Revolution. Stalin attended in the uniform of Generalissimo. He did not wish to look old, but he was seventy-three. Though he was only 1·67 m. tall, he looked big. His shoemakers added a few centimetres to his heels, as was done for Louis XIV. He had put on weight since his photos were taken, when he was young, dark and still thin, and his eighty-four kilos gave his face, which was pockmarked, a gentle, grandfatherly look. And yet . . . We are looking at the last group photograph taken before the death of the 'great guide of the peoples': on the rostrum beside Stalin was the whole of the new Presidium, both full members and substitutes. The senior members, Beria (who was to be shot less than a year later), Molotov, Kaganovich, Malenkov, Khrushchev, who was to denounce his crimes just over three years later, Voroshilov, Mikoyan and Shvernik and the newest recruits, Kosygin, Suslov and Brezhnev who are still ruling the Soviet Union in 1975. This was another turning point in history. They all posed for it, and behind the lens, they seemed to be looking at a mysterious future, the future which we who are alive in 1975 already partly know.

On the morning of 3rd March 1953, Moscow Radio interrupted its programmes to announce that Stalin was ill. On 28th February, Stalin had invited to Kuntsevo his four closest helpers, his four 'brothers-in-arms' (the 'Soratniki'); Beria, Malenkov, Bulganin and Khrushchev. They had drunk a great deal. On 1st March, Stalin had given no sign of life during the day. Nobody had dared go and see him. In the evening, the officer on guard had telephoned the Soratniki to ask advice. They came to the dacha, opened the bedroom doors, for they did not know which one he was in, and on the 2nd March at 3 a.m., he was found lying dying on the carpet, where he had been for hours.

According to the official communiqués, he died on the 5th at 9.50 p.m., not without pointing to a reproduction of a bad picture (a girl suckling a lamb) which was on the wall. Perhaps he died earlier, and the announcement of his death was delayed in order to make arrangements, or perhaps he was assassinated, as has been suggested sometimes, though without solid proof. It does not make any difference. Historically speaking, he died then, or rather when Levitan, the Moscow Radio announcer, announced that 'Joseph Vissorionovich's heart has stopped beating'.

He still had to be buried. His body was cast in wax and destined to lie next to Lenin's in the Mausoleum. For three days, millions of Soviet citizens were to crowd together near the Hall of Pillars in which his body was on show. There was even to be a 'panic', an uproar which cost dozens of lives.

On 9th March, Stalin's body was taken to the Mausoleum in which he was to lie for all time – in fact it was to be for eight years – by a huge crowd which listened to the orators – Malenkov, Beria and Molotov – and looked at the leaders of all the foreign Communist parties who were present: Duclos (Thorez was ill and could not come), Togliatti, Chou En-lai (Mao did not come), the Czech Gottwald, the Hungarian Rakosi, the German Ulbricht, the Pole Bierut and dozens of others.

Huge demonstrations took place across the world. In Peking, there was an immense procession in the presence of Mao, in Paris there was a great funeral wake at the Vél' d'Hiv.[7]

The Stalin phenomenon did not die with Stalin, but its decline began. In Rome, the Tarpeian Rock was near the Capitol, and the Mausoleum in Red Square was not far from the hall in the Kremlin in which the 20th Congress was held.

NOTES

1. These terms are to be found in the secret protocols of the Yalta Conference. In Teheran Roosevelt had proposed the setting up of five German states and Stalin had not refused.
2. Zhdanov was made the scapegoat of Stalinist policy, hence the often used expression 'the Zhdanovchina' (the Zhdanov period).
3. Zhdanov, *On Literature, Music and Philosophy*, London 1950, pp. 26–7.
4. For example, Suzanne Labin in *Staline le Terrible*, Paris, 1948, or Brzezinski in *The Permanent Purge*, Harvard University Press, Cambridge, 1956.
5. It was as a result of the 'pigeon plot'. Several leaders of the French Union of Republican Youth (The Communist Youth Movement) had been arrested, others spent months in hiding.

6. The French Communist Party, the Italian Communist Party, the Communist Party of the Soviet Union, the Bulgarian Workers' Party, the Hungarian Communist Party, the Polish Workers' Party, the Albanian Communist Party, the Yugoslav Communist Party and the Romanian Communist Party.

7. The Vélodrome d'Hiver, a covered stadium in Paris (translator's note).

7 Some Economic and Social Aspects of the Stalin Phenomenon

The Stalin phenomenon was complex and contradictory, so it is not easy to analyse, let alone explain. Up until now we have been trying to give a historical approach, because as a matter of principle, and not for professional reasons, it seems of decisive importance to us. However, this is not enough, and that is why we considered it indispensable to study its various aspects in order to try to define and explain it better.

The economic and social changes which the Soviet Union had undergone since 1922 struck all observers, though some of them tried and are still trying to minimise their significance or distort their meaning. The productive forces grew considerably, all the more so because two facts must be taken account of. Growth did not really begin until 1928, since the 1913 production figures were not reached again until 1927. And it was interrupted by the Second World War which laid waste the Soviet Union.

We have given a precise enough description of the demographic and economic consequences of the war, and there is no point in returning to the subject at length. Let us simply recall that since 1913, the peoples of the Soviet Union had lost at least 45 million lives as a result of war, famine and terror, and that the loss of potential children was of the same order.

In 1953, the population of the Soviet Union was 188 million inhabitants. It should have been about 270 million. It reached 250 million on 9th August 1973. It will only reach 270 million in about 1990, that is to say thirty seven years later. This gives one an idea of the delay which the wars and the Stalin phenomenon itself imposed on the Soviet Union from the demographic point of view, and doubtless in the economic field.

If we examine the results of this period as a whole, we can

say that they are very good as far as heavy industry (energy sources and iron and steel) is concerned, poor in the case of light and consumer industry, and frankly bad in the case of agriculture.

	1913	*1922*	*1928*	*1940*	*1945*	*1953*
Coal	28·4	11·4	35·9	165·9	149·3	320·4
Oil	9·4	3·8	10·9	31·1	19·4	52·8
Electricity	2·0	1·1	5·0	48·3	43·2	134·8
Steel	4·3	1·4	4·2	18·3	12·3	38·1
Cotton	1·9	0·7	—	3·9	1·6	5·3
Grain	80·1	43·0	73·0	95·6	47·3	92·2
Cattle	54·1	—	60·0	47·8	47·6	56·6
Population	159·2	—	—	194·1	171·0	188·0

Oil
Coal
Steel } in millions of tons
Grain
Cotton

Electricity: in millions of kWh.

Cattle: in millions of heads of stock

Population: in millions of inhabitants (on the present territory of the U.S.S.R.)

These results require comment. They cannot be compared to those of the great capitalist states which had started at an incomparably higher level and had experienced infinitely less problems since 1913. This is one of the great problems raised by the history of socialism. As it has only triumphed in insufficiently or slightly developed countries (except in Czechoslovakia, but it is a small country), in all objectivity comparison cannot be valid. If it does indeed exist, and we believe it does, the superiority of socialism can only be demonstrated in a conceptual, basically abstract manner. It cannot be measured, hence the interminable debates in this field and the intellectual effort necessary in order to perceive it.[1] This is why one of the characteristics of the Stalin phenomenon, and a harmful one, however understandable, was systematic lying about what the developed capitalist countries were really like, instead of explaining in a comprehensible way the deep-seated reasons why the Soviet Union was still far behind the United States and the developed capitalist states of Western Europe in 1953.

Nevertheless, the Soviet Union had made up part of its deficit, despite historical conditions infinitely less favourable than those of the United States.

	1913	*1951*	*(1973)*
Electricity (in milliards of kWh.)			
U.S.S.R.	2	103	915
U.S.A.	25·8	370	1,853
Coal (in millions of tons)			
U.S.S.R.	29·2	281	668
U.S.A.	517·8	523	532
Oil (in millions of tons)			
U.S.S.R.	10·3	42	421
U.S.A.	34	309	467
Steel (in millions of tons)			
U.S.S.R.	4·3	31	131
U.S.A.	31·5	95	123·5

As far as the output of consumer goods and the standard of living was concerned the gap was still enormous (vehicles, household appliances, plastics, etc.). In 1955 output per thousand inhabitants was as follows:

	U.S.S.R.	*U.S.A.*
Radios	66	974
Refrigerators	5	288
Television sets	4	318
Washing machines	1	216
Small domestic appliances	2	211
Motor vehicles	2	300

The Soviet Union had given priority to developing a certain numbers of sectors which it considered basic: sources of energy, iron and steel, the armaments industry and socio-cultural resources (firstly education). Let us bear in mind that the Soviet Union had the atom bomb by 1949 and the hydrogen bomb by 1953. In 1957, it launched the first 'sputnik', that is to say the first space ship in orbit around the earth. There was no other way to ensure that the U.S.S.R. remained independent. The socialisation of the means of production and exchange made this possible by directing investment to certain sectors and not to others. This was quite clear, and only utopians and dreamers who knew nothing of the facts of history could dispute it, because the country involved was predominantly agrarian, still poor, insufficiently developed and culturally backward.

These options cannot be the subject of debate, but what can be is the way in which they were achieved, and, at this stage of our analysis, the question raised is no longer simply economic or even social but political. They implied enormous sacrifices in terms of living standards and consumption. As we pointed out in connection with the 1929–30 period, this choice could have been made democratically; it was not easy, for it would have required political and ideological consciousness of a very high level, something which did not exist on a wide enough scale in the Soviet Union in 1929. The stages in which these goals were achieved could have been slower, this was the opinion of Bukharin, and could have combined both economic incentives and democratic processes. These aims could have been achieved relatively fast, but, in the absence of democracy, that implied recourse to coercion and terror. The Soviet Union chose the latter way for reasons which were due to the history of the Russian Empire, the Soviet Revolution and the Soviet Union up until 1929, and that is why the Stalin phenomenon developed. We are not so much questioning the need to develop the economy as the way in which it was done. To put it another way, the culprit is not 'economism',[2] but the bureaucratic distortions of a workers' state in which the lack of political democracy was bound up with the very conditions under which the transition to and building of socialism took place. Yet if we are to seek a deeper, more scientific and pluri-disciplinary historical explanation of why the Stalin phenomenon appeared and flourished, we must first look at the political economy of socialism.

The development of the forces of production is a necessity for a socialist state, like the Soviet Union in 1922. It cannot solve every problem, but without it nothing can be done: it is a necessary but not sufficient condition for the building of socialism. It is necessary to improve productivity. These are historical facts which confronted socialism in an acute manner. This is precisely what Lenin taught in 1922, as well as the corollaries of the fight against bureaucracy and the cultural revolution.

We will come back to this. For the time being, let us remain in the economic and social field. If the forces of production do not grow, and there is no scientific and technical revolution and productivity is not improved, socialism cannot be built. The Stalin phenomenon does not arise from these requirements, for what kind of socialism is possible on the basis of backwardness and poverty?

Let us proceed. Either the U.S.S.R. is not a socialist state but a 'special kind of capitalist state' – as some maintain – in which socialist relations of production do not exist, but where capitalist relations of production have survived in another form, and along with them capitalist exploitation, or it is a socialist state in which socialist relations of production exist; it is this aspect of the matter which needs to be looked at in detail. Socialism is not communism, far from it. In contrast to the hopes and to some extent to the utopian views of the founders of scientific socialism, including Marx, the least utopian of all, contemporary history itself demonstrates that socialism constitutes a very long 'period of transition' from capitalism to communism, a period which has already lasted almost sixty years and will certainly last decades more, because communism requires extremely highly developed productive forces, a new social consciousness, and the previous triumph of socialism in every country – since the state and the market economy are to disappear, something which will take longer still. We do not say this to show that it is impossible, but to show how difficult it will be for our present societies to reach that stage. We can state that this problem is not on the agenda, even for those

children born in 1975. That which was originally only going
to be a transition from capitalism to communism has proved
to be an economic and social formation which enjoys considerable autonomy in relation to capitalism, from which it
sprang, and communism, to which it is proceeding. It is a mode
of production and an economic and social formation which will
span a historical period at least as long as that of capitalism. If
you like, it is a transition, but in a very loose sense, as the
feudal mode of production was a transition between the mode
of production based on slavery and the capitalist mode of
production in certain European societies.

As Marx pointed out in a letter to Annenkov as early as
28th December 1846, 'all economic forms are transient and
historical'. Now, this economic and social formation which is
different from capitalism proves, however, to be akin to it, so
much so that it may appear to some good souls that it is
identical; in the case of the U.S.S.R., this similarity was all
the greater because the conditions under which socialism was
born and developed were, for historical reasons, particularly
difficult. What does this mean? In a socialist economy, the
sphere of action of the law of value remains intact: 'The value
of each commodity is determined . . . by the working time
necessary, under given social conditions, for its production'
(*Capital*, Vol. 1). Socialism is still dominated by the market
economy. Money, prices, wages, investments, capital and its
creation and circulation all still exist. The difference, and it
is fundamental, between it and capitalism comes from the
system of ownership. On the one hand, ownership is private,
on the other it is collective. Surplus value as such no longer
exists and no capitalist profit is created, but prices are still
determined by the law of value and the product of labour is
shared between the producer (the worker) and the collective,
represented by the state; the latter estimates the sum of
products according to the needs of the collectivity as it under-
stands them, taking into account historical requirements (for
example, investment for the atomic, space and computer
industries, for cultural development, education, etc.). Such
an economy is closer to capitalism than to communism.

The Stalin phenomenon made its appearance in the situation created by the emergence of this socialist mode of

production and this form of economy and society. Let us observe the social consequences of these economic changes. Thanks to the growth of the productive forces, a working class emerged (which did not exist in 1922, and which was small in number in 1913). In 1950, there was a total of 40,400,000 workers and clerks, and in 1955 there were 50,300,000 (about 45 million in 1953). The number of workers (in heavy industry, building and transport) can be put at about 25 million in 1953.

By 1935, private ownership of the means of production and exchange had completely disappeared from industry and there was no private commerce; only craftsmen's co-operatives – artels – remained. Just as important changes had taken place in agriculture, by 1937 small peasant holdings had disappeared: 30 million peasants had formed kolkhozes (farmers' production co-operatives, collective farms), and 5 million people were in sovkhozes (state farms). By 1953, the intellectuals has become a sizeable stratum of the Soviet population.

In 1913, the total number of students at university or in specialist higher education colleges was 112,000. A total of 1,500,000 Russians and other citizens had gone beyond primary education.

In 1940, there were 811,700 students of whom 585,000 were full-time, and in 1953 the total was 1,562,000 of whom 1,042,700 were full-time. These figures give one an idea not only of the cultural transformation but, by the same token, of the fantastic social changes which the U.S.S.R. underwent during this period.

As the country was industrialised, so the urban population grew, the following table shows this:

	Total population (in millions)	Town dwellers in % (in millions)		Country dwellers in % (in millions)	
1913	159·2	28·5	18	130.7	82
1940	194·1	63·1	33	131	67
1953	188	80·2	43	107·8	57

(*Statistical Yearbook* – 'The National Economy of the U.S.S.R. in 1972', p. 7)

So, from 1913 to 1953, the towns had seen their populations rise by 15,500,000. Industrialisation and urbanisation had been carried out 'at full speed', as Stalin had suggested, particularly if we take into account the wars and all the events in the history of the U.S.S.R. which we have mentioned. In fact, these huge changes had come about in a thirty-six year period (1917–53), nine years of which had been spent at war, thus in twenty-seven years, or even in twenty years if one takes into account war damage and reconstruction.

As Isaac Deutscher quite rightly pointed out in 1954: 'None of the great Western nations carried through its industrial revolution in such a short period nor under conditions bristling with so many obstacles' (*La Russie après Staline*, Paris, p. 52).

By 1936, the capitalists had vanished, and even the most subtle of minds finds it hard to make them appear in an analysis of Soviet society in 1953. So, the problem of 'bureaucrats' and the bureaucracy is raised at this juncture.

For a certain number of historians (Bettelheim is merely the most recent example), the U.S.S.R. is allegedly not a socialist or workers' state, but a bureaucratic state in which a new class, the bureacracy, supposedly oppresses and exploits the workers and peasants. This is why Bettelheim defines it as: 'a special kind of capitalist state'. The Stalin-phenomenon is alleged to have its roots in this class. In 1921, the Workers' Opposition had already advanced this view through the writings of Kollontai and Shliapnikov. Lenin, on the other hand, had stated that the Soviet state was a workers' state with a bureaucratic distortion, which was not the same thing at all. The Trotskyites expressly adopted the idea. As early as 1929, when he was in exile in Siberia, Rakovsky wrote about it (*The Opposition Bulletin*, Nos. 15–16, 1930). In *The Revolution Betrayed*, Trotsky himself did not seem sure whether to characterise the Stalin phenomenon in this way. The idea was also put forward by Boris Souvarin in his book *Stalin* (published in 1935). It was Rizzi, an Italian Trotskyite, who gave the clearest emphasis to this theory in a book published in 1939: *The Bureaucratisation of the World*.

Rizzi wrote as follows: 'In Soviet society, the exploiters do not appropriate surplus value directly, as does a capitalist when he pockets the dividends from his company. They do so indirectly, by means of the state which receives the total sum of the nation's surplus value and then shares it out among its functionaries.' According to Rizzi, this was an inevitable stage in social development, 'a historical step forward', and on the basis of this he demonstrated the similarity between Hitlerism, Stalinism and the Roosevelt 'New Deal'. Trotsky replied (in *The U.S.S.R. at War*), saying quite rightly that, whatever similarities there might be between the methods of government of Nazism and Stalinism, in the economic and social fields they were qualitatively different.

According to Trotsky, 'Soviet bureaucracy was still a parasitic outgrowth of the working class, as dangerous as such an outgrowth can be; but it was not an independent body.' It was 'an aberration from the revolutionary course' (Deutscher, *Trotsky*, Vol. 3, p. 465).

Rizzi's theories, which led him to deny that the U.S.S.R. was socialist in character, caused him to talk of the 'convergence' of the capitalist and socialist systems, a thesis which we find in Burnham's work – in *Science and Style, a Reply to Comrade Trotsky* and above all in *The Managerial Revolution*. According to Burnham, managers will have the task of running industrial companies. Similar ideas can be found in the works of Raymond Aron (in *Eighteen Lectures on Industrial Society*), Djilas and many others since.

But what is the truth about this 'bureaucratic class'? For its existence to be confirmed as a fact, the 'surplus value' would have to be accumulated and inherited. This was certainly not the case. In the U.S.S.R., posts in the Party, Civil Service, management, unions etc. were not occupied by successive generations of the same families. These posts could not be bequeathed. It is true that a large number of these posts brought with them the right to certain benefits and privileges. Those who worked full-time for the Party, the 'apparatchiki', were often better paid than even the most highly skilled workers. Some of them had the benefit of a car or the right to shop in special shops. Since the N.E.P., the wage range was fairly wide (from 1–12 on average). It may be conceded that a – minimal – part of the product of labour which was not shared out among wage-earners (in the form of wages) and which the state took was monopolised to a disproportional extent by the state and Party functionaries. Indeed, this is a consequence of the phenomenon of bureaucracy, but the difference between this and talk of surplus value and a bureacratic class is huge.

Besides, these non-bequeathable benefits went with the post, and were thus subject to recall. They could hardly be turned into fixed or movable property, for, though 'personal' private property did exist, this was only within certain limits. So, they enabled some people to live better than the other Soviet citizens, perhaps to live too well compared with the majority, but, for all that, this does not constitute the creation of a 'bureaucratic class'. Social injustice does exist under Socialism, that is true, but how utopian it was to have thought it could not! This is precisely because it is socialism and not communism. Besides, such an argument assumes that civil servants and bureaucrats are the same, which is not the case. It is true that the Stalin phenomenon was bureaucratic, but that means that the role played by offices was more important than that of the masses and that administrative decisions outweighed economic stimuli. This meant that the economy could be mismanaged, the towns badly administered and the kolkhozes badly run, because decisions were taken by civil servants who were incompetent, irresponsible, or who either did not face up to their responsibilities or who were corrupt. At the 21st Congress of the C.P.S.U., Khrushchev admitted it: 'Faulty methods had spread to the leadership of the Party, the state and the economy: there was bureaucracy, concealment of weaknesses and cowardice. In this environment, a good number of sycophants, flatterers and people who bluffed their way through had emerged.'

This evil is not specifically socialist. In contemporary society, it is linked with the growth in the functions and role of the state. It is to be observed in all the capitalist countries, including the most 'liberal' of them, namely the United States. In France, are there not considerable examples of bureaucracy in a good few ministries?

Let us take as examples the Ministry of Education or the Treasury. This ailment can be cured, but it is eating away at our society. Historical tradition and the growth in the functions of the state in a socialist country, and more particularly in the

Soviet Union, can add to the danger. If we study the U.S.S.R. in 1953, we observe that everything is owned by the state and it concerns itself with everything. The distinction between state and civil society tends to disappear, which had traditionally been the case in Russia, and socialism accentuated this trait which was already characteristic of Tsarism.

There are only two remedies against the all-powerful state and its bureaucratic consequences, these are economic stimuli and democracy. The economic stimulus is provided by using the mechanisms of the market economy. The bureaucrat gives way when faced with financial requirements of the factory, group or ministry, and material incentives for individuals can even play a decisive role in the struggle against the bureaucracy. This is true of the big capitalist firm. Tendencies towards bureaucracy are annulled by the requirements of the cost price and by the fact that it is financially advantageous for the firm's managers to eliminate them. Well, in contrast to what a number of writers have said, Stalinist policy made little use of these economic stimuli after 1929. Stalin was content to create a wide range of salaries, but the principle of material incentives was hardly applied in commerce, agriculture or even in industry. Enterprises did not enjoy financial autonomy, and the highly centralized planning system had become extremely bureaucratic. Distant and meddling decisions were made for the enterprises, trusts and groups by departments of the ministries involved (the 'Glavki'). This often led to considerable delays in the supply of raw materials and parts and considerable disorder in the transport and distribution network. The number of civil servants working in Moscow was enormous, if one thinks that in the next few years two million of them, who were working in the Moscow Glavki, were to be given new jobs. Besides, the Glavki worked in an empirical fashion, as did the Gosplan offices (the state planning body), to which they were loosely linked. This is what bureaucracy meant. The system of management was 'anti-economic' from top to bottom. To this we can add the fact that the problems were seriously underestimated. There were no training schools for management specialists, nor schools of commerce, administration or financial skills. Sociology was not taught. Political economy was subject to such strict ideological and police supervision that progress was blocked in most of the useful areas. For example, the use of mathematics in economics was prevented. Kantorovich's work *Mathematical Methods of Organising and Planning Production*, which was published in 1939, was only used at the end of the fifties, and other works he wrote in 1941 were not published until 1959. The credit system was still primitive. Statistics were falsified. From 1933 to 1953, they only made public proportional figures, indexes or even inflated, that is to say false, figures. In order to cover up the problems in agriculture, the Soviet authorities gave the figures of the standing harvest of grain (the biological harvest), and not, as had been the case in the U.S.S.R. (as everywhere else), the amount actually got in. Thus, the bureaucratic system led to a denial of economic laws and a refusal to take account of reality. The economic potential of socialism was thus seriously underestimated, and this makes the results achieved all the more remarkable – but they are the result of the rationality of socialism itself.

To turn to democracy, it constitutes another way of struggling against bureaucracy. It is not certain that it is in itself sufficient to combat the phenomenon of bureaucracy, but it makes a great contribution. We do not simply mean political democracy in general, for example the right to vote every five years to elect an M.P. or every seven years to elect a President of the Republic, we are thinking of social and economic democracy, of control and initiation by the masses, of trade union activity, of opportunities for democratic management of enterprises, of the right to express oneself in the press, on the radio or on the television, of freedom in literature, the theatre, the cinema and art.

Well, what we observe is quite the opposite. Of course, a real effort was made to develop a new attitude towards work, to improve its productivity and organisation thanks to a mass movement based on the initiative and enthusiasm of the people. This movement emerged with the 'Communist Saturdays', developed with the shock workers, the 'udarniki', then with the stakhanovites. Stakhanov was a miner from the Donbas region who shattered output records. His example was widely popularised, and in November 1935 there was even a conference of stakhanovite workers which was held in the Kremlin with 3,000 delegates present.

Photographs of the best workers were displayed in factory entrance halls. They were given certain privileges (bonuses, holidays, etc.). The stakhanovite movement had evident didactic aims which should not be underestimated. There was a 'mystique' of industrialisation which even the most anti-Soviet observers noted at the time.

Since the resolution adopted at the 16th Party Congress in 1930, the trade unions had been given the task of encouraging production and taking part in management. The right to strike did not exist and strikes were severely punished by law. In 1933, the People's Commissariat for Labour was merged with the trade unions.

On 20th December 1938, work record books, which made strict supervision of the labour force possible, were introduced. The following comments were found in *Izvestia*: 'From now on, when starting a new job, workers will have to present their work record book, which reflects all the facts about the work of its bearer, about his moves from one concern to another and the reasons for these moves.' Unjustified absences ('progul') were punished by six months' corrective labour, which was undertaken on the spot but with a 25 per cent reduction in wages.

On 26th June 1940, there was a decree forbidding wage-earners to change jobs or move to another workplace. Was this a step to prepare for war? Apparently not, since it merely rubberstamped a situation which already existed and was to be maintained until 1953. Only the manager of an enterprise could authorise a worker to change jobs or move to another enterprise.

Wages were fixed by the central offices of the ministries. The law of 2nd October 1940 on 'labour reserves', determined that each year one million young people would be directed into industry for at least four years, having received a maximum of two years professional training. This 'ukase' remained in force until after 1953.

In certain professions, for example the railways and the armaments industry, the rules were even more draconic. People who were repeatedly absent without good reason became subject to the law on 'the abandoning of work'. Their punishment was from two to four months in prison and they lost their accommodation.

As for the inhabitants of the kolkhozes and sovkhozes, they could not leave their place of work without express permission from the authorities.

As far as the rest, that is to say political democracy, is concerned, we know that it only existed in the constitution and not in fact. So, the results achieved in the economic and social fields were achieved at the cost of enormous efforts and sacrifices. The choices made in 1929 (more rapid industrialisation and collectivisation of the land) still had an effect on the use of coercion and bureaucracy against the people. They had led to terror and to Stalin's dictatorship. A heavy price was paid for these changes. The Stalin phenomenon helped in the growth of the productive forces and radical transformation of society, but at the same time it slowed this growth and these changes. Here, the fundamental socialism/despotism contradiction expresses itself fully. On the one hand, the mechanisms of the socialist economy function, on the other, despotism impedes the use of the full potential of socialism and hides its considerable advantage in terms of rationality, concentration of effort and taking into account the general interest. One sometimes hears sincere defenders of the Soviet Union state that the Stalin phenomenon was necessary, even though they condemn its most dreadful consequences. It seems to me that such a point of view arises from insufficient knowledge about the real situation in the Soviet Union at the time of Stalin. If the Terror had only meant the execution of a few thousand counter-revolutionaries or even the execution of a few Communists as a result of judicial errors, such an argument would not be totally wrong – but this was not the case.

For example, forced labour played a relatively important economic role. We noted this in connection with the Baltic–White Sea Canal, but the system spread from 1936 on. More and more forced labour camps were set up in the Northern and Eastern regions. Concentration-camp labour was used in the coal, precious and base metal mines, to build railway lines like the Turksib and even on the big building sites in Moscow or the big towns (for the first skyscrapers, for example) and the Metro. Whole regions were controlled by the Gulag (the Central Management of the Camps); this was the case, for example, of the Dalstroy (a huge area in the Far East). A proportion of the deportees were sentenced to settle in poor areas where life was particularly uncomfortable because of the cold. These camps were not extermination camps, but life in them was hard and the death rate was high because of the climate and working conditions. Apart from the accounts of camp survivors (Ginsberg's *Into the Whirlwind*, Shalamov's *Tales of Kolyma*, Solzhenitsyn's *A Day in the Life of Ivan Denisovich* and the precious first-hand evidence of *The Gulag Archipelago*), we have an important document on concentration camp labour: *The State Plan for the Development of the National Economy for 1941*. This text, which was not intended for publication, was found by the Nazis when they invaded, as were the Smolensk Archives. In it, we read that the N.K.V.D. received 6,810 million roubles out of a total of 37,655 million roubles for investment, that is to, say about 18 per cent of the total. Calculations made by Jasny indicate that in 1941 the N.K.V.D. controlled about 1,172,000 workers on building sites, to which must be added the labour force in the Dalstroy region, the mines, the arms factories and the timber producing forests. Jasny arrives at the plausible figure of 3,500,000 deportees in 1941. We must of course take into account the fact that this figure was higher in 1937–8, as well as after the war. So, the overall figure for the 1930–53 period could be estimated as more than 12 million. As for the death rate, the lack of precise information makes it hard to estimate, but it was very high.

Great and scandalous though the use of forced labour was, it was however 'a factor which is marginal to the system' (Deutscher, *La Russie après Staline*, Paris, p. 56), since it represented barely a tenth of the industrial labour force.

From a Communist standpoint, there can be no justification for the Stalin phenomenon. It arose from a series of different causes, economic, political and ideological, among which personal factors played a considerable part.

The opponents of socialism use the Stalin phenomenon to combat socialism itself in countries where the causes which gave birth to it do not exist, and where the historical environment is radically different. The Stalin phenomenon must be dissociated from socialism. The aspects of Soviet socialism which are worth defending are not its deviations and distortions, or the specific and circumstantial forms it happened to take, but its basic economic mechanisms, its social and cultural consequences and its rationality.

What is the relationship between the Stalin phenomenon and class struggle? In Stalin's view, his policy expressed the interests of the working class and was explained by the heightening of class struggle as a result of the attitude of the bourgeoisie. But, the latter only had scattered forces in the Soviet Union of 1928. Of course, there were the Nepmen and the kulaks, but they did not represent a coherent political force. Moreover, the socialist state had a firm grip on the army and the police, as well as the commanding heights of the economy. Stalin used the real activities of foreign imperialism, first French, British and American, then German and Japanese, then American and British, to justify his policy. Equally, he used the pretext that it was necessary to combat the kulaks to gradually widen the scope of repression, which affected the middle and even the poor peasants. The soil in which the Stalin phenomenon grew was indeed that of class struggle, but Stalin quickly went beyond it and carried out a policy which was only indirectly related to it. In 1937, the kulaks and Nepmen no longer existed. They had all been destroyed, most of them deported and killed. In 1929, there might have seemed to be a certain danger from within, but not in 1937. In the name of the theory 'of the heightening of class struggle as socialism is built', Stalin unleashed repression against Communists themselves, accusing them of being the agents of foreign imperialism. Within the logic of the system, this can be explained, for, in the Soviet Union of 1934, the Communist Party constituted the only real force in opposition to Stalin. So, class struggle was no longer anything more than a political and ideological cover intended to justify the Stalin phenomenon.

In my opinion, any explanation of this phenomenon in terms of class struggle tends willy nilly to come back to the Stalinist thesis which was used to justify the Terror. The only objective basis of the latter came from the historical soil in which the Stalin phenomenon flourished. The interests of the working class or the requirements of class struggle offer neither the slightest explanation nor the slightest justification. Whether concealed under the veil of humanism or not, the Stalin phenomenon has nothing in common with the political practice of the 2nd International of petty bourgeois humanism. Neither Kautsky, Hilferding, Bernstein, Kant nor Bentham are in the dock, entirely new circumstances which had arisen from the conditions under which the first socialist experiment in history developed. In particular, the 'expansion' of production and productivity were a necessity for a socialist economy; without them, it could not be built, especially in the 1922 situation. As for freedom, for Stalin it was merely an ideological cloak intended to conceal a totally unjustified policy of terror. The patient is not responsible for the cancer eating away at him, and economic growth and productivity were not the cause of the Stalin phenomenon. The historical conditions of Russia and the Revolution created a particular type of socialist state, with structures, traditions, circumstances and men which made the Stalin phenomenon possible and gave it the appearance we know. It is not by chance that Bettelheim to some extent justifies it.[3] I do not deny that Stalin had certain good points. Socialism in one country was the only possible path just after the defeat of the Revolution in Europe. Priority for heavy industry was a requirement for economic growth. In October–November 1941, Stalin managed to keep calm and patient when the Nazi troops were 20 km. from Moscow. But we are not discussing the good and bad points of an individual, but the way in which socialism was built in the Soviet Union and the reasons why it was built in this way.

Some people characterise the Stalin phenomenon as arising from a war economy; this is the case with Oskar Lange: 'It is a war economy *sui generis*.' This is an interesting idea, because it seems to us that it contains a profound truth from the historical point of view. The history of the U.S.S.R. up until 1953 is the history of the wars being waged, wars being prepared for, or war-wounds being dressed. This could not fail to influence economic growth and the methods of running the economy, as well as the political system. Stalin himself considered the economic sector to be a real battle front, and all the terms used show this clearly. There would have to be more detailed studies of the vocabulary used, but in his speeches he uses the terms 'front', 'battle', 'mobilisation' and 'army'. The requirements of the period and the long-lasting habits which resulted increased the military aspects of Stalinist economic policy, as is shown by the importance of 'work discipline', one of the favourite themes of the Soviet press at the time. Many characteristics of the Stalin phenomenon are explained by the part played by war in Soviet history. The Soviet Union was a 'besieged fortress', and must have looked like a huge beleaguered camp. This is why, for example, foreigners were forbidden to travel about, to take photographs and even to ask questions. Until 1953, everything was a military secret. There were no telephone directories or town plans. Spy-itis was rife everywhere: 'Keep quiet, be on your guard, enemy ears are listening to you', was one of the favourite themes of the Soviet press. On this basis, the worker had to stay in his factory, the collective farmer in his field and the soldier in his unit, and they all had to be disciplined since, as is well known, discipline is the main strength of armies. The whole of the U.S.S.R. was thus a veritable army within which all criticism was banned because it might threaten the army's unity and therefore its discipline.

However, Lange's definition is still inadequate in as much as what is involved is a socialist war economy, a fact which in some respects increases its rigidity because of the virtually exclusive role of state ownership, but which, on the other hand, may facilitate its disappearance. It was an actual state of affairs, forced upon the country by circumstances, rather than a deliberate aim which arose from an economic structure and a political doctrine. For example, it had nothing in common with Nazism where the militarisation of the economy played a vital role. For Hitler, the militarisation of the economy and militarism constituted the essential means to achieve the goal he had set himself, that is to say German domination of the world. For Stalin, they were simply the quickest, simplest and most effective response to a specific situation: Soviet backwardness in face of the capitalist world and the threat of aggression to which it exposed the Soviet Union.

We know that the shortest way from one point to another is not necessarily a straight line. The most effective method today is not necessarily the one that will give the best results tomorrow, and the simplest method at a given time may make things more complicated in the future. To use force to collectivise the land, to whip the peasants into the kolkhozes, was a simple, rapid and effective solution, but what difficulties such a policy was to create in the future!

In 1941, Soviet agriculture had not recovered from it. The situation was made worse by the war and the destruction caused by the Germans, and it was no better in 1953. It was correct to build a great scientific and mechanised agricultural industry on the basis of co-operatives, but in 1930 the Soviet Union did not have the means to do so. It did not possess the chemical industry necessary to produce adequate quantities of fertilisers, or a large enough engineering industry to produce agricultural machinery in sufficient quantity or quality; nor were there enough agronomists to ensure that the crops, varieties and rotation of crops would be suitable for the soil and climatic conditions, which varied a great deal across the Soviet Union and were often very difficult.

The fatal haste – which Lenin had mentioned with reference to Stalin on a completely different matter (relations with the non-Russian nationalities) – made itself felt here in a tragic way, but Stalin did not choose this line alone. Without seeing the consequences of this policy, most Communists thought it was correct, and they were the very ones who were to pay for this fatal error with their lives in their hundreds of thousands.

The wilfulness and subjectivity of this policy are striking. It is sufficient to read what Sabsovich or Strumilin wrote in the years 1929–30. The former, who was an economist working for the Gosplan, predicted an annual growth rate of 40 to 50 per cent in industrial output. According to him, the Soviet Union would catch up with American output in 1936. As for Strumilin, he criticised the notion of economic laws: 'Our job is not to study economics but to change it. We are bound by no laws. There is no fortress that the Bolsheviks cannot storm. The question of speed is subject to human decisions' (*The Planned Economy*, No. 7, 1927, p. 11). At the 18th Congress in 1939, Kosygin, People's Commissar for the Textile Industry, spoke of overtaking American output in a few years, and it was not just the Second World War which prevented this utopian goal being achieved. Even today, it is a long way off.

All this enables us to better understand the economic and social balance sheet of 1953. The U.S.S.R. had become the second greatest power in the world. It possessed a rapidly expanding heavy industrial sector, but light industry was still very poor and inadequate. Agriculture produced less per inhabitant than in 1913. Society had been transformed from top to bottom. All industry and commerce had been socialised. All agriculture had been collectivised. Cultural backwardness had almost totally disappeared. Some social classes had survived, workers and collective farmers, and intermediate social strata had emerged.

To some extent – to a considerable extent – the consequences of the Second World War explain the persistence of problems after 1946, but only to some extent. The Stalin phenomenon, that is, bureaucratic, despotic and arbitrary management, bears a heavy responsibility for a situation which became harder to explain as the war receded into the past. The economic successes had limitations which arose from the conditions under which they had been achieved. The socialist economy and planning had made possible the development of heavy industry, but the Stalin phenomenon made it more difficult to solve the problems in the other sectors of the economy (light industry and agriculture) and to improve productivity.

Back in the 18th century, when people protested about the way in which Peter the Great had built St. Petersburg – 100,000 serfs died building it – Voltaire replied: 'Yes, but the town does exist!'

It is true that in 1953 socialism existed in the U.S.S.R., and at the same time it had assumed a face which could be explained historically, but not justified. The Stalin phenomenon constituted an obstacle to further progress at home and abroad. At the same time, a new situation tending to reject it had emerged. Barbarity had fallen back, both materially and spiritually. The Stalin phenomenon constituted a system of government and economic management which was less and less suited to the requirements of its period and in conflict with the real situation in the Soviet Union.

NOTES

1. The situation is no longer the same in 1975. The Soviet economy has made progress. The Soviet Union is ahead of the United States for coal, cast-iron and iron. The gap in output of consumer goods is decreasing at a time when the capitalist economy is heavily affected by crisis, inflation and unemployment.
2. Cf. L. Althusser, *Réponse à John Lewis*, pp. 88, 89.
3. 'Stalin made serious mistakes [*sic*] . . . The errors made were doubtless inevitable.' *Class Struggles in the U.S.S.R.*, Vol. 1, p. 38 (*Les luttes de classe en U.R.S.S.*).

8 The Socialist State and Democracy

Socialism does not solve the problems of governing men with a wave of a magic wand. And they are infinitely more difficult and more complicated to solve than economic problems. Proudhon was not right to give preference to the struggle against 'control over man' as against the struggle it was important to wage against 'the exploitation of man by man'. But Marx put these two fights in an order of priority. By putting an end to the exploitation of man, you created conditions conducive to ending control of men by other men. When communism comes, the state is destined to wither away, but socialism is a long way from communism. The state remains and will remain for a long time. Its role is perhaps destined to diminish as socialism develops. This was not and could not have been the case in the Soviet Union. Because of the threats of imperialism and the requirements of the economy, there was a considerable need for a state. The traditions of the Russian state only added weight to these requirements and they were a real danger, as the future was to show. It is precisely at the level of the superstructure that we must seek the key to understanding the Stalin phenomenon. Class phenomena, the relationships between social classes and their struggles, constitute the backdrop to this extraordinary tragedy of history, but there is no direct, instantaneous relationship between the various elements which make up basis and superstructure. The state is always the tool by which one class maintains its dominance, but it is formed and develops on the basis of specific historical situations, not independently of them.

So each state has its own characteristics which have been accentuated by the present extent of the phenomenon of nationalism. Despite the fact that it is now easier for peoples to communicate, national factors have acquired such importance that there is a greater difference between states than there was in the 17th or 18th centuries. At the same time, technical and scientific progress has given the state an increased potential for informing, supervising and intervening in everyday life, and at a time when the functions of the state were growing. Stalin had at his disposal infinitely greater means of government than did Alexander, Julius Caesar, Peter the Great or Napoleon. Thanks to the telegraph and the radio, he knew what was going on in the farthest corner of the Soviet Union practically as it happened. Thanks to the aeroplane, representatives of central government were on the spot in a few hours, or the local leaders were summoned to Moscow. Thus, every state becomes more popular in the sense that, even in dictatorships, the basis of power is as much popular support as the force which those in control of the state machine have at their disposal. The state is a modern Leviathan and tends to absorb everything, swallowing up previously autonomous institutions, interfering with everyone's private life and controlling what everyone does from the cradle to the grave.

The anarchists fought a rearguard action against the state. They saw the danger, but all they could muster against it were broadsides of moral condemnation and examples of a few exceptional individuals who tried to live outside the established rules, rather by reverting to the life style of their ancestors than by organising contemporary life in a new way. Marx was correct to combat anarchists, like Proudhon and Bakunin, who refused to give priority to the struggle against the exploitation of man by his fellows and to use the state to combat and abolish it. He was also aware of the need to smash the capitalist state and to set up a workers' state of a new kind, and he saw the government of the Paris Commune as the model for this. In *The Civil War in France*, he stressed that it was necessary for this workers' state to abolish the special bodies of the army and police and to have elected civil servants who were paid a worker's wage and subject to recall. At the same time he stressed how important it was for the working class to have its own organisations, firstly a political party independent of the bourgeoisie. However, he was faithful to the origins of communism and socialism and only really envisaged a democratic political programme. For him, the 'dictatorship of the proletariat' was a theoretical concept which he contrasted with the 'dictatorship of the bourgeoisie' in order to define the class

G

content of the new state which had to be set up. It is significant that he does not use this expression in *The Civil War in France,* and is content to talk of the 'working-class government', for which he saw a model in the Paris Commune. He had of course spoken of the 'dictatorship of the proletariat' in a letter to Wedemeyer in 1852, and he returned to it at greater length in the *Critique of the Gotha Programme* in 1875, but it is still a theoretical concept which he uses in a very precise context and still only to define the class content of the government in contrast with the capitalist state dominated by the 'dictatorship of the bourgeoisie'.

Next came the period of the 2nd International and the building of social-democratic parties, which arose from the democratic movement itself in the Western democracies. The political programme of the Paris Commune was very similar to the Belleville Radical Programme adopted by Gambetta's voters in 1869. The Commune, which was elected by universal suffrage, abolished the standing army, reduced the number of police, separated Church and State, cut the salaries of high-ranking civil servants and made a certain number of posts subject to election. There was nothing specifically socialist in these measures, apart from the fact that they were carried out by 'the working-class government'. The Social-Democratic parties played a decisive part in spreading socialism among the masses, more from the social and political standpoint than from a theoretical one. Using bourgeois democracy to set up many strong organisations, they started from the people's aspirations for more equality and social justice and linked democratic activity with a socialist consciousness. Though there were no decisive electoral victories, the results were still honourable in many countries, and the parties became mass parties solidly rooted in the life of the nation. The German Social-Democratic Party was the standard bearer of the 2nd International. In 1914, it had a membership of 1,700,000, 35 per cent of the vote and 110 Members of Parliament and 4,000 full-time workers, and it was the biggest party in Germany and the most powerful Socialist party in the world.

In France, the S.F.I.O. had over 100 members of parliament and played an important role in French political life. In Britain, the Labour Party became a force in Parliament whilst the trade unions' influence grew. In Italy, as well as in Austria-Hungary, the Socialist Party was powerful.

The First World War marked the failure of democratic socialism in Western and Central Europe. Not without justification, Lenin was to talk of 'the bankruptcy of the 2nd International'. No doubt a left trend here and there tried its best to fight the nationalism which had swept away the socialist parties and led them each to ally themselves with their own national bourgeoisie and to fight each other. The Soviet Revolution came flooding out of the First World War. After the failure of the German and Hungarian revolutions, the centre of gravity of the labour movement shifted to Russia. With hindsight, one can find profound reasons for this, which already existed and which supposedly explain it as an immanent fact of history. To me, it appears to be more the consequence of a succession of circumstances in which individuals and the masses played a decisive part. To have fostered within Marxism a historical dogmatism which impoverished and made it barren, is not the least of the crimes of Stalinism.

In *The German Ideology*, Marx and Engels criticised the speculative distortions, according to which later history is made the goal of earlier history, e.g. the goal ascribed to the discovery of America is to further the eruption of the French Revolution. Thereby, 'history receives its own special aims . . .' (*The German Ideology*, London, 1970, p. 57). The German Revolution could have been victorious and the Soviet Revolution could have been defeated. The Soviet state built just after the Civil War constitutes a very original system which was very different from the one Marx described with reference to the Paris Commune and even from that imagined by Lenin in *The State and the Revolution* and his writings of 1917. Then he wrote of 'the Soviets, a new kind of state with no bureaucracy, with no police, with no standing army.'

In 1922, as we have noted, the bureaucracy dominated the state. The political police was all-powerful. There were five million soldiers in the Red Army. There were excellent reasons for all this. Without the Red Army, the 'Red Terror' and 'War Communism', the Bolsheviks would have been defeated, and each year we would piously celebrate the memory of their defeat, just as we commemorate that of the Communards who were crushed by the armies of Versailles in May 1871. At the same time, the tools with which the victory of Soviet Power was achieved and the circumstances in which it took place set it formidable problems from which the Stalin phenomenon was eventually to draw its substance. The tentacular role of the state was further increased by the Tsarist tradition in which the Russian state had acquired powers which were all the greater since they encountered neither social classes nor individuals capable of restricting them.

In France and the West, the thick fabric of democracy dates from the Renaissance. It was woven over centuries of historical experience, with periods of ebb and flow, and, since Hitler, we know that it still remains fragile and under threat.

What is known as bourgeois democracy 'was to a large extent imposed' by the working class after the 1848 Revolutions. On the other hand, history developed quite differently in Russia. The fabric of democracy was extremely thin and had hardly been woven in opposition to Tsarism, whilst in France it had been formed through the bourgeois revolution of 1789 and 19th century democratic socialism. As Lenin noted, capitalism had given 'a democratic culture and organisation to all men, however humble'.

The isolation of the Soviet Union after 1922, the ever greater role of the state in economic, social and cultural matters, the growth in the means at its disposal, and the existence of a single, all-powerful party all made the situation worse.

The vicissitudes of Soviet history which led to the growth of the Stalin phenomenon are now well known. It is impossible to lay sufficient emphasis on the crushing weight of the state, for we feel that this leads us to the very heart of the Stalin phenomenon. The new class content of this state and its economic and social base tend to hide the seriousness of the phenomenon from us, and did so for decades. Also, we must remember that the capitalist countries experienced this just as much and sometimes even more, and that they are still threatened by a flashback against which there is no guarantee. The state is both necessary and dangerous. Soviet history demonstrates this quite unequivocally. We can see this even at the level of the life of the Communist Party. A slow, subtle but

effective process gradually emptied it of its democratic substance. Let us take a specific example. At the 10th Congress in
1920, the decision to ban factions was accompanied by measures
towards developing democratic debate within the Party. The
publication of a 'discussion' journal was to enable the debate
to flow horizontally (within a particular organisation) and
vertically (from the bottom to the top and from the top to the
bottom). Without democracy, democratic centralism gradually
becomes dictatorship, and that is what took place in the Soviet
Union in the late twenties and early thirties. Any criticism of
Stalin became an offence. In the early twenties, the 'opponents'
were given appointments far from Moscow, and from 1926 on
they were expelled from the Party. By the 14th Congress (in
December 1925), Stalin was shouting to his critic Riazanov:
'Riazanov is home-sick for Turkestan', and one Bolshevik declared: 'No one wishes to attack the General Secretary, and
for this get sent to Murmusk and to Turkestan.' From 1932
on, these opponents were arrested, from 1936 on they were
tried and executed and from 1938 on they were executed
without trial.

Step by step, this situation spread from the Party leadership
to the whole Party and to other organisations which were
still in existence: the trade unions, the Komsomol and to
the state machine itself. The total absence of freedom of
expression made it impossible to exercise any control over the
activities of the authorities, and the latter gradually extended
their sphere of control and repression to the whole of society.
The state comprehended every phase of the individual's life –
school, work and leisure. Taken individually, none of the
elements which gave rise to and characterised the Stalin
phenomenon was dangerous, the danger arose from them all
coming together.

The omnipotence of the state became confused with that of
the Party, and that of the Party with that of Stalin. The part
he played, his character, his methods and his mentality
accentuated certain aspects of the phenomenon. Nevertheless
he did not create it. All he did was to crystallise and hyper-
trophy things which existed before him, and which arose from
the specific history first of Russia then of the Soviet Union, and
from the Soviet state, just as Hitler crystallised and hyper-

trophied the specific characteristics of German history and the
German state, though under the fundamentally different and
contrary conditions of big capitalism.

Capitalism has produced states and political forms which
have varied considerably according to the time, place and
nation concerned. The same is true of socialism. The autonomy
of politics and ideology in relation to the economic and social
aspects is much greater than is imagined because of Stalinist
dogmatism itself. We must see all the consequences of this.
Though 'economic necessity always prevails in the end'
(letter from Engels to Starkenburg, 25th January 1894), the
relationship is not always direct and immediate. In a letter
written to Mehring on 14th July 1893, Engels admitted that
Marxism had been wrong to neglect 'the form for the substance',
and he stressed the need for knowledge of reciprocal action in
history, for people tended to forget 'the fact that as soon as a
historical factor is engendered by other economic facts, it
reacts in turn and can affect its environment and even its own
causes'.

Still, the Stalin phenomenon is linked to the development of the structures of the Soviet socialist state and of its
mechanisms in ways determined by history.

Cultural backwardness and capitalist encirclement were
added to the weight of history (that is to say the resurgence of
the Russian Tsarist state and the consequences of the Civil
War). The cult of the leader makes it possible to gain a better
understanding of what happened. It took over a whole tradition
which was not uniquely Russian, but there can be no doubt that
it was localised. It seems quite clear that such a phenomenon is
universal and seems if anything to have become more so in the
20th century. It does not seem to be specifically socialist, it is
found well before socialism, ever since the state has existed. As
far back as Antiquity its existence may be ascertained in
Egypt and Mesopotamia. As the state increased its control
over the lives of individuals, so the cult of the leader gave a
popular basis for the political regime constituted by the society.
In the Hellenistic kingdoms, the King was the 'sôter' (saviour),
'poliocete' (protector of the city), 'phylax' (guardian) and
'evergete' (man who turns away evil).

It may be objected that the *Internationale* proclaimed that there was 'neither God, nor Caesar nor supreme Saviour', a piece of wishful thinking which seems derisory when compared to the facts of contemporary history. In China, the cult of Mao has developed to a similar extent to that of Stalin (though it has not been so bloody). The same causes produce the same effects. At the same time, the forms assumed by the Mao cult are not the same as those of the Stalin cult, for they exist in a different national situation and in a different historical environment. In Stalin's case, the 'Guide' ('vojd') was honoured like a living God. He punished the wicked, protected the weak and personified the socialist state. He was the saviour, the guarantor and the cement of the unity of the Soviet peoples; this enables us better to understand the reasons for Stalin's popularity, his charismatic quality, despite the fact that he subjected the Soviet peoples to widespread terror for about twenty years.

When he died, though they numbered friends and relations among the victims of the repression, millions of Soviet citizens mourned the dead guide. The cult of the leader was an important element of the Stalin phenomenon. It broke up into a large number of regional cults. In the Smolensk region, the cult of the Regional Party Secretary Rumantsyev was just as real. Photographs of him were to be found next to those of Stalin in public places and Party offices. Factories were named after him. Until his arrest in 1937, his speeches were solemnly quoted by the press. The cult grew in the Communist and Workers' Parties where they were in power. In Hungary we find the cult of Stalin and Rakosi, in Czechoslovakia that of Gottwald together with Stalin, etc. Even the Western Communist Parties practised it in a milder form, but everywhere Stalin's seventieth birthday was celebrated in a spectacular fashion.

Even the Lenin Mausoleum served to transfer religious feelings to the secular and socialist field. Soviet society was a society without God, but was scarcely or not at all ready for this situation, so it created rituals, ceremonies, buildings and a vocabulary which are not unreminiscent of defeated Orthodoxy. Fundamentally, it was different, since materialism had prevailed and Marxism could use the state to spread it, but the forms were similar.

At the heart of the Soviet state we find the Communist Party. The distinction between the Party and the state no longer meant much in the Soviet Union by the end of the Civil War. There was an osmosis. The leading role of the Party was such that it got what it wanted in the matter of appointments to posts of responsibility. As the years went by, the 'Nomenklatura', that is to say the list of posts only filled with the permission of the leading bodies of the Party or for which they alone appointed, grew longer, and increasingly strict control was exercised. To attain one of these posts enabled you to share power, but, from 1935 on, to be removed meant not just the loss of power, but also that of freedom and often of life. Eventually, to attain certain posts meant playing double or quits. So, the small ruling group in the state had no more protection than ordinary militants. In fact it was affected more by repression than the ordinary members of the Party, and they were more affected than non-members. This is the strange thing about a system which is often studied in reverse.

Being omnipotent, the Stalinist state – the form assumed by the socialist state in the U.S.S.R. – took no notice of the laws which it itself had enacted. In the economic field, economic stimuli could have made an effective contribution to the struggle against bureaucracy. In the political field, this was clearly quite impossible. Only really democratic practices were capable of opposing the despotic tendencies of the state. It is precisely the total absence of political democracy in the Soviet Union after 1922 which enables us to understand the truth about the Stalin phenomenon. Here we are dealing with a crucial problem in contemporary history.

The experience of the Bolsheviks, the conditions under which they carried on their clandestine struggle, the circumstances of the Revolution and Civil War and their lack of experience in this field led them to misunderstand democratic processes and mechanisms. There was to be nothing to counterbalance a state conducive to bureaucracy and despotism, so anything could happen. We can see that even in the culturally and democratically advanced countries of Western Europe, there was a threat of totalitarianism and it was eventually to triumph in Germany. In these circumstances, how can we be surprised that, despite the existence of socialism – but we have seen how weak and uncertain it was because of the conditions – despotism should have flourished in the Soviet Union under the guise of the Stalin phenomenon.

The single party and the total lack of freedom of expression, association and assembly did not only have minor, marginal consequences. Arbitrariness grew in this environment and no force was capable of opposing it.

The complete absence of criticism within the Party itself and its leadership became really tragic from 1925 on. To criticise any act of the Party leadership and the Central Committee was to risk losing one's post. Henceforth, it was no longer possible to criticise. In contrast to what Lenin said, democracy is not merely a political category the need for which can be questioned. It constitutes a structure, organisation and practice in the absence of which contemporary societies may move towards totalitarianism, because of the technical and scientific foundations upon which they rest, and the increased influence of the state on everyday life. Socialism is not immune to this modern illness to the extent to which it does not develop on the foundation of preponderantly democratic procedures and does not bring about a growth of democratic mechanisms. The socialist economy does not *ipso facto* create democratic mechanisms. This is precisely what the history of the Stalin phenomenon shows. Socialism does not necessarily prevent despotism. It does not necessarily create it either.

To restrict the Stalin phenomenon to these aspects would, however, be to make a serious historical misinterpretation. Its economic and social content is really socialist. This dual character of the phenomenon is too often neglected. Only to see one side is to condemn oneself to fail totally to comprehend Soviet history.

The means used often run counter to the descried aim (here we are not adopting a moral standpoint), but this aim still exists and proceeds through all the obstacles. Cultural and educational progress is one of the best examples of this contradiction. During the whole period, it was considerable. We shall let the figures speak for themselves. By 1939, every child attended school until the end of the 'seven year school' (to about the age of thirteen):

1914   9,656,000 schoolchildren
1939   31,517,000 schoolchildren

Among young people below 20 illiteracy had disappeared. In 1953, secondary education took in more than half the children in each age group. The number of students had gone from the 1914 total of 127,400 to 1,562,000 (of whom 1,042,700 were full-time university students). It is important not just to study the increase in student numbers, but to note the social consequences of this growth. Masses of workers and collective farmers sent their children to secondary school and to the university, and themselves often attended evening classes or took correspondence courses. Thousands of buildings for pioneers and young people and cultural associations were set up. The masses made considerable cultural advances and the idea of this spread to the West from the Soviet Union. Malraux and Aragon brought back the idea of Houses of Culture from their trip to the U.S.S.R. in 1934. It is true that a large number of officials' children undertook higher education and that this led to a degree of social reproduction. Soviet society was not egalitarian. There were still class and socio-cultural differences, nevertheless more than half the students were the children of collective farmers and workers. In 1953, the Soviet Union was the country where social mobility and promotion were greatest. Masses of children of moujiks went to university. As a symbol of this cultural development, Moscow University, which was built in 1952 on the Lenin Hills, dominated the city.

By 1953, the Soviet Union had ended cultural backwardness and made up a great deal of ground on the West. It had trained millions of technicians and hundreds of thousands of scientists and researchers. Thus, the basis for democracy had been widened. Based as it was on a socialist economy, the Stalin phenomenon created the very conditions for its own abolition.

We have already observed the state's attitude to research, science and the creative arts. As A. Tvardovsky was to write in the Soviet magazine *Novy Mir* in 1965, it was a period of 'falsification and distortion of actual truth'. Yet this period cannot be reduced to this authoritarian policy. In every field, a new, large and cultivated public was created. Soviet scientists and engineers perfected their own nuclear research and their own aero-space industry. High-quality works of literature were published and good films made. The contradictions within the Stalin phenomenon reveal themselves strikingly in the cultural field. Eisenstein produced 'Alexander Nevsky' and 'Ivan the Terrible', but had to make numerous concessions to do so.

Marxism, which had become the official state philosophy, was taught as dogma to the youngest children. Lessons in 'Diamat' (dialectical materialism) and 'Hismat' (historical materialism) were organised at every level of education. This dogmatism led to a grave 'theoretical deviation': Stalinism.

With due allowance made, we see here the same phenomenon which Christianity underwent after becoming the state religion in the Roman Empire when the Emperor Constantine was converted to Christianity at the beginning of the 4th century. Marxism, which is a critical philosophy, was transformed into a dogmatic structure designed to provide an ideological framework for tens, or even hundreds of millions of people. What was a research methodology became ossified and partly sterile as a result of a system which banned all free research and criticism.

This dogmatism had tragic consequences in the Soviet Union and the whole international Communist movement. The influence of Stalinism in the foreign Communist Parties is explained by reasons we have analysed. For twenty-five years, the Soviet Union was the only socialist state on earth. The Comintern obliged the Communist parties to defend it, come what may. As the only victorious revolution in history, the Soviet Revolution seemed to Communists to be a model that had to be copied, even taking into account national variations. Until 1934, one of the French Communists' main slogans was: 'Soviets everywhere!'

The construction of Socialism in the U.S.S.R. became a model in its turn, and events after the Second World War led to it being copied in the Eastern European socialist states. The very successes of the Revolution, of socialist construction and the Second World War gave the Stalin phenomenon a formidable impact in all countries, including those where the situation in the economic, cultural and political fields was radically different from that in Russia in 1917 and the U.S.S.R. in 1945.

The need to defend the Soviet Union and its achievements partly obscured the Communist parties' theoretical consideration of the paths to socialism and the forms the latter should take in the various countries, taking into account the precise historical and geographical circumstances of each period and each country. Stalin's influence led them to generalise one particular experience and to move dogmatically from the particular to the general. In the case of the socialist states of Eastern Europe, this was not always voluntary. In the case of the other Communist parties, it can be explained by the fact that what was involved was an experience unique in history which had taken place in a great country, whilst socialism had failed comprehensively in the West. Now, the Soviet Revolution and the building of Socialism in the U.S.S.R. do comprise general features, but they find expression in real history through the intermediary of specific features. This is true of the seizure of power and the socialisation of the means of production and exchange, which were all ensured by the Soviet Revolution. For these reasons, it was not realised – or not sufficiently so – that the historical conditions in the great, economically and culturally developed capitalist states were radically different, and the road to socialism, as well as the forms it would assume, would necessarily differ according to circumstances and country, even if the general features did remain the same. As for the Bolsheviks, despite Lenin's warnings, under Stalin's influence they came to consider their own experience as a model which should be copied everywhere and always. This was true, for example, of the one-party system.

The tragic experience of Germany in 1933 helped France in 1934. With the Anti-Fascist Alliance and the Communists' affirmation that they were fighting for democracy ('Democracy or Fascism'), we witness a radical change of direction, which the Popular Front later developed further. The 7th Congress of the Comintern in 1935 confirmed this approach. Unfortunately the Stalin phenomenon hindered the application of this new policy and largely prevented it being given the required theoretical dimension.

The international situation spoilt any hope of pursuing this path, whose importance for contemporary history should not be underestimated. It had to wait until after the war.

In his London *Times* interview of 19th November 1946, Maurice Thorez, General Secretary of the French Communist Party, declared that it was possible to 'envisage other roads to socialism than that followed by the Russian Communists. Anyway, the road is of necessity different for every country.' This statement, which was criticised by Zhdanov and Malenkov at the inaugural meeting of the Cominform and rather shelved because of the Cold War, nevertheless marked a crucial date in the rejection of Stalinist theory by the General Secretary of one of the most powerful Communist parties in the capitalist world. Stalinist dogmatism, which was contrary to the evolution of science in so many ways, was coming up against the facts and needs of its time. Although it was convenient for teaching – a quality which could be useful – it was nevertheless the source of sclerosis, not only within the Soviet Union but in all the Communist parties. It would be unfair only to see this aspect of things. For example, the French Communist Party played a considerable part in spreading Marxism and developing Marxist theory. At its instigation, the first groups of Marxist intellectuals were formed and the first serious French translations of Marx were published. In philosophy and literature, there were new and interesting experiments which were the precursors of the experimental work carried out in the post-Stalin period. Marxism entered the academic and artistic worlds. In this connection, the names of Eluard, Aragon, Picasso, Joliot-Curie, Langevin, Politzer and Henri Wallon tell us a lot. This took place within the phenomenon itself, whose contradictions were to get worse as the years went by. The economic and social foundations of the Soviet system grew stronger, whilst the authoritarian, bureaucratic system of government became more oppressive. As time went by, it became clearer that this system was not suited to the requirements of the economy (growth of light industry and agriculture), scientific research or technical progress. Though it was obscured by the charisma of the victorious leader and fear of a third world war, this inadequacy remains tragic. The refusal of contact with abroad and the instability of leaderships constantly threatened by the Damocles' sword of bloody purges both slowed down economic expansion, made it impossible to take advantage of the benefits of a socialist economy in terms of planning and production on the national scale, and made Soviet culture, which had been so full of promise just after the Revolution, barren.

Socialism emerged damaged from this situation, but was not destroyed; on the contrary, paradoxically, it continued to progress.

Stalin had tens of thousands of the leaders of the non-Russian Soviet Republics arrested, deported or executed. In these republics, he carried on a vigorous campaign against 'bourgeois nationalism' and imposed a policy of Russian centralism, but, at the same time, the study of the national languages increased in quality and quantity. In Asia new literatures were born and old ones re-emerged. Backwardness declined everywhere. Women threw off the veil which generations of them had worn for centuries. All levels of education spread to every part of the Soviet Union, to places where there had not previously even been primary schools. Thus, the base which added to the fragility of the Stalinist system was being built. Terror still dominated the country and, though to a lesser extent than before the war, personal security was still greatly threatened by the omnipotence of the M.V.D., denunciations, violations of socialist legality and sometimes by the law itself, as in the case of the OSSO. 'One day Lara went out and did not come back.' This tragic sentence from the conclusion to Boris Pasternak's novel *Doctor Zhivago* was still topical in 1953.

The key to understanding the Stalin phenomenon is to be found in the study of the state. Dictatorship was necessary in order to consolidate a revolution that had been born from an insurrection and followed by a merciless civil war. Let us re-read what Rosa Luxemburg said about it: 'But the remedy which Trotsky and Lenin have found, the elimination of democracy as such, is worse than the disease it is supposed to cure; for it stops up the very living source from which alone can come the correction of all the innate shortcomings of social institutions. That source is the active, untrammelled, energetic political life of the broadest masses of the people' (*The Russian Revolution*, p. 62). This is both true and false. False because without this dictatorship the Revolution would have been defeated. True because it was indeed possible for the Stalin phenomenon to emerge from this dictatorship.

'Freedom only for the supporters of the government, only for the members of one party – however numerous they may be – is not freedom at all. Freedom is always and exclusively freedom for the one who thinks differently. Not because of any fanatical conception of justice, but because all that is instructive, wholesome and purifying in political freedom depends on this essential characteristic; and its effectiveness vanishes when "freedom" becomes a special privilege' (*ibid.*, p. 79).

Under the capitalist system, this freedom and democracy are constantly restricted and attacked by social inequality and the rule of profit. However, socialism does not of itself create this freedom and democracy. Dictatorship was a two-edged sword. It was necessary from 1917 to 1922, contrary to Rosa Luxemburg's view, but it still constituted a danger in as much as it did not then create democracy and did not really guarantee freedom for everyone. This is what happened. In the absence of democracy, terror became a system of government in a more and more powerful state, which was thus more and more intrusive, and had become totalitarian in the literal sense of the word, since it took in every sphere of the individual's life.

Nevertheless, the U.S.S.R. was the first socialist state in history, and was exposed to the hostility of all the other states in the world, perpetually menaced by foreign imperialism, constantly threatened with destruction, which it in fact underwent to some considerable extent. One can and must deplore the mistakes made along the road to Socialism and strongly and unhesitatingly condemn the Stalin phenomenon, but at the same time one must state that it was one form in which socialism existed.

9 The Soviet Union after Stalin

Stalin's death did not mean that the Stalin phenomenon perished with him, for it could certainly not be reduced to the mere personality of the 'Guide'. Despite everything, despite the political police, the forced labour camps and the draconic economic and social measures taken, a huge crowd mourned the dead leader and accompanied his corpse to the Red Square Mausoleum. For the Soviet people, he symbolised their own tragic and glorious fate, and the families of those who had been victims of his policy were seen to mingle their sobs with the greater number of the relatives of victims of the Second World War.

The problem of a successor still had to be solved, for Stalin, who apparently thought himself immortal, had made no plans. Under cover of the commotion caused by his death, there was an attempt by Malenkov, probably supported by Beria, to seize power.

On 6th March there was a sudden announcement – the leading bodies had not been convened – that Malenkov had been appointed First Secretary of the Party and President of the Council of Ministers. Thus, he seemed to be Stalin's successor. The Presidium was reorganised and now only had 10 full members (as against 24) and 4 candidates (as against 11). On 10th March 1953, *Pravda* published a 'faked' photograph of Stalin, Mao and Malenkov.

Beria, who was Vice-President of the Council, was also Minister of the Interior. The new Presidium was made up of the 8 members of the old Politbureau as it existed before the 19th Congress: Malenkov, Molotov, Khrushchev, Voroshilov, Mikoyan, Kaganovich and Bulganin, and two new members (who had been elected in 1952): Pervukhin and Saburov.

Suslov, Kosygin and Brezhnev were removed from the Presidium. On 21st March, there was a surprise development. It was announced that Khrushchev had replaced Malenkov as

First Secretary of the Party. The decision was dated 14th March. From then on, there were big changes in the policy of the Communist Party and of the state.

As early as 16th April, *Pravda* stressed the principle of collective leadership. On 28th March, a decree of amnesty provided for the release of prisoners sentenced to less than five years in prison, and a 50 per cent reduction of their sentence for others. Mothers, young people under 18 and old people were released. The penal code was to be revised and economic offences were no longer to be treated as criminal offences.

On 4th April, *Pravda* announced that the 'doctors' plot' was a fabrication by the political police and confessions had been gained by the use of torture.

On 10th July 1953 came the announcement of the arrest of Beria (it was officially decided on 26th June, and, according to Khrushchev, it was carried out on the same day).[1]

These measures all attacked essential characteristics of the Stalinist system. The role of the political police was reduced. Many of the top M.V.D. officials were arrested and executed. The forced labour camps began to empty, and the international situation became somewhat less tense when the Korean Armistice was concluded on 27th July 1953.

The revelations about the 'doctors' plot' forced public opinion to face the question of the repression which had taken place in the preceding period. Had the same thing as happened in 1952–3 not also taken place in 1936–8? The validity of the great political trials of the previous decades was called into question.

So, by July 1953, the Stalin phenomenon had already retreated. The death of Stalin had deprived the cult of the leader of its object. The attempt to provide a substitute failed right at the beginning, partly because it was impossible to fabricate a new Stalin in a few days, and partly because the environment was not favourable.

The insistence on a collective leadership was clear proof that there was no readiness to return to the dictatorship of one man. There were still forced labour camps, but there was a fall in the scale of absolutism for the first time for twenty years, and this took place in public.

The thaw (the title of a novel by Ilya Ehrenburg which

was published at the time) was really beginning. The decline
of the Stalin phenomenon, which was speeded up by Stalin's
death, was explained by the new historical environment, which
it had helped create.

The Soviet Union had emerged from cultural backwardness. It was the second most powerful industrial nation in the
world, with a powerful heavy industry and a technically
advanced armaments industry. The fact that a bureaucratic
management and planning system was maintained slowed
down the development of the socialist economy, particularly in
the fields of light industry and agriculture. Everything was
decided at the top. There was very strict discipline in the
factories and kolkhozes, and there was more frequent recourse
to repression than to material incentives for the wage-earners
and collective farmers. All the draconic measures taken before
and during the war were still in operation and had not been
significantly changed. Workers could not leave their factories,
nor collective farmers their fields without permission and this
was rarely given. Travel was still restricted and strictly
controlled.

Though a large number of technicians and engineers had
been trained, labour productivity was still poor, and output
low. The system was often efficient as far as setting up big steel
plants, building canals, railways and big dams and bringing
new oil-wells and coal mines into service was concerned. It
was for other things that it was the least suitable.

On 10th June 1953, *Pravda* first referred to the 'cult of the
personality', though only in general terms.

In September 1953, the Central Committee discussed the
problems of agriculture on the basis of a report by Khrushchev
which made a realistic analysis of the catastrophic situation.
The quotas for obligatory deliveries were reduced and the
prices of agricultural produce were put up.

Gradually, all the policies followed during the last years
of Stalin's life were called into question. For example, the
Soviet Union resumed diplomatic relations with Yugoslavia
and Khrushchev went to Belgrade (in June 1955), where he
admitted that the U.S.S.R. had been wrong and said that
Beria was responsible.

After Malenkov had resigned from his post as President of

the Council in January 1955, his successor Bulganin tackled the problems of industry. Between 1953 and the beginning of 1956, many steps were taken which changed the situation in the Soviet Union and laid the basis for the 20th Congress of the Communist Party of the U.S.S.R.

For example, the M.V.D. was deprived of the right to use forced labour-camp labour, and it was given to the relevant industrial ministries. The camps began to empty and the first rehabilitations took place. This new policy caused many problems both at home and abroad. Within the Soviet Union, it encountered furious opposition in the leading circles of the Party. We have no detailed knowledge of the internal struggles, but the extent of the changes in the leadership which occurred after 1956 gives some idea of the struggles within the Party leadership. A number of the leading comrades were afraid that if a lot of the characteristics of the Stalin phenomenon were questioned, this would compromise the positive achievements of the preceding period and the balance upon which the Soviet Union depended. They had been tied to the Stalin phenomenon by their own habits and practice, but could the same not be said of those who, like Khrushchev, were in favour of a more rapid, brutal and thorough-going destruction of the negative aspects of the past? In 1956, the dividing line was not established by recalling the attitude of one leader or another in the past, but on the basis of his views on contemporary problems like improving the virgin lands of Central Asia (mainly in Kazakhstan). It is possible, indeed certain, that past attitudes could have played a role in contemporary struggles, but they could not be decisive. Whatever their attitudes in the past, Khrushchev and many other leaders deserve no little credit in historical terms. They brought the political police to heel, emptied the concentration camps, tackled the great economic problems by trying to reduce bureaucracy, conducted a determined foreign policy of peace and peaceful coexistence and resumed relations with Yugoslavia. For Soviet citizens, work became freer and personal security greater; this is the significance of the 20th Congress of the Communist Party of the Soviet Union.

It is true that a considerable proportion of the public were still under the influence of Stalin's charisma; this varied from region to region, being larger in his home area Georgia, for example, than in Leningrad.

Abroad the situation was not simple. In the People's Democracies, the Stalin phenomenon had grown vigorously. The political system had often been copied, or even imposed by the Soviet Union. Stalin had conducted a policy based on unequal relations between the various socialist countries. The attack on the Stalin phenomenon in the Soviet Union could not fail to have serious consequences in countries where, in most cases, fascism had ruled not long before (less than eight years) and where the bourgeoisie was still strong, and in a world where imperialism was lying in wait. This was seen as early as 1953, when there were strikes and demonstrations in the German Democratic Republic, in Berlin and in many other towns, and in Poland at Wroclaw. For the Communist parties in capitalist countries, this raised many problems, though they were restricted to the fields of politics and ideology since it was in these fields that the Stalin phenomenon had had some influence.

In the case of China the situation was doubtless even more complex. The successful Chinese Revolution had taken a course quite independent of the Soviet Union. The Soviet Revolution had played an important part in the birth of Chinese Communism, but afterwards the latter had developed along original paths by keeping closely to the facts of the Chinese situation. Circumstances had forced the Chinese Revolution to assume a national, peasant character. Relations between Stalin and Mao had not been easy, but in 1950 they had achieved a sort of compromise which governed mutual relations and set up a united anti-imperialist policy which had been demonstrated during the Korean War. Because of the policy of peaceful co-existence, did the re-evaluation of the Stalin phenomenon in the U.S.S.R. not risk undermining this compromise, dividing the two great Communist states and even setting them against each other?

From 1953 to 1956, Khrushchev's method was to make a series of modifications rather than deep and spectacular transformations. In practice, these modifications added up to a considerable change and helped to eliminate the bloodiest and most restrictive aspects of the Stalin phenomenon. Until the

20th Congress of the C.P.S.U., there was little discussion of the fundamental issues and there were not even any direct personal attacks on Stalin. It was both difficult to act otherwise and necessary to go further.

At the 20th Congress of the C.P.S.U. in February 1956, Khrushchev announced in his public report that 'socialist legality' had been re-established, the administrative machine of the Soviets cut down (750,000 civil servants had been redeployed) and many innocent people rehabilitated. Again, he ascribed responsibility for past errors to 'Beria's gang', and stressed the need for collective leadership.

We know that a large number of Presidium members were opposed to a direct and radical critique of the Stalin phenomenon. On two points, Khrushchev put forward ideas which, if not new, were at least fairly daring. He showed that, contrary to the early 20th-century Marxist analysis, war was no longer inevitable, because of the changes which had taken place in the world. The emergence of numerous socialist states had reduced imperialism's sphere of action, and the disintegration of the colonial system meant that its rear was threatened. So, peaceful coexistence could be widened after the Great Power Conference held in Geneva in 1955, the end of the war in Korea, and the signing of a peace treaty with Austria.

Next, Khrushchev adopted the theses put forward by Maurice Thorez in 1946 and admitted that 'the forms of transition to socialism will be more and more varied' and that this transition could be peaceful, that is to say without a civil war. Numerous speakers like Furtseva, Suslov and Kirichenko criticised the 'cult of the personality', bureaucracy and dogmatism, but in fairly general terms.

Mikoyan (a candidate member of the Central Committee since 1922, candidate for the Politbureau in 1927, and a full member since 1935) was the first person to attack Stalin. He admitted that 'for almost twenty years we have had no collective leadership', and he criticised the theses on the inevitability of wars between capitalist countries and on 'under-production' by industry in capitalist countries, which Stalin had put forward in 1952 in *Economic Problems of Socialism in the U.S.S.R.* He condemned 'bad use of statistics' and stressed the need for a return to Leninism.

The Stalin Phenomenon

A historian, A. Pankratova, demonstrated how far historical research and the whole field 'of theoretical work' had fallen behind. For example, she admitted 'that scarcely any interest was taken in the importance of denouncing the national and colonial oppression carried out by the Tsarist autocracy'.

It was on the evening of 24th February that Khrushchev read his 'secret report', denouncing the 'cult of the personality' to a closed session of the Congress; it was then conveyed to the members of the Communist Party of the U.S.S.R. and to the leaderships of the brother parties in the socialist countries. The report was never published in the U.S.S.R., but on 5th July 1956 the *New York Times* published a translation which was never challenged. Together with the resolution dated 30th June 1956 adopted by the Central Committee of the C.P.S.U., it constitutes one of the two key documents in what the Western press called 'destalinisation'. In the early hours of 25th February 1956, the Congress delegates emerged distressed and dumbfounded from the historic session of Congress.

As for the leaders of the Western Communist parties, they found out what had been said later.

Despite the new measures adopted since 1953, Soviet public opinion was scarcely ready for the report. Internal struggles within the Party were probably the reason for this shock effect, but it simply made the contents of the report all the more traumatic. In it were documents which were already known (but not in the Soviet Union) and thus received the stamp of authenticity, as well as new documents like Stalin's telegram to Politbureau members about repression, the Central Committee resolution on the use of torture and the letters of the murdered leaders Eikhe and Rudzutak.

The report contained figures, for example the number of Central Committee members elected in 1934 and later shot, and a critical account of Stalin's attitude on many problems, for example about the Yugoslavian affair. Most of the facts quoted are correct, even if the tone is sometimes a bit forced, as in the description of Stalin directing the military operations of the Second World War with the use of a globe.

On the other hand, there was little explanation of what had given rise to the phenomenon. The very expression 'cult of the personality' reduced the Stalin phenomenon to a relatively secondary aspect: the cult of the leader. In terms of history and theory, the analysis of the fundamental problem was still superficial. No mention was made of the conditions under which collectivisation had taken place, the problems concerning freedom to create and research and the critique of Stalin's Russian nationalist policy. What was recognised was only the personal, authoritarian, bureaucratic and often bloody character of Stalin's rule. One observes an attempt to put all the problems in the past down to Stalin, and to explain past events solely in terms of his personal characteristics.

The 30th June 1956 resolution, which was much more political and theoretical in tenor, identified two kinds of causes: 'the objective and concrete historical conditions under which socialism was built in the U.S.S.R.' and 'the subjective factors linked to Stalin's personal characteristics'. It is of course essential to study the historical conditions. The resolution gives a good picture of the internal and external problems that the Socialist Revolution and the building of socialism had encountered. The internal and external circumstances demanded iron discipline, ever growing vigilance and rigorously centralised leadership, which was bound to have a negative effect on the growth of certain forms of democracy. These 'restrictions of democracy were to be considered as temporary'.

These considerations are fundamental, but they were not taken any further, and their scope was restricted by vague historical references. So, whilst the 20th Congress and the decisions taken after it raised a certain number of questions very directly, they did not adequately tackle the fundamentals, that is to say the deep-seated causes of the Stalin phenomenon.

The most obvious and most dangerous parts of the Stalin phenomenon were eliminated, but without discussion in depth of the whole phenomenon itself. The new policy adopted at the 20th Congress had contradictory consequences. The lives of Soviet citizens improved, working conditions got better, workers began to be able to change factories without hindrance and repressive measures within the factory were abolished. The trade unions played a more active role in defending the interests of wage-earners. The lowest wages were increased and bureaucracy combated. Thus, over two million civil servants were eliminated from the central bodies where they had been working. Personal security was better protected. Though it was not officially recognised, freedom to research and create became incomparably greater than during the Stalin period. The 'Special Commission' of the M.V.D. was abolished.

Nevertheless, the economic reforms were still incomplete. Many organisational steps were taken to combat bureaucratic centralisation, for example the often disorganised setting up of sovnarkhozes (regional economic councils), but management methods were not questioned and they continued to make little use of economic stimuli and to underestimate the role of the law of value in price formation. The U.S.S.R. recorded real economic successes, but the consumer goods sector and above all agriculture still experienced problems.

Furious resistance to the policy adopted by the 20th Congress made its presence felt at the level of the Party leadership itself. In June 1957, Khrushchev was outvoted in the Presidium which had been elected at the 20th Congress.[2] He had to hastily convene the Central Committee in order to rectify the situation and eliminate his opponents.

In the new Presidium, the new full members included Brezhnev and Marshal Zhukov and among the candidates were Kosygin and Mazurov. Yet, no 'administrative measures' were taken against the opponents. However, we may assume that there was still considerable disagreement within the Party after 1957, this is why 'destalinisation' remained limited in scope and proceeded in fits and starts. For example, the victims of the great Moscow trials were not rehabilitated, although it seemed quite clear that they were legally innocent. Though the Soviets were to some extent reactivated, the political structures of the U.S.S.R. were hardly changed. For example, freedom of expression, like freedom to create, was still dubious and subject to the goodwill of the authorities. Indisputably, the question of democracy could not be posed in the Soviet Union of 1956 in the same way as in the capitalist countries of the democratic West. Since 1922, the U.S.S.R. had laid the foundations of economic and social democracy. Cultural development had given everyone access to knowledge and so the basis for political democracy had been strengthened, but political democracy still did not exist.

In the U.S.S.R., the one-party system was an irreversible

fact, the product of a history we have studied, which there was little chance of changing. Political democracy had no choice but to grow from the actual situation with a single leading Party. There can be no doubt that it was in this field that there was the greatest difficulty. It is not surprising that it was in the field of literature that the contradictory trends which appeared in the U.S.S.R. after 1953 confronted each other with the greatest pugnacity. In this field the ill effects of the Stalin phenomenon were still to be felt. It was characterised by a predominance of administrative and even repressive measures rather than political and ideological debate. Men and structures play no small part in these manifestations of 'neo-stalinism' which found practical expression in the banning of publication of many works of literature, history and philosophy, and sometimes even the arrest of writers who were given heavy prison or deportation sentences, and in some cases internment in mental hospitals.[3]

The 22nd Congress of the C.P.S.U. in 1961 reopened the debate on the Stalin phenomenon. At it, fresh revelations were made, in particular about the assassination of Kirov. The Congress took the decision to remove Stalin's body from the Mausoleum[4] and to change the name of Stalingrad to Volgograd. Khrushchev talked of making public the findings of the commission of enquiry into the death of Kirov, but this was never done. Finally, he proposed the building in Moscow of a monument to the victims of the Stalinist Terror, but the matter was not raised again after the 22nd Congress.

Thus, the Soviet political system hardly underwent any changes after 1956. The Soviet Constitution of 1936 was still in many cases a formal framework which was inadequately reflected in political practice.

It would be contrary to the facts to describe the contemporary U.S.S.R. as Stalinist. The manifestations of 'neo-stalinism' which are to be found there are survivals from the past, manifestations which recur as a result of habits, established administrative structures and of mental attitudes which, as is well known, are hard to change. I do not claim that the seriousness of these manifestations should be underestimated. They still to some extent tarnish the Soviet Union's image in the world, and consequently the image of socialism which it represents before history. There can be no doubt that they constitute a brake on the economic and cultural growth of the country. There are still after-effects of the Stalin phenomenon.

Though it cannot and must not be taken as a model, Soviet Socialism nevertheless constitutes the first and most important socialist experiment in history. However tragic the Stalin phenomenon was, it remains limited in terms of time and place. The fact that it existed and the consequences which it had beyond the frontiers of the U.S.S.R. and beyond the period during which it was dominant, should not hide the richness of socialism although all the hopes it raised have not yet been fulfilled. It now remains for us to build socialism on the basis of a developed Western capitalist economy.

NOTES

1. Beria's execution was announced on 23rd December 1953, after a trial presided over by Marshal Koniev and held in camera.
2. Bulganin, Voroshilov, Kaganovich, Malenkov, Molotov, Pervukhin and Saburov, that is to say seven of the eleven full members, opposed him. Suslov, Mikoyan, and Kirichenko as well as Brezhnev, Zhukhov and two other candidates supported him.
3. For example, this happened to the writers Sinyavsky and Daniel in 1965, and to the biologist Medvedev who was arbitrarily shut up in a mental hospital.
4. His ashes are now lodged in front of the Kremlin wall near the tombs of many other Soviet leaders. A small bust marks the spot for passers-by.

Index

of Principal Themes, Persons and Authors Quoted